GCSE Edexcel
French

Salut! Welcome to your one-stop shop for everything GCSE French.

This CGP book covers every topic on the Edexcel course, including all the vocab and grammar you'll need to know. There are also exam-style questions, full practice papers and even some handy exam advice to get you fully prepared.

On top of that, there's lots of revision in the CGP RevisionHub. You'll find quick quizzes, summary tests, audio, Q&A videos and more in the Hub, all matched to your book. It's tasty stuff — *bon appétit*!

Unlock **CGP RevisionHub**

Just scan a QR code in the book to access the CGP RevisionHub.
Or go to **cgpbooks.co.uk/revise** and enter this code!

Revision Hub

0836 5475 9569 1147

By the way, this code only works for one person. If somebody else has used this book before you, they might have already claimed the code.

Complete
Revision & Practice
with new **CGP RevisionHub**

Published by CGP

Editors:
Elliott Garraway
Nathan Mair
Ilana Pearce
Anna Stringer
Alex Thompson
Matt Topping

Contributors:
Ben Ffrancon Dowds
Sarah Sweeney

With thanks to Marc Barnard, Tom Carney, Eleanor Claringbold, Marie-Laure Delvallée, Natalie Pomier, Véronique Robine, Hannah Roscoe and Jack Tooth for the proofreading.

With thanks to Alice Dent for the copyright research.

Acknowledgements:

Audio produced by Voice Talent Online.

Questions throughout are based on Pearson Edexcel type questions.

ISBN: 978 1 83774 128 1
Printed by Elanders Ltd, Newcastle upon Tyne.
Clipart from Corel®

Based on the classic CGP style created by Richard Parsons.

Contents

Contents

Theme 4: Media and Technology

Section Seven — Social Media and Technology

Theme 5: Studying and My Future

Section Eight — School

Section Nine — Future Opportunities

Theme 6: Travel and Tourism

Section Ten — Travel and Tourism

Contents

Grammar

Section Eleven — Nouns, Articles and Linking Words

Section Twelve — Adjectives and Adverbs

Section Thirteen — Verbs and Tenses

Pronunciation in French

Exam Advice

Practice Papers

How to Use this Book

This isn't a book. Or rather, this isn't *just* a book. It's full of online resources designed to help you get top marks. To learn how it all works, read these pages or scan the QR code for a walkthrough.

Video

This book follows the Edexcel specification

1) The content for Edexcel GCSE French is divided into six themes:

My personal world	Lifestyle and wellbeing	My neighbourhood
Media and technology	Studying and my future	Travel and tourism

There's also a 'General Stuff' topic in the book and online with content that's useful across the course.

2) In this book, these six themes have been split into ten sections to make things more manageable.
3) There are also three grammar sections that cover the grammar you need to know.
4) The resources on the CGP RevisionHub are split up in the same way as the book.

The CGP RevisionHub is full of resources

- You can use the online resources on the CGP RevisionHub alongside this book as you're revising.
- There's audio, quick quizzes and summary tests, as well as printable vocab lists, transcripts and practice papers.

There are resources for Foundation tier and Higher tier on the CGP RevisionHub. The Hub is automatically set to Higher, but you can switch to Foundation to only see Foundation content.

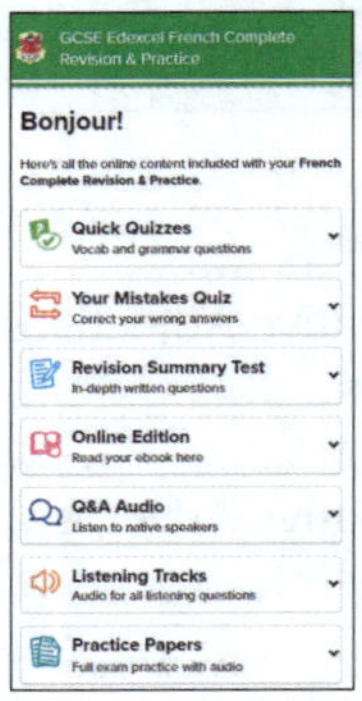

Revision Hub

Scan this QR code to access the CGP RevisionHub, or if you're on a computer, go to www.cgpbooks.co.uk/Merci.

Get exam-style practice

1) In your exams, you can sit Foundation-tier or Higher-tier papers.
2) In each tier, there are four papers: Listening, Speaking, Reading and Writing. You have to choose the same tier for all four papers.

For more about the exams, see p.185-188.

- In Foundation tier, there's less vocabulary and less grammar to learn and the questions are slightly easier. In this tier, you can earn up to Grade 5.
- In Higher tier, you can achieve Grades 4-9, but you'll need to learn more vocab and more complex grammar.

3) Throughout this book, there's practice for all the question types in the exam. Plus, there are full Higher-tier practice papers on pages 189-223. These can also be found on the CGP RevisionHub alongside Foundation-tier practice papers.

Practice Papers

4) Most of this book is helpful for both tiers, but some vocab and questions have been marked with a bracket if they only apply to one tier.

Higher		
	le public	*public, audience*
	représenter	*to represent*
	la critique	*criticism, review*

H		
	le lieu	*place*
	la bibliothèque	*library*

5) If you aren't sure which tier to take, trying out the questions should help you and your teacher make a decision.

Learn the set vocabulary

- The Edexcel specification contains a list of words you could be tested on in your Listening and Reading papers, depending on your tier.
- This vocab will also help you in your Speaking and Writing papers. In these two papers, you can use non-specification vocab, too.
- The key vocab is on the main pages of each section. At the end of each section, there's a list of all the vocab relevant to the topic. Every word on the specification is on at least one of these lists.
- There are printable versions of these lists on the CGP RevisionHub.

Practise your listening skills

1) In this book, you'll find questions and example answers:

Q&A Audio

Question	Simple Answer	Extended Answer
Qu'est-ce que tu penses de la musique classique ? *What do you think of classical music?*	J'adore ça — c'est extraordinaire. *I love it — it's extraordinary.*	Je ne m'intéresse pas à la musique classique parce qu'à mon avis, c'est ennuyeux. *I'm not interested in classical music because, in my opinion, it's boring.*

Scan the QR code to hear the sentences out loud and to practise your pronunciation.

2) There are also QR codes that take you to Listening Tracks. Each track comes with questions that test you on what you've heard.

Test your knowledge

Quick Quizzes

- The QR codes at the top of the page take you to a quick quiz.
- These quizzes test you on the vocab (or the grammar in Sections 11-13) on that page.
- They're a great way to keep your knowledge fresh.
- You can easily revisit questions that you answer incorrectly by doing the 'Your Mistakes' quiz.

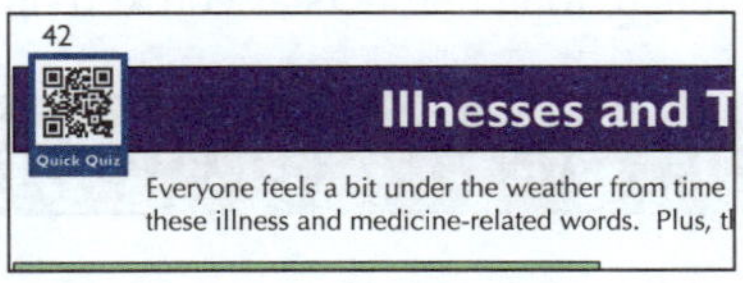

Revision Summary Tests

- For more of a challenge, try a revision summary test. These are found at the end of each section.
- These tests cover the most important information in a topic and are a good way to see how much you can remember.
- You can do these tests on paper or you can complete them online. Online, you can find sample answers, assess your progress, and look at previous topics to see the areas you need to work on.

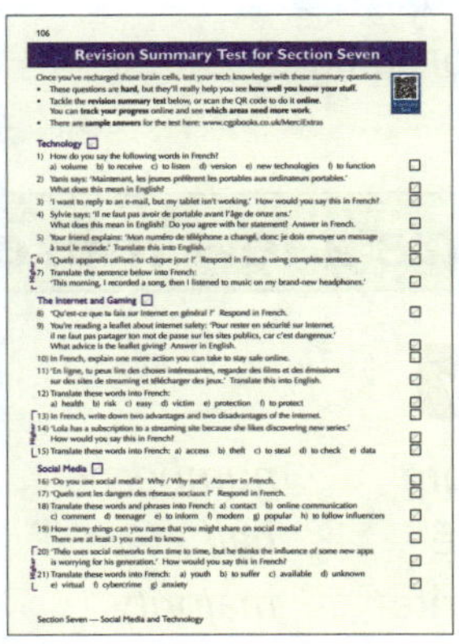

Fun fact — if you rearrange the letters of 'RevisionHub', you get...

...'SnoivierUbh', which makes no sense. But do you know what *does* make sense? Using the RevisionHub alongside this book — it'll help you to get the most out of your revision and impress all those examiners.

Numbers and Times

Quick Quiz

Knowing how numbers and times work in French is important — they're not as simple as in English.

Remember there's also lots of online content here: www.cgpbooks.co.uk/Merci

Un, deux, trois — One, two, three

Vocabulary

0	zéro	*10*	dix
1	un	*11*	onze
2	deux	*12*	douze
3	trois	*13*	treize
4	quatre	*14*	quatorze
5	cinq	*15*	quinze
6	six	*16*	seize
7	sept	*17*	dix-sept
8	huit	*18*	dix-huit
9	neuf	*19*	dix-neuf

11 to 16 all end in 'ze'. But 17, 18 and 19 are 'ten-seven' etc.

Except 'vingt', most of the 'tens' end in 'nte'. Also, '70' is 'sixty-ten', '80' is 'four-twenties', and '90' is 'four-twenty-ten'.

20	vingt
30	trente
40	quarante
50	cinquante
60	soixante
70	soixante-dix
80	quatre-vingts
90	quatre-vingt-dix

21	vingt et un
22	vingt-deux
23	vingt-trois

In-between numbers are formed like English ones, but add 'et un' for numbers ending in '1'.

Grammar — 'un' / 'une'

For feminine nouns, use 'une' and 'et une' instead of 'un' and 'et un':

Il y a vingt et une filles et vingt et un garçons.
There are twenty-one girls and twenty-one boys.

71	soixante et onze	*91*	quatre-vingt-onze
72	soixante-douze	*98*	quatre-vingt-dix-huit

For the 70s and 90s, add 11-19 to 'soixante' and 'quatre-vingt' (like 'quatre-vingts' (*80*) but without the 's'). '81' and '91' miss out the 'et', e.g. quatre-vingt-un (*81*).

100	cent	*10 000*	dix mille
1000	mille	*1 000 000*	un million

In French, long numbers are broken up by full stops or spaces instead of commas.

623	six cent vingt-trois
1947	mille neuf cent quarante-sept

For hundreds and thousands, put cent, deux cent, mille (etc.) before the number.

Add '-ième' to the number to say second, third, etc.

Use 'premier' for masculine nouns and 'première' for feminine ones.

Numbers ending in 'e' lose the e.

A 'u' is added to 'cinq'.

The 'f' in 'neuf' changes to a 'v'.

1st	premier / première	*4th*	quatrième	*7th*	septième	*10th*	dixième
2nd	deuxième	*5th*	cinquième	*8th*	huitième	*99th*	quatre-vingt-dix-neuvième
3rd	troisième	*6th*	sixième	*9th*	neuvième	*100th*	centième

Here are a few more handy number words...

Vocabulary

le nombre	*number*
la moitié	*half*
la majorité	*majority*
la plupart (de)	*most (of)*
une dizaine	*about ten*
une centaine	*about a hundred*
environ	*about, approximately*
compter	*to count*

(Higher: la plupart (de) – compter)

J'ai compté environ six chiens.	*I counted about six dogs.*
Le nombre d'habitants a augmenté.	*The number of residents has increased.*
Il a une dizaine de tableaux.	*He has about ten paintings.*
Un tiers des étudiants étudient l'anglais. Un quart étudient les sciences.	*A third of the students are studying English. A quarter are studying science.*

Quelle heure est-il ? — What time is it?

1) There are different ways to tell the time in French. Make sure you learn all of them. To say 'it's...o'clock', use 'il est...heure(s)'.

Il est une heure.	*It's 1 o'clock.*	Il est vingt heures.	*It's 8 pm.*

The French use the 24-hour clock a lot — so make sure you can use it.

2) To say '...minutes past', you say the hour, then the number of minutes. You don't need any extra words.

Il est trois heures douze.	*It's 03:12.*
Il est vingt heures trente-trois.	*It's 20:33.*

To say 'in the evening' without referring to a specific hour of the day, just say 'le soir'. E.g. 'Le soir, j'ai dormi.' (*In the evening, I slept.*) The same rule applies for 'in the morning' and 'in the afternoon'.

3) Use 'moins...' (*less*) to say '...to'.

Il est onze heures moins dix.	*It's ten to eleven.*

Grammar — 'à' with times

You use 'à' with times to say 'at'.

à dix heures ***at ten o'clock***

4) Use this vocab to say 'quarter past', 'half past' and 'quarter to'.

Vocabulary

et quart	*quarter past*
et demie	*half past*
moins le quart	*quarter to*
du matin	*in the morning*
de l'après-midi	*in the afternoon*
du soir	*in the evening*
le midi	*midday, lunchtime*
la nuit	*night*
minuit	*midnight*
la minute	*minute*
la seconde	*second*

Il est deux heures et quart.	*It's quarter past two.*
Il est deux heures et demie.	*It's half past two.*
Il est trois heures moins le quart.	*It's quarter to three.*
Il est six heures du soir.	*It's six in the evening.*
Je reviens dans une minute.	*I'll be back in a minute.*

'Demi' needs to agree with the gender of the noun before. 'Heures' is feminine, so you add an 'e' to make it 'demie'.

Practice Questions

Q1 Read this activity board for a summer camp, then answer the questions in English. READING

Foot : *quinze heures quarante-cinq*
Musique : *treize heures trente*
Théâtre : *dix-neuf heures quinze*
Natation : *seize heures cinquante*
Cours de cinéma : *vingt heures*

a) At what time does swimming start? *[1 mark]*
b) Which activity happens last? *[1 mark]*
c) Which activity starts before football? *[1 mark]*
d) Which activity happens in between swimming and film class? *[1 mark]*

Q2 Listen to these four sentences and write down ***in French*** *exactly what you hear.* *[8 marks]* LISTENING

Listening Track 1

Don't forget to be on time for your exams...

Being able to use numbers and times in French will prove really handy — it's the kind of thing that comes up again and again in a lot of topics. They can seem daunting at first, so practise them until they get easier.

Quick Quiz

Days and Dates

Dates are essential for your exam — make sure you know how to talk about them in French.

Les jours (m) de la semaine — The days of the week

In French, the days of the week are always lower case. They're also all masculine.

Vocabulary

lundi	*Monday*
mardi	*Tuesday*
mercredi	*Wednesday*
jeudi	*Thursday*
vendredi	*Friday*
samedi	*Saturday*
dimanche	*Sunday*
aujourd'hui	*today*

Grammar — 'le lundi' (Mondays)

To say something happens regularly on a certain day, use the masculine definite article ('le') with the day — not a plural.

Le lundi, je fais du sport.

On Mondays, I do sport.

To say something happened on one specific day, you don't need the article.

Jeudi, j'ai acheté un vélo.

On Thursday, I bought a bike.

le jour / la journée	*day*
demain	*tomorrow*
hier	*yesterday*
la semaine	*week*
le week-end	*weekend*
la veille (Higher)	*the night before, eve*
le lendemain (Higher)	*next day*
quotidien(ne) (Higher)	*daily*

À mardi ! — *See you on Tuesday!*

Vendredi, j'ai fait mes devoirs, donc aujourd'hui je peux me relaxer. — *On Friday, I did my homework, so today I can relax.*

Je vais à la synagogue avec ma mère le week-end. — *I go to the synagogue with my mother at the weekend.* (*during the week* — pendant la semaine)

Elle voit son père le dimanche. — *She sees her father on Sundays.* (*every day* — tous les jours)

Les mois (m) de l'année — The months of the year

Months and seasons are masculine and don't begin with capital letters.

Vocabulary

janvier	*January*	juillet	*July*
février	*February*	août	*August*
mars	*March*	septembre	*September*
avril	*April*	octobre	*October*
mai	*May*	novembre	*November*
juin	*June*	décembre	*December*

l'an (m) / l'année (f)	*year*
il y a (cinq ans)	*(five years) ago*
la saison	*season*
le printemps	*spring*
l'été (m)	*summer*
l'automne (m)	*autumn*
l'hiver (m)	*winter*

To say 'in + a season', you say 'en hiver', 'en été', and 'en automne'. But watch out — 'in spring' is 'au printemps'.

Q&A Audio

Question

As-tu une saison préférée ?

Do you have a favourite season?

Simple Answer

Oui, j'aime l'hiver parce que j'adore la neige.

Yes, I like winter because I love snow.

Extended Answer

Oui, je trouve l'hiver très agréable parce que j'aime beaucoup les traditions de cette période. Mon anniversaire est en janvier, donc c'est une saison que j'apprécie beaucoup.

Yes, I find winter really nice because I like the traditions of this period a lot. My birthday is in January, so it's a season that I really appreciate.

Quelle est la date ? — What's the date?

In French, you say 'the nine April' or 'the seventeen November'. The exception to this rule is the first day of a month, where you use 'le premier' (*the first*), like you would in English.

Aujourd'hui c'est le quinze mai.	*Today is the 15th May.*
Mon frère est né le vingt-cinq février deux mille dix.	*My brother was born on the 25th February 2010.*

the 1st August — le premier août

in the 90s — dans les années quatre-vingt-dix

in 2006 — en deux mille six

Faire des projets (m) — Making plans

These words are really useful for making arrangements... and for your exams.

Vocabulary

le matin	*morning*
le midi	*midday, lunchtime*
l'après-midi (m)	*afternoon*
le soir	*evening*
la nuit	*night*

Grammar — forming adverbs

To form adverbs in French, you normally add '-ment' to the feminine form of the adjective (see p.159):

seule ➔ **seulement** ***(only)***

générale ➔ **généralement** ***(generally)***

Qu'est-ce que tu fais ce matin ?	*What are you doing this morning?*
Le soir, je vais souvent au cinéma.	*In the evening, I often go to the cinema.*
La semaine prochaine, je vais danser.	*Next week, I'm going to dance.*
Je suis rarement en retard.	*I am rarely late.*

this weekend — ce week-end

This afternoon — Cet après-midi

Practice Questions

Q1 *Write to your friend about your week.*
*Write between 80 and 90 words **in French**.*
*You **must** include the following points:*

- *what you are doing today*
- *your opinion of winter with reasons*
- *what you did last weekend*
- *what you will do tomorrow.* *[18 marks]*

WRITING

Top Tip for Higher Students
✓ Use the proper future tense to talk about what you will do tomorrow.

Higher

Q2 *Listen to these announcements made in a French school, then answer the questions in English.*

LISTENING

a) On what date will the show take place? *[1 mark]*
b) In which month do the exams finish? *[1 mark]*
c) On which days do language classes take place? *[1 mark]*
d) When was the school established? *[1 mark]*

Listening Track 2

In French, you say 'the four June' instead of 'the fourth of June'...

Adding in a day or a date can be a great way to make your answers more detailed. But be sure to match your tenses to your time phrases — if you say something happened last week, you'll need the past tense.

Quick Quiz

Questions

Knowing how to ask questions is key in any language. And it's not just the words that matter...

Poser des questions (f) — Asking questions

Vocabulary

la question	*question*	combien ?	*how much / many?*
quand ?	*when?*	qui ?	*who?*
pourquoi ?	*why?*	quoi ?	*what?*
où ?	*where?*	que / qu' ?	*what?*
comment ?	*how?*	quel / quelle ?	*which?*

These are known as interrogatives.

'It's behind you!'

Qui vient avec moi ? *Who's coming with me?*

Où est la plage ? *Where is the beach?*

Ask questions by changing your tone of voice

1) The easiest way to ask a question in French is to say a normal sentence, but make your voice go up at the end.

Le pain coûte combien ? *How much is the bread?*

C'est loin ? *Is it far?*

In writing, the only difference between this question and the statement 'C'est loin.' (*It's far.*) is the question mark.

Higher

2) To answer 'yes' to a question containing a negative, use 'si'.

Tu n'as pas faim ? — Si, j'ai faim. *Aren't you hungry? — Yes, I'm hungry.*

Ask questions by putting the verb after the question word

When the sentence starts with a question word, you can also swap the verb and the subject (the person or thing doing the action) around. Don't forget to add a hyphen between the verb and the subject pronoun.

Pourquoi es-tu en retard ?	*Why are you late?*
Où travailles-tu ?	*Where do you work?*
Qui est-il ?	*Who is he?*
Qu'as-tu mangé ?	*What did you eat?*

If the verb ends in a vowel and is followed by 'il', 'elle' or 'on', you add a 't' to make it easier to say.

Quand a-t-il fini ses devoirs ?
When did he finish his homework?

Ask questions using 'est-ce que' or 'qu'est-ce que'

1) You can turn a statement into a yes or no question by using 'est-ce que'.

Est-ce que tu as des frères et sœurs ? *Do you have any brothers or sisters?*

Est-ce que tu aimes jouer au tennis ? *Do you like playing tennis?*

2) You usually use 'qu'est-ce que' if your question starts with 'what'.

Qu'est-ce que tu fais le samedi ? *What do you do on Saturdays?*

Qu'est-ce que c'est ? — What is it?

Here are some useful questions that you might want to ask:

Quelle heure **est-il** ?	*What time **is it**?*
Pendant **combien de temps** ?	*For **how long**?*
D'où vient votre famille ?	*Where is your family from?*
Qu'est-ce que vous avez **dit** ?	*What did you **say**?*
À quelle heure tu voudrais aller à la fête ?	***At what time** would you like to go to the party?*

how many days — combien de jours

do — fait
ask — demandé

Grammar — prepositions

You can use a preposition before a question word, e.g.

Avec qui habites-tu ?
Who do you live with?

'C'est' can also be used to form lots of different questions:

C'est de quelle couleur ?	*What colour is it?*
C'est **combien** ?	***How much** is it?*
C'est quelle date aujourd'hui ?	*What is the date today?*
C'est quel jour **de la semaine** ?	*What day **of the week** is it?*

When — quand
Who — qui
Where — où

Q&A Audio

Question
D'où viens-tu ?
Where are you from?

Simple Answer
Je viens de Millom.
I'm from Millom.

Extended Answer
Je viens de Millom, dans le nord-ouest du pays. J'habite dans une petite ville tranquille.
I'm from Millom, in the north-west of the country. I live in a small, quiet town.

Practice Questions

Q1 Imagine you are at a restaurant with your friend. Ask the following questions out loud in French. SPEAKING

- *Ask what time the restaurant closes.*
- *Ask your friend if they want chips.*
- *Ask how much an ice cream costs.*
- *Ask where the toilets are.* *[4 marks]*

Higher

Q2 You are interviewing some teachers for a school project. Write a list of questions in French that you will use for the interviews. You should find out: WRITING

- *how long they have been a teacher for*
- *where they work*
- *what subject they teach*
- *why they like being a teacher*
- *what their favourite part of the school day is.* *[10 marks]*

You'll have to ask questions in the role-play part of the exam...

...so make sure you know how to form them in French. This page covers lots of different ways to ask questions — practise coming up with some for all the topics until you've got them down. Fantastique.

Quick Quiz

Being Polite

Politeness makes a big difference — not everyone you talk to will be a friend. Here's a run-down of how to adjust your speech in different situations to make it more or less formal.

Bonjour...au revoir — Hello...goodbye

Learn these phrases — they're crucial.

Vocabulary

bonjour	*hello*	ça va (bien)	*I am good / well*
salut	*hi, bye*	voici	*here*
bonsoir	*good evening*	monsieur	*sir, mister, Mr*
au revoir	*goodbye, bye*	madame	*madam, Mrs*
(comment) ça va ?	*how are you?*	à bientôt	*see you soon*

Stephen practised his French by greeting himself every morning.

Comment ça va ? — How are you?

Comment ça va ?	*How are you? (informal)*
Je me sens super bien.	*I feel super.*
Pas mal.	*Not bad.*
Félicitations pour votre succès !	*Congratulations on your success!*
Bienvenue à l'hôtel.	*Welcome to the hotel.*
Voici votre chambre.	*Here is your room.*
À bientôt !	*See you soon!*
À tout à l'heure.	*See you later.*
Bonne journée !	*Have a good day!*

How are you? (formal) — Comment allez-vous?

awful — très mal

well — bien

Grammar — using 'tu' and 'vous'

There are two ways of saying 'you' in French.

- 'Tu' is singular and informal. You should use it with a friend or family member.
- 'Vous' is for more than one person, or for one person in a formal situation, e.g. a stranger or someone older than you.

The conversation below shows some common phrases in use:

Madame Rollet:	Bonjour Nour, comment ça va ?	*Hello Nour, how are you?*
Nour:	Ça va bien. Comment allez-vous ?	*I'm fine. How are you?*
Madame Rollet:	Pas mal, merci.	*Not bad, thanks.*
Nour:	Est-ce que je peux vous présenter Sahil ?	*May I introduce Sahil?*
Madame Rollet:	Enchantée. Ça va ?	*Pleased to meet you. How are you?*
Sahil:	Ça ne va pas très bien.	*I'm not very well.*
Madame Rollet:	Pourquoi ?	*Why?*
Sahil:	Je me sens un peu triste aujourd'hui.	*I feel a bit sad today.*

Nour uses the polite 'vous' form — Madame Rollet is older than her.

If you're talking to someone you call 'tu', say 'est-ce que je peux te présenter' — it's informal.

Je voudrais... — I would like...

1) '<u>Je voudrais</u>' (*I would like*) is <u>more polite</u> than '<u>je veux</u>' (*I want*).

Je voudrais un verre d'eau.	*I would like a glass of water.*
Je voudrais du pain.	*I would like some bread.*

He would like — Il voudrait
She would like — Elle voudrait

'Je voudrais' is in the conditional tense — see p.173 for more.

2) '<u>Est-ce que je peux...</u>' means '<u>Can I...</u>' or '<u>May I...</u>'.

Est-ce que je peux m'asseoir ?	*Can I sit down?*

See p.8-9 for more about forming questions.

S'il vous plaît — Please

Don't forget these useful <u>polite words</u> — they could make all the difference...

Vocabulary

s'il te plaît	*please (informal)*	d'accord	*OK*
s'il vous plaît	*please (formal)*	attention	*attention*
merci (beaucoup)	*thank you (very much)*	désolé(e)	*sorry*
de rien	*you are welcome*	H (quel) dommage	*(what a) pity*

Don't forget to say 's'il te plaît' instead of 's'il vous plaît' if you're talking to someone you call 'tu.'

Grammar — 'désolé' or 'désolée'?

'désolé' has to <u>agree</u> with the <u>subject</u>.
Je suis désol<u>é</u>. *I'm sorry.* (male)

You add an extra '<u>e</u>' if you're female:
Je suis désol<u>ée</u>. *I'm sorry.* (female)

Practice Questions

Q1 *Read the following email that Amelia has written to her party planner, then answer the questions below.*

READING

Bonsoir ! Je voudrais organiser une grande fête pour l'anniversaire de mon mari. Je voudrais de la musique, un gâteau et des tables dans le jardin pour l'événement. Est-ce qu'on peut aussi danser à la fin de la soirée, s'il vous plaît ? Merci !

a) What occasion is the party celebrating? *[1 mark]*
b) What food would Amelia like to order for the party? *[1 mark]*
c) Where does Amelia want the tables to be put? *[1 mark]*
d) What will happen at the end of the party? *[1 mark]*

Q2 *Write a script about two people informally meeting and introducing themselves for the first time. Write about 50 words in French. Then edit your script to make it more formal. Make sure your two characters:*

WRITING

- *greet one another*
- *introduce themselves*
- *ask one another how they're doing.* *[10 marks]*

Top Tip for Higher Students
✓ Try to include some Higher-only adjectives to show off your vocabulary.

Knowing how to use 'tu' and 'vous' correctly is important...

You don't want to begin every conversation on the wrong foot. Being able to adjust the politeness and formality of your language depending on who you're talking to is a useful skill to have under your belt.

Quick Quiz

Opinions

Having an opinion is a great way to pick up lots of marks in the exam, so don't hold back on giving your views. Just make sure that you use a cracking variety of phrases to really impress the examiner.

Qu'est-ce que tu penses de... ? — What do you think of...?

There are lots of ways to ask someone their opinion in French.

Vocabulary

l'opinion (f)	*opinion*
l'avis (m)	*opinion*
le côté	*side*
l'idée (f)	*idea*
la pensée (Higher)	*thought*
selon (Higher)	*according to*
d'un côté (Higher)	*on one hand*
d'un autre côté (Higher)	*on the other hand*

Qu'est-ce que tu penses de cette chanson ?	*What do you think of this song?*
Quel est ton avis sur cette émission ?	*What's your opinion of this TV show?*
Est-que je peux te poser une question sur le sport ?	*Can I ask you a question about sport?*
Selon toi, quelle est la meilleure saison ?	*In your opinion, what is the best season?*

Speak your mind — it'll sound impressive

Vocabulary

oui	*yes*	aimer	*to like*
non	*no*	préférer	*to prefer*
absolument	*absolutely*	détester	*to hate*
peut-être	*maybe, perhaps*	apprécier (H)	*to appreciate*
ça m'est égal	*I'm not bothered*	exprimer (H)	*to express*
adorer	*to love*		

Be careful — 'j'aime Pierre' can mean 'I like Pierre' OR 'I love Pierre'. If you only like him, it's safer to say 'je trouve Pierre sympa' (*I think Pierre is nice*) or 'j'aime bien Pierre' (*I like Pierre*). Otherwise you might be giving out the wrong message...

J'aime bien lire.	*I like reading.*
Je m'intéresse à la musique.	*I'm interested in music.*
Je déteste vraiment danser.	*I absolutely hate dancing.*
Tu es d'accord avec moi ?	*Do you agree with me?*
Non, à mon avis le shopping en ligne est moins pratique qu'aller dans les magasins.	*No, in my opinion online shopping is less practical than going to shops.*

I'm not interested in — Je ne m'intéresse pas à

with that — avec ça

in my view — selon moi

Parce que — Because

The best way to justify your opinion is to give a reason.

Vocabulary

parce que	*because*
car	*because*

J'aime ce film parce que les acteurs sont formidables.	*I like this film because the actors are terrific.*
Je trouve ce film nul car l'histoire est ennuyeuse.	*I think this film is rubbish because the story is boring.*

Use describing words to explain your opinions

Here are some describing words that you can use to explain your opinion. If you don't have an opinion on something, just make one up. There aren't any marks available for shrugging...

Vocabulary

bon(ne)	*good*	étonnant(e)	*surprising, amazing, incredible*
génial(e)	*great*	ennuyeux / ennuyeuse	*boring*
préféré(e)	*favourite*	triste	*sad*
excellent(e)	*excellent*	mauvais(e)	*bad*
passionnant(e)	*exciting*	seul(e)	*alone, lonely, only*
amusant(e)	*funny, fun*	H bref / brève	*brief*
intéressant(e)	*interesting*	H précédent(e)	*previous, preceding*
certain(e)	*certain*		
clair(e)	*clear*		

Je pense que c'est très intéressant. — *I think that it's very interesting.*

J'aime bien cette série. Je trouve l'histoire passionnante et elle me touche beaucoup. — *I like this series. I find the story exciting and it moves me a lot.*

Grammar — 'ce'/'cette'/'cet'

'Ce' (*this / that*) becomes 'cette' in front of feminine nouns. For masculine nouns starting with a vowel, you use 'cet'. See p.157 for more info.

Q&A Audio

Question

Qu'est-ce que tu penses de la musique classique ?

What do you think of classical music?

Simple Answer

J'adore ça — c'est extraordinaire.

I love it — it's extraordinary.

Extended Answer

Je ne m'intéresse pas à la musique classique parce qu'à mon avis, c'est ennuyeux.

I'm not interested in classical music because, in my opinion, it's boring.

Practice Questions

Q1 *Listen to this recording from your French partner school. Blandine and Marc are talking about what they do at the weekend. Decide whether the statements below are true or false.*

LISTENING

Listening Track 3

a) i) Blandine has fun with her sports team. *[1 mark]*

ii) Marc dislikes all sports. *[1 mark]*

b) i) The book Marc is reading is boring. *[1 mark]*

ii) Blandine often reads novels. *[1 mark]*

c) i) Blandine likes different kinds of films. *[1 mark]*

ii) Marc enjoys watching action films. *[1 mark]*

Q2 *Answer the following questions out loud in French. You should talk for about 20 seconds for each question.*

SPEAKING

- *Quel est ton film préféré et pourquoi ?*
- *Que penses-tu de ton école ?*
- *Qui est ton chanteur ou groupe préféré ?* *[6 marks]*

Top Tips for Higher Students
✓ Give two details for each answer.
✓ Use Higher-tier adjectives.

Always make sure you can justify your opinions...

Giving your opinion is a fantastic way to pick up extra marks. You can use adjectives to support your opinions with reasoning — if you say you like or dislike something, try to explain why that's the case.

Speaking Questions

Here are four pages of brilliant exam practice that will prepare you for each of the GCSE French papers.

For the Speaking Question pages, you'll need a friend or a parent to read the teacher's role. Before the conversation starts, read through the candidate's material and think about what you're going to say.

Candidate's Material

Myriam has sent you some information about her life.
Read out the text below to your teacher.

Foundation

Je visite une université dans le nord de l'Angleterre.

Je veux devenir étudiante ici.

La majorité des professeurs sont géniaux.

L'année scolaire commence le neuf septembre.

Les bâtiments sont beaux mais ils sont assez petits.

Higher

Lundi prochain, c'est le premier jour du mois de mars.

Je préfère le printemps à l'hiver car il fait généralement moins froid.

Il y a un parc à environ dix minutes de chez moi,
où nous apprécions toujours les fleurs.

J'ai l'intention d'y aller tous les jours, même s'il pleut.

- Once you have read the text, you will then be asked two questions related to what you have read.
- You are expected to say a few words or a short phrase/sentence in response to each question. One-word answers will not be sufficient to gain full marks.

Teacher's Material

- Start by asking the candidate to read the text by saying '*Please read the text*'.
- Allow the candidate to read the text aloud, then ask the following two questions for their tier.
- Allow the student to develop their answers as much as possible.

F

- Qu'est-ce que tu aimes faire le week-end ?
- Qu'est-ce que tu penses de tes professeurs ?

H

- Est-ce que tu préfères quand il fait beau ou quand il fait froid ?
- Quel est ton avis sur l'été ?

Listening Questions

1 You are talking to your penfriend Nathan on the phone about his weekend. Listen to the recording and complete the following table.

Listening Track 4

		Number	
1 a	How many bags Nathan bought	....	*[1 mark]*
1 b	How many letters he sent	....	*[1 mark]*
1 c	How much money he spent	....	*[1 mark]*
1 d	How old his best friend turned	....	*[1 mark]*
1 e	How many presents his best friend received	....	*[1 mark]*

Higher

2 Listen to these two people giving their opinions on a celebrity. For each person, tick the correct statement.

Listening Track 5

2 a Sabrina is Léa's...

	A favourite actor.
	B favourite singer.
	C favourite rapper.

[1 mark]

2 b Léa says Sabrina's shows are always...

	A long.
	B loud.
	C extraordinary.

[1 mark]

2 c Rachid is not interested in Sabrina because he thinks that...

	A her work is not original.
	B her work is not appropriate.
	C she doesn't treat people well.

[1 mark]

2 d Rachid thinks that the main goal of all celebrities is to...

	A get famous.
	B follow their passions.
	C make money.

[1 mark]

Reading Questions

Foundation

1 Read these emails sent to a clothing company.

Eva: Est-ce que vous avez ce pantalon dans une plus grande taille ?
Luis: Est-ce qu'on peut acheter en ligne ? Vous acceptez les retours ?
Toni: Il y a une réduction pour les étudiants ?

What is each question about? Choose the correct answers.
Put a cross in the correct column for each question.

	Who...	**Eva**	**Luis**	**Toni**	
a)	... asks for a student discount?				*[1 mark]*
b)	... wants to know about returns?				*[1 mark]*
c)	... needs a bigger size?				*[1 mark]*
d)	... wants to shop online?				*[1 mark]*
e)	... is buying trousers?				*[1 mark]*

Higher

2 Read what Ana has written about her free time.
Put a cross in the correct box for each question.

Je fais souvent du sport pour garder la forme. Le mardi après-midi, je fais de la natation — je commence à dix-sept heures. J'aime aussi la musique. Dimanche prochain, je vais rencontrer mon groupe car nous donnerons un grand concert le dix-huit août. Je passe une grand partie de mon temps à lire. Aujourd'hui, j'ai fait une liste de quatorze livres que je veux acheter. Je lis environ quarante livres par an.

2 a Ana goes swimming...

	A on Saturday mornings.
	B on Tuesday afternoons.
	C at seven o'clock.

[1 mark]

2 b On 18th August,...

	A she will go to band practice.
	B she will watch a concert.
	C she will perform.

[1 mark]

2 c She says she...

	A reads fourteen books each month.
	B buys around forty books each year.
	C spends most of her time reading.

[1 mark]

Writing Questions

Foundation

1 Translate the following five sentences **into French**.

Use words to write out the full form of any numbers.

1 a I am organising a party on Sunday.

.... *[2 marks]*

1 b What time is it?

.... *[2 marks]*

1 c The party starts at 7pm on 12th June.

.... *[2 marks]*

1 d My friends are late — where are they?

.... *[2 marks]*

1 e How much does a cake cost?

.... *[2 marks]*

2 Write a letter to your French penfriend about your likes and dislikes.
You **must** include the following points:

- what you like to do in the evenings
- your opinion of reading with reasons
- what sports you have done recently
- what hobby you will take up next and why.

Write your answer **in French**. You should aim to write between 80 and 90 words. *[18 marks]*

Higher

3 Translate the paragraph **into French**.

> May I introduce my neighbour? She is ninety-nine years old. Previously, she didn't speak to me often. But recently she has started to come to see me each morning, and she invited me to a dinner party. She often tells me stories about her life, and I want to know more about her family and friends.

[10 marks]

General Stuff — Vocabulary

These pages are full of useful vocab that you'll find yourself using all the time, so make sure you've nailed the basics.

Numbers

le nombre	*number*
le numéro	*number*
zéro	*zero*
un	*one*
deux	*two*
trois	*three*
quatre	*four*
cinq	*five*
six	*six*
sept	*seven*
huit	*eight*
neuf	*nine*
dix	*ten*
onze	*eleven*
douze	*twelve*
treize	*thirteen*
quatorze	*fourteen*
quinze	*fifteen*
seize	*sixteen*
dix-sept	*seventeen*
dix-huit	*eighteen*
dix-neuf	*nineteen*

'Number' can be translated as 'nombre' or 'numéro', depending on the context. E.g. you say 'elle habite au <u>numéro</u> sept' (*she lives at number 7*), but 'le <u>nombre</u> de personnes a augmenté' (*the number of people has increased*).

Remember to add 'et un' to numbers ending in '1'.

vingt	*twenty*
vingt et un	*twenty-one*
vingt-deux	*twenty-two*
trente	*thirty*
quarante	*forty*
cinquante	*fifty*
soixante	*sixty*
soixante-dix	*seventy*
quatre-vingts	*eighty*
quatre-vingt-dix	*ninety*
cent	*a hundred*
mille	*a thousand*
le million	*a million*

premier / première	*first*
second(e)	*second*
deuxième	*second*
troisième	*third*
quatrième	*fourth*
cinquième	*fifth*
sixième	*sixth*
septième	*seventh*
huitième	*eighth*
neuvième	*ninth*
dixième	*tenth*
centième	*hundredth*
la moitié	*half*
le quart	*quarter*
la majorité	*majority*

Higher:

la plupart (de)	*most*
une dizaine	*about ten*
une centaine	*about a hundred*
le tiers	*third*
environ	*about, approximately*
compter	*to count*

Times

la période	*period*
l'heure (f)	*hour, o'clock*
(trois) heures (f)	*(three) o'clock*
et quart	*quarter past*
et demie	*half past*
moins le quart	*quarter to*
le matin	*morning*
le midi	*midday, lunchtime*
l'après-midi (m)	*afternoon*
le soir	*evening*
la nuit	*night*
minuit	*midnight*
la minute	*minute*
la seconde	*second*
tard	*late*

en retard	*late*
toujours	*always*
maintenant	*now*
en ce moment	*at the moment*
après	*after, afterwards*
avant	*before*
pendant	*during*
souvent	*often*
quelquefois	*sometimes*
de temps en temps	*from time to time*
normalement	*normally, usually*
généralement	*generally*
finalement	*finally*

longtemps	*a long time, a long while*

Higher:

la soirée	*evening, dinner party*
le moment	*moment*
enfin	*finally*
parfois	*sometimes*
d'habitude	*usually*
presque	*nearly*
immédiatement	*immediately*
auparavant	*previously, before, formerly*
désormais	*from now on*

Dates

la date	*date*
lundi	*Monday*
mardi	*Tuesday*
mercredi	*Wednesday*
jeudi	*Thursday*
vendredi	*Friday*
samedi	*Saturday*
dimanche	*Sunday*
aujourd'hui	*today*
le jour / la journée	*day*
demain	*tomorrow*
hier	*yesterday*
la semaine	*week*
le week-end	*weekend*
l'an (m) / l'année (f)	*year*
il y a (cinq ans)	*(five years) ago*

la saison	*season*
le printemps	*spring*
l'été (m)	*summer*
l'automne (m)	*autumn*
l'hiver (m)	*winter*
janvier	*January*
février	*February*
mars	*March*
avril	*April*
mai	*May*
juin	*June*
juillet	*July*
août	*August*
septembre	*September*
octobre	*October*
novembre	*November*
décembre	*December*
le mois	*month*

la fois	*time*
le présent	*present*
le passé	*past*
l'avenir (m)	*future*
le futur	*future*
bientôt	*soon*
dernier / dernière	*last*
prochain(e)	*next*
récent(e)	*recent*
récemment	*recently*
la veille (Higher)	*the night before, eve*
le siècle (Higher)	*century*
le lendemain (Higher)	*the next day, following day*
quotidien(ne) (Higher)	*daily*

Questions

la question	*question*
quand ?	*when?*
pourquoi ?	*why?*
où ?	*where?*
comment ?	*how?*
combien ?	*how much / many?, how long? (time)*

qui ?	*who?*
quoi ?	*what?*
que / qu' ?	*what?*
quel / quelle ?	*which?*
est-ce que, est-ce qu'	*expression put before a verb that makes a sentence into a question*

Being Polite

bonjour	*hello*
salut	*hi, bye*
bonsoir	*good evening*
au revoir	*goodbye, bye*
(comment) ça va ?	*how are you?*
ça va (bien)	*I'm good / well*
bien	*well, a lot*
mal	*badly*
voici	*here*
monsieur	*sir, mister, Mr*

madame	*madam, Mrs*
s'il te plaît	*please (informal)*
s'il vous plaît	*please (formal)*
merci (beaucoup)	*thank you (very much)*
de rien	*you are welcome*
d'accord	*OK*
désolé(e)	*sorry*
attention	*attention*
à bientôt	*see you soon*
H (quel) dommage	*(what a) pity*

General Stuff — Vocabulary

Opinions

l'opinion (f)	*opinion*
l'avis (m)	*opinion*
le côté	*side*
l'idée (f)	*idea*
oui	*yes*
ouais	*yeah*
bien sûr	*of course*
non	*no*
la raison	*reason, right, correct*
le tort	*wrong, incorrect*
l'espoir (m)	*hope*
le plaisir	*pleasure*
la grâce	*grace*
probablement	*probably*
absolument	*absolutely*
peut-être	*maybe, perhaps*

'Right' and 'wrong' are adjectives in English, but they're nouns in French. They're used with 'avoir', e.g. 'il a tort' (*he is wrong*).

malheureusement	*unfortunately*
ça m'est égal	*I'm not bothered, I don't mind*
parce que	*because*
car	*because*
Higher:	
si	*yes (in response to a negative question)*
la pensée	*thought*
le doute	*doubt*
la peur	*fear, fright*
contraire	*contrary (adj.)*
selon	*according to*
d'un côté	*on one hand*
d'un autre côté	*on the other hand*
c'est-à-dire	*in other words, that is to say*

Opinions — Verbs

adorer	*to love*
aimer	*to like*
préférer	*to prefer*
détester	*to hate*
s'intéresser à	*to be interested (in)*
penser (à)	*to think (of)*
poser	*to pose (a question)*
trouver	*to find*
H: apprécier	*to appreciate*
H: noter	*to note, notice*
Higher: concerner	*to concern, be relevant to*
Higher: raconter	*to tell*
Higher: exprimer	*to express*
Higher: s'exprimer	*to express oneself*

Useful Adjectives

bon(ne)	*good*
génial(e)	*great*
préféré(e)	*favourite*
parfait(e)	*perfect*
excellent(e)	*excellent*
passionnant(e)	*exciting*
extraordinaire	*extraordinary*
amusant(e)	*funny, fun*
intéressant(e)	*interesting*
heureux / heureuse	*happy, lucky, fortunate*
content(e)	*glad, pleased, happy*
certain(e)	*certain*
clair(e)	*clear*
étonnant(e)	*surprising, amazing, incredible*
ennuyeux / ennuyeuse	*boring*
triste	*sad*
mauvais(e)	*bad*
nul(le)	*rubbish, bad*
terrible	*terrible*
seul(e)	*alone, lonely, only*
gros(se)	*big, large, lots of*
large	*large, wide, big*
double	*double*
maximum	*maximum*
minimum	*minimum*
final(e)	*final*
inclus(e)	*included*
H: bref / brève	*brief*
H: précédent(e)	*previous, preceding*

Useful Nouns

l'affaire (f)	*matter*
les affaires (f)	*belongings, things*
le cas	*case*
la chose	*thing*
le début	*beginning, start*
la décision	*decision*
la définition	*definition*
le détail	*detail*
la difficulté	*difficulty, issue, problem*
l'émotion (f)	*emotion, feelings*
l'exemple (m)	*example*
la fin	*end*
l'importance (f)	*importance*
l'instant (m)	*instant, moment*
le lien	*link*
la liste	*list*
la manière	*manner, way*
le moyen	*means, way*
l'ordre (m)	*order*
la partie	*part*
la possibilité	*possibility*
le sens	*sense, meaning, direction*
la situation	*situation*
la sorte	*sort, kind, type*
le système	*system*
le truc	*thing*
la vérité	*truth*

Higher:

l'accent (m)	*accent*
l'article (m)	*article*
l'aspect (m)	*aspect*
l'expression (f)	*expression*
la façon	*way*
l'intention (f)	*intention*
la mémoire	*memory*
l'origine (f)	*origin*
la parole	*speech, word, speaking*
la perte	*loss, waste*
le reste	*rest, remainder*
le sourire	*smile*

Useful Verbs

changer	*to change*
croire	*to believe*
décrire	*to describe*
dépendre de	*to depend on*
devenir	*to become*
dire	*to say, tell*
espérer	*to hope*
finir	*to finish*
laisser	*to let, leave behind*
mettre	*to put*
oublier	*to forget*
prononcer	*to pronounce*
proposer (de)	*to propose (to), suggest*
rendre	*to return, hand in, give back*

Higher:

appartenir	*to belong*
apporter	*to bring (something)*
s'asseoir	*to sit*
créer	*to create*
décevoir	*to disappoint*
s'occuper (de)	*to look after, take care (of)*
oser	*to dare*
produire	*to produce*
remercier	*to thank*
signifier	*to mean*
souhaiter	*to wish*
sourire	*to smile*
tenir	*to hold*
toucher	*to touch, affect*

Useful Phrases

il y a	*there is / there are*
il y aura	*there will be*
il y avait	*there was / there were*
il faut	*it is, it's necessary, must*
je suis d'accord avec	*I agree with*
grâce à	*thanks to*
avoir...ans	*to be...years old*
vouloir dire	*to mean*
qu'est-ce qui ne va pas ?	*what's wrong?*
à l'arrière plan	*in the background*
au premier plan	*in the foreground*

Higher:

il est (difficile) de	*it is (difficult) to*
il manque	*it is missing*
il vaut la peine de	*it is worth*
il vaut mieux	*it is better (to)*

Revision Summary Test for Section One

Put your knowledge of the basics to the test with these summary questions for Section One.

- These questions are **hard**, but they'll really help you see **how well you know your stuff**.
- Tackle the **revision summary test** below, or scan the QR code to do it **online**.
  You can **track your progress** online and see **which areas need more work**.
- There are **sample answers** for the test here: www.cgpbooks.co.uk/MerciExtras

Summary Test

Numbers and Times

1) In words, write the numbers 0-20 in French.
2) Write down the French for these numbers:
   a) fifty-two b) seventy-four c) ninety-three d) five hundred and eighty e) six thousand
3) How would you say the following words in French? a) first b) fourth c) ninth d) tenth
4) Say the current time in French. Then write the French for each of these times:
   a) 11:30 am b) 18:00 c) 20:47 d) 10 pm e) 00:00
5) Translate this sentence into French: 'It is four in the afternoon, so I must leave now, or I am going to be late.'
6) What do the words below mean in English?
   a) une centaine b) immédiatement c) environ d) la plupart (de) e) compter f) parfois

Days and Dates

7) List the days of the week in French. Then list them again, backwards.
8) Give all of the months of the year in French, then list the four seasons.
9) What do these words and phrases mean in English?
   a) l'avenir b) la fois c) il y a quatre ans d) hier e) la semaine f) prochain
10) 'C'est quand, l'anniversaire de ton meilleur ami ?' Write your answer in words and in French.
11) What is the French for these words and phrases?
    a) century b) the next day c) the night before d) daily e) dinner party f) from now on

Questions

12) Your French friend is hosting a party. Ask them some questions to find out where and when the party is, who is coming, and what you should bring.
13) What do these questions mean in English?
    a) Pourquoi tu manges ?
    b) Où est-ce que tu manges ?
    c) Qu'est-ce que tu manges ?
    d) Quand est-ce que tu manges ?
    e) Avec qui manges-tu ?
    f) Quel légume manges-tu ?

Being Polite

14) What's the French for the following phrases? a) see you soon b) see you tomorrow c) I'm sorry
15) Write down a short conversation between two people in French. Have them say hello to each other, ask each other how they are and then say goodbye.
16) What's the English for these phrases? a) merci beaucoup b) bonsoir monsieur c) s'il vous plaît
17) Translate these words and phrases into French: a) hi b) you are welcome c) OK

Opinions

18) In French, give five adjectives you could use to express a positive opinion and five adjectives you could use to express a negative opinion.
19) Translate these phrases about opinions on sport into French:
    a) I love playing sport.
    b) I prefer sport to music.
    c) I'm interested in sport.
    d) I don't like sport.
    e) She plays football well.
    f) I find football exciting.
20) Answer this question in French: 'Quel est ton avis sur les films d'action ?'

About Yourself

Quick Quiz

Learning to tell the examiner about yourself is really important. Make sure you have a few key facts about your identity under your belt so that you can describe yourself confidently.

Don't forget you can access your online content here: www.cgpbooks.co.uk/Merci

Je m'appelle... — My name is...

Vocabulary

le nom	*name, surname*	gay	*gay*
s'appeler	*to be called*	lesbien(ne)	*lesbian*
(être) né(e)	*(to have been) born*	hétéro	*straight*
la langue	*language*	non-binaire	*non-binary*
français(e)	*French*	transgenre	*transgender*
anglais(e)	*English*	le handicap	*disability*
britannique	*British*	le fauteuil roulant	*wheelchair*
canadien(ne)	*Canadian*	se présenter (Higher)	*to introduce oneself*
européen(ne)	*European*	l'allié(e) (Higher)	*ally*
bi(sexuel) / bi(sexuelle)	*bi(sexual)*	la foi (Higher)	*faith*

Grammar — saying your age

In French, you don't say how old you are — you say how many years you have. This means you need to use the verb 'avoir' (to have).

Quel âge as-tu ? → **J'ai seize ans.**

How old are you? → ***I am sixteen.***

For more on numbers and dates, see p.4-7.

Je m'appelle Sara et j'habite à Natland.	*I'm called Sara and I live in Natland.*
J'ai quinze ans, et je suis né(e) le neuf juin 2010.	*I'm fifteen years old, and I was born on the ninth of June 2010.*
Mon anniversaire, c'est le deux février.	*My birthday is on the second of February.*
Je suis britannique mais ma famille est d'origine canadienne.	*I'm British but my family is of Canadian origin.*
J'ai un handicap et j'utilise un fauteuil roulant depuis mon enfance.	*I have a disability and I have used a wheelchair since my childhood.*

near to Kendal — près de Kendal

'Né(e)' needs an extra 'e' on the end if you're female (see p.155).

English — anglais(e)
Welsh — gallois(e)
Scottish — écossais(e)
Irish — irlandais(e)

Practice Question

Q1 Read the following text out loud, then answer the questions below in French.

SPEAKING

Je m'appelle Sophie et j'ai quinze ans. Je suis née le dix-sept mars. J'habite avec ma famille à Manchester, en Angleterre. Cependant, je suis française. Mes parents sont nés à Nice.

[8 marks]

a) *Comment t'appelles-tu ?*
b) *Quel âge as-tu ?*
c) *Quand es-tu né(e) ?*
d) *Où habites-tu ?* *[4 marks]*

Top Tip for Higher Students
✓ Develop your answers by using different tenses, e.g. talking about where you would like to live in the future.

You only get one chance to make a good first impression...

The vocab on this page will help you answer questions about yourself. And if you run out of things to say about yourself, you could add extra detail about where your parents are from or what your town is called.

Quick Quiz

My Family and Friends

You need to be able to describe your family and friends as well as yourself. These pages have lots of useful words for family members, as well as some key verbs you can use to talk about them.

La vie de famille — Family life

When you're talking about something or someone that belongs to you, e.g. 'my sister', you need to use a possessive adjective (see p.157).

Vocabulary

la famille	*family*	unique	*unique, only (child)*	le chien	*dog*
le parent	*parent*	le frère	*brother*	le cheval	*horse*
le père	*father, dad*	la sœur	*sister*	le chat	*cat*
la mère	*mother, mum*	le demi-frère	*half-brother, step-brother*	le lapin	*rabbit*
le beau-père	*step-father*	la demi-sœur	*half-sister, step-sister*	garder (Higher)	*to take care of, look after*
la belle-mère	*step-mother*	l'oncle (m)	*uncle*	jumeau / jumelle / jumeaux / jumelles (Higher)	*twin (adj.)*
le grand-père	*grandfather*	la tante	*aunt*		
la grand-mère	*grandmother*	l'animal (m)	*animal, pet*		
le fils	*son*				
la fille	*daughter*				

Parle-moi de ta famille — Tell me about your family

Q&A Audio

Question

Est-ce que tu as une grande famille ?

Have you got a big family?

Simple Answer

J'ai une petite famille — nous sommes quatre.

I've got a small family — there are four of us.

Extended Answer

J'ai une grande famille — j'ai un frère qui est plus jeune que moi et une sœur jumelle. Nous avons aussi un chien qui s'appelle Félix.

I've got a big family — I have a younger brother and a twin sister. We also have a dog called Felix.

The photographer forgot to tell the Grey family to say 'cheese'.

Grammar — comparisons

To compare one person or thing to another, use 'plus / moins...que' (*more / less...than*) with an adjective in the middle. See p.158.

Elle est plus jeune que moi.
She is younger than me.

Dans ma famille, il y a neuf personnes.	*In my family, there are nine people.*
J'ai une grande famille car mes parents sont séparés et j'ai un beau-père et une belle-mère.	*I have a big family because my parents are separated and I have a step-father and a step-mother.*
J'ai deux demi-frères qui sont plus grands que moi.	*I have two step-brothers who are taller than me.*
Le partenaire de ma mère vient de Madagascar, donc j'ai de la famille à l'étranger.	*My mum's partner comes from Madagascar, so I have some family abroad.*
Ma mère a trois sœurs, mais mon père est fils unique.	*My mum has three sisters, but my dad is an only child.*

don't live together — ne vivent pas ensemble
are divorced — sont divorcés

older — plus âgés
younger — plus jeunes

isn't British — n'est pas britannique

my grandmother is an only child — ma grand-mère est fille unique

Tu t'entends bien avec... ? — Do you get on well with...?

Vocabulary

l'ami(e)	*friend*	comprendre	*to understand*
s'entendre (avec)	*to get on(with)*	échanger	*to exchange*
rencontrer	*to meet (up)*	écouter	*to listen*
connaître	*to know, be familiar with*	l'amitié (f) (Higher)	*friendship*
passer	*to spend time*	soutenir (Higher)	*to support*
parler	*to speak, talk*	encourager (Higher)	*to encourage*
discuter	*to discuss, talk about, chat*	s'excuser (Higher)	*to apologise*
aider	*to help*	le souvenir (Higher)	*memory*

Je connais beaucoup de gens dans ma ville. — *I know lots of people in my town.*

I've made friends — Je me suis fait des amis

Tu t'entends avec ta famille ? — *Do you get on with your family?*

Je m'entends bien avec mes grands-parents. — *I get on well with my grandparents.*

I have a good relationship — J'ai un bon rapport

Mon amie n'est pas gentille, parce qu'elle ne s'excuse jamais après une dispute. — *My friend is unkind because she never apologises after a dispute.*

Mes amis me soutiennent toujours — nous avons des liens très forts. — *My friends always support me — we have a very strong bond.*

spend a lot of time together — passons beaucoup de temps ensemble

Practice Questions

Q1 *Write a description of your family and friends. You should write about 80-90 words in French. Describe:* WRITING

- *the size of your family*
- *the members of your family*
- *whether you get along with your family and friends*
- *what activities you like to do with your friends.* *[18 marks]*

Top Tips for Higher Students
✓ Use plural reflexive pronouns, e.g. 'nous <u>nous</u> entendons bien'.
✓ Add more detail to your sentences using relative pronouns like 'qui' and 'que'.

Q2 *Read this email that your penfriend Manon wrote about her family and answer the questions below in English.* READING

> *Dans ma famille, il y a trois personnes — ma mère, mon père et moi. Je n'ai ni frères ni sœurs, mais j'ai un lapin qui s'appelle Marcel. J'ai aussi deux oncles et une tante — nous passons souvent du temps ensemble. Le week-end dernier, par exemple, nous sommes allés au cinéma car nous essayons d'aller voir un film ensemble tous les mois. C'est une tradition familiale.*

a) Who is in Manon's immediate family? *[1 mark]*
b) What animal does Manon have as a pet? *[1 mark]*
c) What did Manon do last weekend? *[1 mark]*
d) Why did Manon choose to do this? *[1 mark]*

Don't just list your family members — add in details as well...

Describing the members of your family will help score you extra marks, so keep a few handy adjectives in your pocket that you can use to add interest to your answers. That's where the next page comes in...

Quick Quiz

Describing People

Now you know how to name people in French, you can begin to describe them. These pages will help you to gain marks by describing people accurately with lots of fancy vocab. Read on for more...

Décrire les autres — Describing others

Vocabulary

les yeux (m)	*eyes*	noir(e)	*black*	bleu(e)	*blue*
les cheveux (m)	*hair*	blanc(he)	*white*	rose	*pink*
long(ue)	*long*	blond(e)	*blond*	marron	*brown*
court(e)	*short*	rouge	*red*	châtain	*brown*
grand(e)	*great, big, tall*	roux	*red, ginger*	gris(e)	*grey*
petit(e)	*small, little*	orange	*orange*	[Higher] ressembler à	*to look like*
la taille	*size*	jaune	*yellow*	[Higher] moyen(ne)	*medium, average size*
clair(e)	*clear, light, bright*	vert(e)	*green*		

Ma tante est assez grande et jolie. Elle a les yeux bleus et les cheveux longs. — *My aunt is quite tall and pretty. She has blue eyes and long hair.*

fat — grosse
slim — mince

Mon meilleur ami a les yeux verts et les cheveux noirs. — *My best friend has green eyes and black hair.*

a beard — une barbe
wears glasses — porte des lunettes

Je ressemble à mon père car je suis petit et j'ai les yeux verts comme lui. — *I look like my dad because I am small and I have green eyes like him.*

average height — de taille moyenne

Mon père avait les cheveux bruns quand il était jeune, mais maintenant il a les cheveux gris. — *My dad had brown hair when he was young, but now he has grey hair.*

curly — bouclés
straight — raides

Grammar — agreements

Adjectives agree with the person or thing they're describing — if it's feminine, you need to add an 'e' onto the end of the adjective. If it's plural, add an 's'. If it's feminine and plural, add 'es'.

Ma sœur est très petite. — ***My sister is very small.***

Elle a les cheveux longs. — ***She has long hair.***

Watch out for irregular adjectives though, e.g. 'blanc' becomes 'blanche' when it follows a feminine noun.

Décris-toi — Describe yourself

Q&A Audio

Question

À quoi ressembles-tu ?
What do you look like?

Simple Answer

Je suis grand(e) et j'ai les yeux bleus.
I am tall and I have blue eyes.

Extended Answer

Je suis grand(e) mais je suis plus petit(e) que mon frère. Comme ma mère, j'ai les yeux verts. Mes cheveux sont courts et blonds. Pourtant, je voudrais changer la couleur de mes cheveux, car je trouve que les cheveux châtains sont plus beaux.

I am tall but I am smaller than my brother. Like my mother, I have green eyes. My hair is short and blond. However, I would like to change the colour of my hair because I think that brown hair is more beautiful.

La personnalité — Personality

Vocabulary

sympa	*nice, kind*	spécial(e)	*special*	Higher	fier / fière	*proud*
agréable	*pleasant, nice*	patient(e)	*patient*	Higher	fidèle	*loyal, faithful*
calme	*quiet*	ennuyeux / ennuyeuse	*boring*	Higher	se sentir	*to feel*
fort(e)	*strong, loud, good at*	respecter	*to respect*	Higher	la colère	*anger*
sérieux / sérieuse	*serious, responsible*	responsable	*responsible*	Higher	inquiet / inquiète	*worried, anxious*
travailleur / travailleuse	*hard-working*			Higher	prudent(e)	*prudent, careful, cautious*
strict(e)	*strict*					

Grammar — imperfect tense

To describe someone in the past, use the imperfect tense (see p.171).

Elle était sympa et patiente. ***She was kind and patient.***

Mes parents sont très sympas et très prudents. — *My parents are very nice and very cautious.*

Mon père pense qu'il est drôle, mais je trouve ses blagues ennuyeuses. — *My dad thinks that he is funny, but I find his jokes boring.*

Mon frère est calme et travailleur, mais il ne pense jamais aux autres. Cependant, je suis très fier / fière de ma famille. — *My brother is quiet and hard-working, but he never thinks about others. However, I'm very proud of my family.*

Mon amie Li est vraiment sympa. Elle est toujours là pour moi quand j'ai un problème. — *My friend Li is really nice. She is always there for me when I have a problem.*

Practice Questions

Q1 *In this extract from a podcast, Fabien is being interviewed about his family.* LISTENING

Listening Track 6

There are two true statements in each list below. Choose the correct statements from each list.

a) **A.** It's never quiet at Fabien's house.
B. Fabien is the youngest child at home.
C. His sisters have blue eyes.
D. Fabien is smaller than his brother. *[2 marks]*

b) **A.** Fabien's mother has short hair.
B. His father is tall.
C. His father has blond hair.
D. Fabien's mother is patient. *[2 marks]*

c) **A.** Fabien's mother has a lot of siblings.
B. Fabien has a lot of uncles.
C. His father has three sisters.
D. Fabien lives near his grandparents. *[2 marks]*

Q2 *Write a description of your best friend for your blog. You should write about 80-90 words in French. Describe:* WRITING

- *the appearance and personality of your friend*
- *why they are your best friend*
- *an activity you recently did together*
- *what you will do with your friend when you next see them* *[18 marks]*

Top Tips for Higher Students
✓ Use a range of tenses, e.g. talk about when you first met your friend.
✓ Include a wide range of adjectives, e.g. superlatives to talk about your friend's best qualities.

Say how people have changed so you can use different tenses...

If you think you've said all there is to say about the people in your life, you can always describe how their appearance or personality has changed over time, or any activities you hope to do with them in future.

Quick Quiz

Relationships and Partnerships

The examiners are also pretty interested in your relationships with other people. Luckily, these pages will give you the chance to practise those pesky reflexive verbs you know and love. Get reading...

Être en couple (m) — Being in a couple

Vocabulary

le / la partenaire	*partner*
le couple	*couple*
seul(e)	*alone*
ensemble	*together*
la communication	*communication*
la conversation	*conversation*
l'amour (m)	*love*
regretter	*to regret*
le problème	*problem, issue*
différent(e)	*different*
la relation	*relationship*
la faveur	*favour*

Higher

le copain	*friend, mate*
la copine	*friend, mate*
le rapport	*relationship*
le conflit	*conflict*
compter (sur)	*to count (on), intend*
se fier (à)	*to rely on (someone)*
s'identifier (à)	*to identify (with), relate (to)*
la confiance	*trust*
se séparer	*to separate*

Grammar — reflexive verbs

Reflexive verbs (see p.174) have an extra part — a reflexive pronoun.

Tu t'entends bien avec...
You get on well with...

In the perfect tense (see p.169), the pronoun goes before the present tense part of 'être' (*to be*).

Je me suis marié(e).
I got married.

J'étais seul(e) pendant deux ans, et puis j'ai rencontré ma femme, Usma.	*I was alone for two years, and then I met my wife, Usma.*
Mon ami va m'aider à trouver un partenaire.	*My friend is going to help me find a partner.*
Je connais ce copain depuis un an. Il m'écoute quand je parle de mes problèmes.	*I've known this friend for a year. He listens to me when I talk about my problems.*

Le mariage — Marriage

Vocabulary

le couple	*couple*
la femme	*wife*
le mari	*husband*
se marier	*to marry, get married*
le mariage du même sexe	*same-sex marriage*
égal(e)	*equal*
la société	*society*

la tradition	*tradition*
traditionnel(le)	*traditional*
le symbole	*symbol*
la promesse	*promise*
prometter (H)	*to promise*
l'union (f) (H)	*union*

À mon avis il est possible d'être un couple fort sans se marier.	*In my opinion it is possible to be a strong couple without getting married.*
Les mariages sont trop chers. Moi, je préférerais acheter une maison.	*Weddings are too expensive. Personally, I would prefer to buy a house.*
Aujourd'hui, le PACS est plus courant.	*Today, civil partnerships are more common.*

I think that — Je pense qu'

In my opinion — Selon moi

These days — De nos jours

Tu voudrais te marier ? — Do you want to get married?

Q&A Audio

Question

Tu voudrais te marier un jour ?

Do you want to get married one day?

Simple Answer

Oui, plus tard, je voudrais me marier et avoir des enfants.

Yes, in the future I'd like to get married and have children.

Extended Answers

Oui, pour moi le mariage est très important, et plus tard, j'espère rencontrer l'homme / la femme de mes rêves et rester avec lui / elle pour toujours. Je ne comprends pas les gens qui ne désirent pas se marier.

Yes, marriage is very important for me, and in the future I hope to meet the man / woman of my dreams and stay with him / her forever. I don't understand people who don't want to get married.

Moi, je ne veux absolument pas me marier. Par contre, pour moi, ce qui est plus important c'est l'amour et la confiance. On peut être avec quelqu'un et avoir des enfants sans se marier.

I absolutely don't want to get married. On the other hand, for me, what's more important is love and trust. You can be with someone and have children without getting married.

Grammar — talking about the future

There are lots of different ways to talk about your future plans. You can use:

The immediate future (see p.172):

Je vais rencontrer quelqu'un. ***I am going to meet someone.***

Or the conditional (see p.173):

Je voudrais avoir une famille. ***I would like to have a family.***

Or use 'j'espère' (*I hope*) + infinitive:

J'espère me marier un jour. ***I hope to get married one day.***

If you're taking Higher tier, you can also use the proper future (see p.172).

Practice Questions

Q1 *Choose one of the photos below. Talk in French about what is in the photo. You should talk for about a minute and describe who is in the photo, where it takes place, and what is happening.*

SPEAKING

[8 marks]

Higher

Q2 *Read these headlines about marriage from a French news website, then answer the questions below in English.*

READING

Les mariages étaient moins chers dans le passé — maintenant, ça coûte trop cher	*Selon les recherches, les couples qui se marient semblent plus heureux que les autres*	*Le nombre de mariages entre personnes du même sexe a récemment augmenté*

a) Give one advantage to getting married mentioned in a headline. *[1 mark]*

b) Give one disadvantage to getting married mentioned in a headline. *[1 mark]*

c) Name one way that marriage has changed according to the headlines. *[1 mark]*

Use 'être' with reflexives in the perfect tense...

Reflexive verbs may look a bit complicated at first, but they're simple once you know how to form them, and they'll be really useful when describing your relationships with other people. So flex those reflexives...

Quick Quiz

Role Models

This page is all about those people you look up to and why they inspire you. It's a great chance to use lots of adjectives and a variety of tenses to talk about them. Here you go — time to get inspired...

Mon modèle est... — My role model is...

Vocabulary

célèbre	*famous*	l'acteur / l'actrice	*actor*
la célébrité	*celebrity*	le personnage	*character*
l'influenceur / l'influenceuse	*influencer*	chanter	*to sing*
inspirer	*to inspire*	regarder	*to watch*
le fan	*fan, supporter*	le concert	*concert*
suivre	*to follow*	le spectacle	*show*
le rôle	*role*	le groupe	*group, band*

la mode	*fashion*
le style	*style*
populaire	*popular*
privé(e)	*private*
[Higher] le public	*public, audience*
[Higher] représenter	*to represent*
[Higher] la critique	*criticism, review*

Mes modèles sont très influents. Ils m'inspirent à travailler dur car je veux être comme eux. — *My role models are very influential. They inspire me to work hard because I want to be like them.*

to help people — aider les gens
to stay motivated — rester motivé(e)

Mon auteur préféré m'inspire beaucoup. Il écrit des romans extraordinaires et il a une vie passionnante. — *My favourite author inspires me a lot. He writes extraordinary novels and he has a fascinating life.*

Q&A Audio

Question

Qui est ton modèle ? Pourquoi ?

Who is your role-model? Why?

Simple Answer

J'aime le joueur de foot Gabriel Bernaut parce qu'il encourage les jeunes à faire du sport.

I like the football player Gabriel Bernaut because he encourages young people to do sport.

Extended Answer

Mon modèle, c'est l'actrice Marianne Perrin. Je l'adore dans tous ses rôles au cinéma comme à la télé, particulièrement dans '*Maurice et Moi*'. Elle est toujours patiente et parle à tous ses fans.

My role model is the actress Marianne Perrin. I love her in all her roles in films and on the TV, particularly in 'Maurice and I'. *She's always patient and talks to all her fans.*

Practice Questions

Q1 *Listen to this extract from a podcast in which two people discuss their role models. There are* **two** *correct statements in each list below. Choose the correct statements in each list.* LISTENING

Listening Track 7

a) **A.** Margot's role model is a singer.
B. She dresses like her role model.
C. Margot wants to be a dancer.

b) **A.** André wants to become president.
B. André shares his role model's views.
C. André has met his role model. *[4 marks]*

Q2 *Write a blog post about someone who inspires you. You should write about 80-90 words in French. Describe:* WRITING

- who they are and what they do
- what you like about them
- when they first inspired you
- what you would like to do to inspire others *[18 marks]*

Top Tip for Higher Students
✓ Use Higher-tier adjectives to describe your role model.

Don't just say who you like — say why you're a fan of them...

Jot down a few role models and some adjectives you can use to describe them to help prepare for the exam.

Celebrations

Quick Quiz

There are lots of occasions to celebrate with your family and friends, so this page has some handy celebration vocabulary and examples of how you could use it. Now... anyone for cake?

Venez à la fête ! — Come to the party!

Vocabulary

la fête	*party, festival*	donner	*to give*
faire la fête	*to party, have fun*	le gâteau	*cake*
l'événement (m)	*event*	inviter	*to invite*
l'anniversaire (m)	*birthday*	réunir	*to gather, meet, reunite*
le Nouvel An	*New Year's Day*	fêter (Higher)	*to celebrate*
la Saint-Sylvestre	*New Year's Eve*	apprécier (Higher)	*to appreciate*
la surprise	*surprise*	surprendre (Higher)	*to surprise*
le cadeau	*present, gift*	offrir (à) (Higher)	*to offer(someone)*
la carte	*card*		

J'ai apprécié la musique à l'événement.	*I enjoyed the music at the event.*
L'année dernière, j'ai reçu un beau cadeau pour mon anniversaire.	*Last year, I received a beautiful gift for my birthday.*
Ma tante a invité ses amis chez elle pour fêter la Saint-Sylvestre, mais je ne peux pas y aller.	*My aunt invited her friends to her house to celebrate New Year's Eve, but I can't go to it.*
Je sais déjà qu'ils vont faire une fête surprise pour mes 20 ans.	*I already know they're going to throw a surprise party for my 20th birthday.*

a tasty cake — un gâteau délicieux
new headphones — de nouveaux écouteurs

wish me a happy birthday — me souhaiter un joyeux anniversaire

Grammar — talking about the (immediate) future

You can use the immediate future to talk about something that is going to happen. Use the present tense form of the verb 'aller' + an infinitive.

Nous allons donner des fleurs à Maman. ***We are going to give some flowers to Mum.***

You can use either 'bon anniversaire' or 'joyeux anniversaire' to say 'happy birthday'.

Practice Question

Q1 *Youssou is describing his birthday celebrations. Choose the correct option to finish each sentence.* LISTENING

Listening Track 8

a) To celebrate his birthday, he...
A. had an enormous party. **B.** ate his favourite meal. **C.** had a small family event. *[1 mark]*

b) His parents gave him...
A. a novel. **B.** a new phone. **C.** a cake. *[1 mark]*

c) The following Saturday, he...
A. went to the town centre. **B.** spent the day alone. **C.** watched a show with friends. *[1 mark]*

Make sure you can talk about past and future celebrations...

Try using different tenses to add some variety to your sentences. For example, you could use the perfect tense to say what you did last year for your birthday or the immediate future to describe next year's plans.

Speaking Questions

It's time to put what you've learnt to the test — have a go at answering these practice questions.

Candidate's Material

- Choose **one** of the pictures below to describe. Make notes on it to use during the test.
- Your teacher will ask you to describe the picture. You should talk for approximately **one and a half to two minutes**. Your description must cover the **people, location and activity** shown in the picture.
- After you have spoken about the content of the picture, your teacher will ask you two questions about your chosen picture. Then, they will ask you some questions related to any of the topics within the theme of **My Personal World**.

Picture 1:

Picture 2:

Teacher's Material

- Begin by asking the candidate which picture they have chosen, then say 'Describe the picture'. Candidates should talk about the picture for approximately **one and a half to two minutes**. They may use any notes they have made during the preparation time.
- When the candidate has finished, ask the questions below that relate to their chosen picture.

Picture 1:

- F Tu habites avec qui ?
- Qu'est-ce que tu penses des fêtes de famille ?
- H Qu'est-ce que tu as fait cette semaine avec ta famille ?

Picture 2:

- F Où aimes-tu passer du temps avec tes amis ?
- Quelles qualités font un bon ami ?
- H Qu'est-ce que tu as fait avec ton meilleur ami récemment ?

- Now ask the candidate the following unprepared conversation questions on the theme of **My Personal World**:

- Parle-moi d'un membre de ta famille.
- Qui t'inspire ? Pourquoi ?
- Qu'est-ce que tu vas faire pour ton anniversaire cette année ?
- À ton avis, qu'est-ce qu'il faut faire pour maintenir de bonnes relations ?

Listening Questions

1 You are going to hear someone talking about their family.

Sentences 1 and 3: Write down the missing words in the gaps provided. In each gap, you will write one word **in French**.

Sentences 2 and 4: Write down the full sentences that you hear in the spaces provided, **in French**.

Listening Track 9

F

1 a **Sentence 1**

Mon .... est .... *[2 marks]*

1 b **Sentence 2**

....

.... *[2 marks]*

Higher

1 c **Sentence 3**

J'habite avec mon frère ...., ma ....

et mon .... *[2 marks]*

1 d **Sentence 4**

....

.... *[2 marks]*

2 You hear this radio show about marriage. Answer the questions in **English**.

Listening Track 10

2 a Why does Sylvie want to stay single?

.... *[1 mark]*

2 b Why does Richard say he isn't married yet?

.... *[1 mark]*

Reading Questions

Foundation

1 Translate these sentences **into English**.

1 a Mon frère s'appelle Tom et il a quinze ans.

.... *[2 marks]*

1 b Mon beau-père est vraiment sympa.

.... *[2 marks]*

1 c Charlie parle plus fort que Lola.

.... *[2 marks]*

Higher

2 Translate the following paragraph **into English**.

> Je suis en train d'organiser une fête pour ma meilleure amie ce week-end. Je voudrais la surprendre pour son anniversaire. J'ai déjà invité toute sa famille et ses amis. Demain, je dois acheter un gâteau et des fleurs. Je pense que ça sera une bonne occasion de lui montrer que je l'aime.

[10 marks]

3 You read this profile on a dating app. Answer the questions below **in English**.

> Je m'appelle Sabrina. Je viens de Nantes, mais j'habite à Lille avec ma petite sœur, Clara. Je suis patiente et mes amis disent que je suis très travailleuse. J'ai besoin d'un homme agréable et fidèle, parce que je n'ai pas pu compter sur mon dernier partenaire. J'aimerais rencontrer quelqu'un qui adore son travail, parce que ma carrière est très importante pour moi. Je suis très sportive, donc mon partenaire idéal devrait être actif aussi. J'espère vous rencontrer bientôt !

3 a How do Sabrina's friends describe her?

.... *[1 mark]*

3 b Why does Sabrina want a partner who is loyal?

.... *[1 mark]*

3 c What is **one** trait that Sabrina's ideal partner would have?

.... *[1 mark]*

Writing Questions

Foundation

1 Describe the photo.

Write **four** short sentences **in French**.

1 a .... *[2 marks]*

1 b .... *[2 marks]*

1 c .... *[2 marks]*

1 d .... *[2 marks]*

2 Write to your friend about a recent family wedding.
You **must** include the following points:

- a description of the married couple
- your opinion on marriage with reasons
- what happened at the wedding
- whether you want to get married in the future.

Write your answer **in French**. You should aim to write between 80-90 words. *[18 marks]*

Foundation

3 Translate the following three sentences **into French**.

3 a I have brown hair and blue eyes.

.... *[2 marks]*

3 b I have three brothers and a sister.

.... *[2 marks]*

3 c When I was young, I was very independent.

.... *[2 marks]*

Higher

4 Translate the paragraph **into French**.

I used to spend a lot of time with my grandfather. He has a disability and uses a wheelchair. He was born in France but now he lives in England. He is the oldest member of our family and I am the youngest. We love music and often sing together.

[10 marks]

Identity & Relationships — Vocabulary

Your relationship with vocab may be a bit rocky, but it's important that you know how to talk about yourself and others.

About Yourself

le nom	*name, surname*
appeler	*to call*
s'appeler	*to be called*
l'âge (m)	*age*
la date	*date*
(être) né(e)	*(to have been) born*
l'identité (f)	*identity*
la langue	*language*
français(e)	*French*
francophone	*francophone*
anglais(e)	*English*
britannique	*British*
canadien(ne)	*Canadian*
européen(ne)	*European*
bi(sexuel) / bi(sexuelle)	*bi(sexual)*
gay	*gay*
lesbien(ne)	*lesbian*
hétéro(sexuel) / hétéro(sexuelle)	*straight, heterosexual*
non-binaire	*non-binary*
transgenre	*transgender*
le sexe	*sex, gender*
le handicap	*disability*
handicapé(e)	*disabled*
le fauteuil roulant	*wheelchair*
la religion	*religion*
religieux / religieuse	*religious*
croire	*to believe*
personnel(le)	*personal*

Higher

nommer	*to name*
introduire	*to introduce*
se présenter	*to introduce oneself*
la naissance	*birth*
la jeunesse	*youth*
l'allié(e)	*ally*
la foi	*faith*

My Family and Friends

la famille	*family*
familial(e)	*family (adj.)*
le membre	*member*
le parent	*parent*
le père	*father, dad*
la mère	*mother, mum*
le beau-père	*step-father*
la belle-mère	*step-mother*
le grand-père	*grandfather*
la grand-mère	*grandmother*
le fils	*son*
la fille	*daughter*
unique	*unique, only (child)*
le frère	*brother*
la sœur	*sister*
le demi-frère	*half-brother, step-brother*
la demi-sœur	*half-sister, step-sister*
l'oncle (m)	*uncle*
la tante	*aunt*
l'animal (m)	*animal, pet*
les animaux (m)	*animals, pets*
le chien	*dog*
le cheval	*horse*
le chat	*cat*
le lapin	*rabbit*
l'ami(e)	*friend*
s'entendre (avec)	*to get on (with)*
rencontrer	*to meet (up)*
connaître	*to know, be familiar with*
passer	*to spend time*
parler	*to speak, talk*
discuter	*to discuss, talk about, chat*
aider	*to help*
l'aide (f)	*help, aid*
comprendre	*to understand*
échanger	*to exchange*
entendre	*to hear*
écouter	*to listen*

Higher

la génération	*generation*
adopter	*to adopt*
garder	*to keep*
le souvenir	*souvenir, memory*
soutenir	*to support, sustain*
permettre	*to allow, permit*
encourager	*to encourage*
s'excuser	*to apologise*
l'excuse (f)	*excuse*
fournir	*to provide, supply, give*
l'amitié (f)	*friendship*
meilleur(e)	*better, best*
jumeau / jumelle / jumeaux / jumelles	*twin (adj.)*

Alex and James had the nickname 'Double Trouble' for a reason.

Describing People — Appearance

la personne	*person, people*
l'adulte (m/f)	*adult*
l'enfant (m/f)	*child*
le garçon	*boy*
la fille	*girl*
l'adolescent(e)	*teenager*
l'homme (m)	*man*
la femme	*woman*
jeune	*young*
le / la jeune	*young person*
vieux / vieil / vieille	*old*
le visage	*face*
les yeux (m)	*eyes*

les cheveux (m)	*hair*
long(ue)	*long*
court(e)	*short*
grand(e)	*great, big, tall*
petit(e)	*small, little*
la taille	*size*
beau / bel / belle	*beautiful, handsome*
la couleur	*colour*
clair(e)	*clear, light, bright*
noir(e)	*black*
blanc(he)	*white*
blond(e)	*blond*
rouge	*red*

roux	*red, ginger*
orange	*orange*
jaune	*yellow*
vert(e)	*green*
bleu(e)	*blue*
rose	*pink*
marron	*brown*
châtain	*brown*
gris(e)	*grey*

Higher

ressembler à	*to look like*
moyen(ne)	*medium, average size*
âgé(e)	*old*
aîné(e)	*older, oldest*

Describing People — Personality

la personnalité	*personality*
sympa	*nice, kind*
agréable	*pleasant, nice*
calme	*quiet*
fort(e)	*strong, loud, good at*
sérieux / sérieuse	*serious, responsible*
travailleur / travailleuse	*hard-working*
strict(e)	*strict*
spécial(e)	*special*
patient(e)	*patient*

ennuyeux / ennuyeuse	*boring*
fou / folle	*crazy, wild*
respecter	*to respect, follow*
le respect	*respect*
responsable	*responsible*
l'indépendance (f)	*independence*
indépendant(e)	*independent*
le type	*type, kind, sort*

H

fier / fière	*proud*
fidèle	*loyal, faithful*

Higher

le sentiment	*feeling*
sembler	*to seem*
se sentir	*to feel*
la responsabilité	*responsibility*
la colère	*anger*
inquiet / inquiète	*worried, anxious*
prudent(e)	*prudent, careful, cautious*
l'impression (f)	*impression*
exceptionnel(le)	*exceptional*

Relationships and Partnerships

le / la partenaire	*partner*
le couple	*couple*
la femme	*wife*
le mari	*husband*
le mariage	*marriage, wedding*
se marier	*to get married*
le mariage du même sexe	*same-sex marriage*
seul(e)	*alone, lonely*
ensemble	*together*
la communication	*communication*
la conversation	*conversation*
l'amour (m)	*love*
regretter	*to regret*
le problème	*problem, issue*
différent(e)	*different*
égal(e)	*equal*
la société	*society*
la tradition	*tradition*
traditionnel(le)	*traditional*

le symbole	*symbol*
la relation	*relationship*
la promesse	*promise*
la faveur	*favour*

'relation' is often used in the plural, e.g. 'j'ai de bonnes relations avec mon père' (*I have a good relationship with my father*).

Higher

le copain	*friend, mate*
la copine	*friend, mate*
le rapport	*relationship*
le conflit	*conflict*
promettre	*to promise*
compter (sur)	*to count (on), intend*
se fier (à)	*to rely on (someone)*
s'identifier (à)	*to identify (with), relate (to)*
désirer	*to desire*
communiquer	*to communicate, pass on*
la confiance	*trust*
séparer	*to separate*
se séparer	*to separate, break up*
la séparation	*separation*
l'union (f)	*union*

Role Models

le modèle	*model, role model*
célèbre	*famous*
la célébrité	*celebrity, star*
la carrière	*career*
l'influenceur / l'influenceuse	*influencer*
l'influence (f)	*influence*
inspirer	*to inspire*
le succès	*success*
le fan	*fan, supporter*
suivre	*to follow*
reconnaître	*to recognise*
les médias (m)	*media*
Internet (m)	*internet, web*
la photo	*photo*
l'image (f)	*picture, image*
la vidéo	*video*
le journal	*newspaper*
la télé(vision)	*TV, television*
la réalité	*reality*
l'émission (f)	*TV programme*
la série	*series*
le film	*film, movie*
le cinéma	*cinema*
l'acteur / l'actrice	*actor*
le rôle	*role*
le personnage	*character*
le chanteur / la chanteuse	*singer*
chanter	*to sing*
la chanson	*song*
la musique	*music*
voir	*to see*
regarder	*to watch*
le concert	*concert, gig*
le spectacle	*show*
le groupe	*group, band*
le sport	*sport*
l'équipe (f)	*team*
jouer (à un sport)	*to play (a sport)*
porter	*to wear, carry*
la mode	*fashion*
à la mode	*fashionable, trendy*
le style	*style*
l'argent (m)	*money*
le prix	*price*
la marque	*brand, mark*
la sécurité	*safety*
la victime	*victim*
le secret	*secret*
annoncer	*to announce*
voyager	*to travel*
public / publique	*public (adj.)*
principal(e)	*main, principal*
réel(le)	*real*
international(e)	*international*
populaire	*popular*
riche	*rich*
la société	*society*
culturel(le)	*cultural*
local(e)	*local*
national(e)	*national*
extraordinaire	*extraordinary*
privé(e)	*private*
positif / positive	*positive*
négatif / négative	*negative*

Higher

le public	*public, audience*
la scène	*stage, scene*
présenter (à)	*to present*
représenter	*to represent*
la voix	*voice*
les paroles (f)	*lyrics*
l'article (m)	*article*
la honte	*shame*
l'inquiétude (f)	*worry, anxiety*
l'occasion (f)	*opportunity, occasion*
tolérer	*to tolerate*
la critique	*criticism, review*
majeur	*major, main*

Celebrations

la fête	*party, festival*
faire la fête	*to party, have fun*
l'événement (m)	*event*
l'anniversaire (m)	*birthday*
le Nouvel An	*New Year's Day*
la Saint-Sylvestre	*New Year's Eve*
la Fête de la Musique	*World Music Day*
le 14 juillet	*Bastille Day*
la surprise	*surprise*
le cadeau	*present*
la carte	*card*
donner	*to give*
recevoir	*to receive*
ouvrir	*to open*
acheter	*to buy*
envoyer	*to send*
le gâteau	*cake*
inviter	*to invite*
venir	*to come*
partager	*to share*
réunir	*to gather, meet, reunite*
rappeler	*to recall, remind*
se rappeler (de)	*to remember*
passer	*to spend time*
se passer	*to happen, take place*

Higher

fêter	*to celebrate*
apprécier	*to appreciate*
profiter de	*to make the most of, take advantage, profit*
surprendre	*to surprise*
offrir (à)	*to offer (someone)*
le bonheur	*happiness*
la joie	*joy*
crier	*to shout*
la fleur	*flower*

Reflexive verbs like 'se passer' take 'être' in the perfect tense. E.g. 'La fête <u>s'est passée</u> hier.' (*The party <u>happened</u> yesterday.*) See p.174 for more.

Mathilde had an unusual method of ensuring she got the entire cake to herself.

Revision Summary Test for Section Two

It's time for some summary questions to test just how well you've got on with this section.

- Yep, these questions are **hard** — they'll really help you see **how well you know your stuff**.
- Tackle the **revision summary test** below, or scan the QR code to do it **online**.
  Use the CGP RevisionHub to **track your progress** and see **which areas need more work**.
- You can find **sample answers** here: www.cgpbooks.co.uk/MerciExtras

Summary Test

About Yourself

1) How many nationalities can you name in French? There are at least 4 you need to know.
2) How would you give your name and age to a French person you've just met?
3) Now tell them where you live and what nationality you are, giving as much detail as you can.
4) How would you say these words in French? a) language b) disability c) identity d) wheelchair
5) List as many French words related to gender and sexuality as you can. There's 7 you need to know.
6) 'Est-ce que je peux te présenter Axel ? C'est un allié de notre communauté.'
   What's Élodie saying? Answer in English. (H)

My Family and Friends

7) How many words for family members can you name in French?
   There are at least 14 you need to know.
8) 'As-tu une grande famille ? Est-ce que tu as des animaux ?' Answer in French.
9) How would you say the words below in French?
   a) to meet b) to understand c) to exchange d) to hear e) to discuss f) to help

Describing People

10) Describe two of your friends. Give details about their personality as well as their appearance.
11) How would you say these words in French? a) pleasant b) boring c) serious d) quiet
    e) hard-working f) responsible g) independent h) strict i) strong
12) 'Je suis fière de ma sœur aînée car elle est très fidèle.' Translate Mari's sentence into English. (H)
13) 'Tu ressembles à tes parents ?' Translate this question into English and then answer it in French. (H)

Relationships and Partnerships

14) How would you say the words below in French?
    a) to get married b) a promise c) to regret d) marriage e) love f) relationship
15) In French, give two arguments for marriage and two arguments against it.
16) 'À mon avis, la confiance est importante dans une relation. Si on ne peut pas se fier à quelqu'un et communiquer de manière ouverte, cela mène au conflit et peut-être à la séparation.'
    Translate Jean's sentences into English. (H)

Role Models

17) In French, describe a role model in your life and explain how they inspire you.
18) Lucien, an actor, is a private person who does not like having his personal life on display.
    Which of the following is he most likely to do? (Higher)
    a) parler de sa vie privée dans un article
    b) avoir un mariage très public
    c) partager des photos sur un site Internet populaire
    d) éviter l'attention des médias

Celebrations

19) Describe your ideal party. Answer in French and try to give as much detail as you can.
20) What do these words mean in English? a) réunir b) le cadeau c) la carte d) le gâteau

Quick Quiz

Physical and Mental Wellbeing

A healthy lifestyle is something that many people aspire to — if only pizza and TV didn't get in the way. For this topic, try to think about the everyday choices you make.

Head to the CGP RevisionHub for all your online content: www.cgpbooks.co.uk/Merci

Le mode de vie — Lifestyle

Vocabulary

la santé	*health*	le danger	*danger*	empêcher (de)	*to prevent (someone from)*
sain(e)	*healthy*	dangereux / dangereuse	*dangerous*	risquer (de)	*to risk (doing something)*
malsain(e)	*unhealthy*	fatigant(e)	*tiring, exhausting*	refuser (de)	*to refuse (to)*
bon(ne)	*good*	essayer (de)	*to try*	la menace	*threat*
mauvais(e)	*bad*	arrêter (de)	*to stop (doing something)*	éviter (de)	*to avoid (doing something)*
rester	*to stay*	difficile	*difficult*	maintenir	*to maintain*
dormir	*to sleep*	se reposer	*to rest*	cesser (de)	*to stop*
se lever	*to get up*	dépendre (de)	*to depend (on)*		
tôt	*early*	le risque	*risk*		
le lit	*bed*				
la drogue	*drug(s)*				

(Higher: empêcher (de) – cesser (de))

Je me lève à 06h30 et je me couche à 22h30. — *I get up at 6:30 am and I go to bed at 10:30 pm.*

wake up — me réveille

Bien dormir est important pour rester en bonne santé. — *Sleeping well is important for staying healthy.*

eating — manger

Grammar — preposition + infinitive

When followed by an infinitive, the preposition '<u>pour</u>' means '<u>to</u>' do something and '<u>sans</u>' means '<u>without</u>' doing something. See p.150-151 for more on prepositions.

Je cours souvent <u>pour rester</u> en forme. — ***I often run <u>to stay</u> in shape.***

Faire de l'exercice — Doing exercise

Vocabulary

l'activité (f)	*activity*	le foot(ball)	*football*	fort(e)	*strong*
actif / active	*active*	courir	*to run*	faible	*weak*
physique	*physical*	marcher	*to walk*	l'équipe (f)	*team*
le sport	*sport*	danser	*to dance*	bouger	*to move*
sportif / sportive	*sporty, sports*	la natation	*swimming*	l'esprit (m)	*spirit*
jouer (à un sport)	*to play (a sport)*	la forme	*shape*	mener	*to lead*

(H: l'esprit (m), mener)

Elle est assez sportive — elle aime courir et faire de la natation. — *She is quite sporty — she likes to run and swim.*

go skateboarding — du skate

Pour rester en bonne forme, il faut faire un effort pour mener une vie active. — *To stay in good shape, you must make an effort to lead an active life.*

healthy — en bonne santé

J'adore jouer au football parce que j'aime bien l'esprit d'équipe. — *I love playing football because I really like the team spirit.*

rugby — au rugby

Le bien-être mental — Mental wellbeing

Vocabulary

triste	*sad*	pleurer	*to cry*	l'inquiétude (f)	*worry, anxiety*
heureux / heureuse	*happy*	stressé(e)	*stressed*	inquiétant(e)	*worrying*
mental(e)	*mental*	H le souci	*worry*	le soutien	*support*

(Higher: l'inquiétude (f), inquiétant(e), le soutien)

La santé mentale est aussi importante que la santé physique. — *Mental health is as important as physical health.*

Quand je me sens triste, j'évite d'utiliser les réseaux sociaux. — *When I feel sad, I avoid using social media.*

anxious — anxieux / anxieuse
overwhelmed — accablé(e)

Q&A Audio

Question

Qu'est-ce que tu fais pour ton bien-être mental ?

What do you do for your mental wellbeing?

Simple Answer

Quand je suis stressé(e), j'essaie de passer du temps dehors — j'adore courir.

When I am stressed, I try to spend time outdoors — I love to run.

Bernard credited his good health to his morning routine.

Extended Answer

J'ai un réseau de soutien — ma famille et mes amis — qui m'aide à maintenir un esprit sain. Pour moi, il est important de parler aux autres quand je ne me sens pas bien.

I have a support network — my family and my friends — who help me to maintain a healthy mind. For me, it's important to talk to others when I don't feel good.

Practice Questions

Q1 *Answer these questions out loud in French.* SPEAKING
- *Qu'est-ce que tu fais pour rester en bonne santé ?*
- *Qu'est-ce que tu penses de la drogue ?*
- *Cette semaine, qu'est-ce que tu as fait pour ton bien-être ?* *[6 marks]*

Top Tips for Higher Students
✓ Explain your answers fully.
✓ Use a wide range of vocab, including some Higher-tier words.

Higher

Q2 *Read this passage and answer the questions below.* READING

> *Le nouveau centre sportif dans ma ville est maintenant ouvert. On peut y faire beaucoup de sports différents. Par exemple, il y a un grand gymnase où on peut s'entraîner. Moi, je me sens heureux quand je fais de la natation — j'oublie tous mes soucis à la piscine. À mon avis, le sport et l'exercice sont de bons moyens de s'amuser et de rester en bonne forme.*

a) What has recently opened in the writer's town? *[1 mark]*
b) Which sport does the writer enjoy? *[1 mark]*
c) Why do they enjoy this sport? *[1 mark]*
d) Give one benefit of physical activity mentioned in the text. *[1 mark]*

Remember to include 'de' after 'faire' when talking about exercise...

When using 'faire' to talk about the kind of sport or exercise you do, you have to include 'de' after 'faire'. And while you're here, don't forget that 'de' combines with 'le' to make 'du' and with 'les' to make 'des'.

Quick Quiz

Illnesses and Treatments

Everyone feels a bit under the weather from time to time, so it's important that you know these illness and medicine-related words. Plus, they'll be useful in a range of contexts.

Je me sens malade — I feel ill

Vocabulary

la maladie	*illness*	l'accident (m)	*accident*	se brûler (Higher)	*to burn oneself*
malade	*ill*	mort(e)	*dead*	souffrir (Higher)	*to suffer, be in pain*
le virus	*virus*	lutter	*to fight, struggle, battle*	conscient(e) (Higher)	*conscious, aware*
tomber	*to fall*	la fièvre (H)	*fever, temperature*	grave (Higher)	*serious, grave*
avoir mal à	*to ache, hurt*	se blesser (H)	*to hurt oneself, injure oneself*	se sentir (Higher)	*to feel*

Elle est tombée malade d'une maladie rare du sang.	*She fell ill with a rare blood disease.*
Deux personnes sont mortes à la suite d'un grave accident.	*Two people are dead as a result of a serious accident.*
Je crois que j'ai attrapé un rhume.	*I think I've caught the cold.*

is fighting — lutte contre
is suffering from — souffre d'

were injured — ont été blessées

flu — la grippe
measles — la rougeole

J'ai mal au corps — My body hurts

Vocabulary

la tête	*head*	la gorge	*throat*	la main	*hand*
les yeux (m)	*eyes*	le corps	*body*	le doigt	*finger*
l'oreille (f)	*ear*	le cœur	*heart*	la jambe	*leg*
la bouche	*mouth*	le ventre	*belly, stomach*	le pied	*foot*
le nez	*nose*	le dos	*back*	la peau (H)	*skin*
la langue	*tongue*	le bras	*arm*	le sang (H)	*blood*

When talking about body parts in French, you often use the definite article ('le' / 'la' / 'les') instead of a possessive adjective. E.g. 'Il s'est brulé la main' (*He burnt his hand*).

J'ai mal à la tête.	*I have a headache.*
Elle s'est cassé les jambes.	*She broke her legs.*
Bilal a mal au dos parce qu'il est tombé de son vélo.	*Bilal's back hurts because he fell off his bike.*

a stomach ache — mal au ventre
pneumonia — la pneumonie

wrist — au poignet

Grammar — avoir mal + au / à l' / à la / aux

The preposition 'à' combines with definite articles (see p.144):

- **à + le = au ⟶ J'ai mal au dos. (*I have backache.*)**
- **à + l' = à l' ⟶ J'ai mal à l'oreille. (*My ear hurts.*)**
- **à + la = à la ⟶ J'ai mal à la main. (*My hand hurts.*)**
- **à + les = aux ⟶ J'ai mal aux pieds. (*My feet ache.*)**

À l'hôpital — At the hospital

Vocabulary

médical(e)	*medical*	traiter	*to treat*
l'hôpital (m)	*hospital*	le traitement	*treatment*
la pharmacie	*pharmacy, chemist*	conseiller (à... de) (Higher)	*to advise, (someone to do something)*
le / la médecin	*doctor*	le conseil (Higher)	*advice*
le rendez-vous	*appointment*	efficace (Higher)	*efficient*
le médicament	*medicine, pill*	l'urgence (f) (Higher)	*emergency*
allergique	*allergic*	le soin (Higher)	*care*
améliorer	*to improve*	le secours (Higher)	*help, aid, assistance (in an emergency)*
sauver	*to save, rescue*		

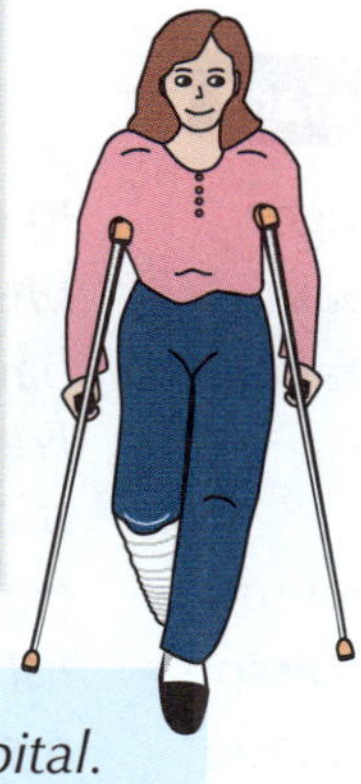

J'ai bénéficié des soins médicaux à l'hôpital.	*I received medical care at the hospital.*
Le médecin m'a donné de bons conseils pendant mon rendez-vous à l'hôpital.	*The doctor gave me some good advice during my appointment at the hospital.*
Pour de nombreux patients le nouveau médicament est efficace, mais j'y suis allergique.	*For lots of patients the new drug is effective, but I am allergic to it.*
Le médicament peut être utilisé par les médecins pour gérer les maladies de longue durée.	*The medicine can be used by doctors to manage long-term illnesses.*

The nurse — L'infirmier / L'infirmière

mental — mentales

Practice Questions

Q1 *Mathieu is talking about visiting the hospital. Read the text, then answer the question below.*

READING

> *Je vais souvent à l'hôpital pour voir ma tante, qui est malade. J'étais triste, mais le médecin lui a donné un nouveau médicament et donc elle va bientôt quitter l'hôpital. À l'avenir, je voudrais étudier les sciences et trouver de nouveaux médicaments pour aider les personnes malades.*

Choose the two correct statements from the list below.

A. Mathieu often goes to the hospital.
B. Mathieu's aunt's health is declining.
C. Mathieu wants to work in medical research when he is older.
D. Mathieu wants to work with old people in the future. *[2 marks]*

Q2 *You are writing an article for a French website.*
You should write about 80-90 words in French. Describe:

WRITING

Top Tip for Higher Students
✓ Use the conditional.

- *the role of a doctor*
- *a time when you were ill*
- *your opinion of medical facilities in your area*
- *whether you would like to be a doctor when you grow up, and why.* *[18 marks]*

You need to know that 'à' + 'le' = 'au'...

... and 'à' + 'les' = 'aux'. It might all seem a bit of a headache, but it's important that you've got this down — you may need it in the exam if you're asked to talk about how you feel and which part of you hurts.

Quick Quiz

Food

Grab a croissant, then munch your way through the tasty vocab on this page.
There's quite a lot of it, but there's a good chance you'll recognise a few words already.

Je vais manger — I'm going to eat...

Vocabulary

manger	*to eat*
le pain	*bread*
la baguette	*baguette, French stick*
l'œuf (m)	*egg*
le poisson	*fish*
la viande	*meat*
le légume	*vegetable*
le fruit	*fruit*
le fromage	*cheese*
les pâtes (f)	*pasta*
le riz	*rice*
les frites (f)	*chips*
la glace	*ice cream, ice*
le chocolat	*chocolate*
le fastfood	*fast food, fast food restaurant*
la pâtisserie	*patisserie, cake shop*
le sucre	*sugar*
boire	*to drink*
l'eau (f)	*water*
le café	*coffee, café, coffee house*
le thé	*tea*
le lait	*milk*
la nourriture (Higher)	*food*
la boisson (Higher)	*drink*
le produit (Higher)	*product*

Je vais au café pour le déjeuner — je mangerai un sandwich au thon, et comme boisson, je prendrais un thé.

I'm going to the café for lunch — I will eat a tuna sandwich and to drink, I will have a tea.

chicken — au poulet
ham — au jambon

Q&A Audio

Question

Qu'est-ce que tu aimes boire ?

What do you like to drink?

Simple Answer

J'adore le café, mais normalement je bois de l'eau.

I love coffee, but normally I drink water.

Extended Answer

J'adore les boissons chaudes, surtout quand il fait froid dehors. J'aime bien le thé, mais ma boisson préférée, c'est le café au lait.

I love hot drinks, especially when it's cold outside. I quite like tea, but my favourite drink is milky coffee.

Faire la cuisine — To cook

Vocabulary

la cuisine	*cooking, kitchen*
le goût	*taste*
végan(e)	*vegan*
végétarien(ne)	*vegetarian*
préparer	*to prepare*
couper	*to cut*
se couper	*to cut oneself*
la recette	*recipe*
délicieux / délicieuse	*delicious*
sentir (Higher)	*to smell*
goûter (Higher)	*to taste, try*
contenir (Higher)	*to contain*
le régime (Higher)	*diet*
frais / fraîche (Higher)	*fresh*
aigre (Higher)	*sour*
sucré(e) (Higher)	*sweet, sugary*
savoureux / savoureuse (Higher)	*tasty*

Pour le repas, je vais préparer du poulet aux légumes. — *For the meal, I am going to prepare chicken with vegetables.*

J'aime le goût du poisson frais. — *I like the taste of fresh fish.*

C'est un plat qui contient du lait. — *It's a dish that contains milk.*

dinner — le dîner
rice — au riz
sugar — du sucre

L'heure du repas — Mealtime

Vocabulary

la faim	*hunger*	recommander	*to recommend*	le verre (Higher)	*glass*
la soif	*thirst*	le reste	*rest, remainder*	le couteau (Higher)	*knife*
le repas	*meal*	les restes	*leftovers*	la fourchette (Higher)	*fork*
le petit-déjeuner	*breakfast*	bon appétit !	*enjoy your meal!*	la cuillère (Higher)	*spoon*
le déjeuner	*lunch*			la bouteille (Higher)	*bottle*
l'entrée (f)	*starter*	le plat (H)	*dish*	supplémentaire (Higher)	*extra, additional*
le dessert	*dessert*	l'assiette (f) (H)	*plate*		

Jun-ho mange des aliments sains en semaine, et va au fast-food seulement le week-end.	*Jun-ho eats healthy food during the week and only goes out for fast food at the weekend.*
Pour le dessert, je recommande de la glace avec du chocolat et des fraises.	*For dessert, I recommend ice cream with chocolate and strawberries.*
Excusez-moi, j'ai besoin d'un couteau et d'une fourchette s'il vous plaît.	*Excuse me, I need a knife and fork please.*
Le plat sentait très bon, mais quand je l'ai goûté, c'était trop sucré.	*The dish smelt very good, but when I tasted it, it was too sweet.*

cake — du gâteau

napkin — d'une serviette
menu — d'une carte

salty — salé

Grammar — hungry & thirsty

In French, you don't say that you are hungry or thirsty. Instead, you say that you have hunger or thirst.

J'ai faim. — ***I'm hungry.***
Elles ont soif. — ***They are thirsty.***

Calliopée wasn't going to let a little spilt milk ruin her day.

Practice Questions

Q1 *Listen to Selina, Ahmed and Élodie talking about food. Choose the correct answer to complete each statement.* LISTENING

	A.	B.	C.	
a) Selina likes to eat...	**A.** cheese	**B.** fish	**C.** bread	*[1 mark]*
b) Ahmed likes...	**A.** rice	**B.** chips	**C.** cheese	*[1 mark]*
c) Élodie's sister eats...	**A.** healthy food	**B.** unhealthy food	**C.** fast food	*[1 mark]*
d) Ahmed doesn't eat...	**A.** meat	**B.** ice cream	**C.** vegetables	*[1 mark]*

Listening Track 11

Q2 *Answer these questions out loud in French.* SPEAKING
- *Qu'est-ce que tu aimes manger pour le déjeuner ?*
- *Qu'est-ce que tu penses des fast-foods ?*
- *Décris-moi ton repas préféré.* *[6 marks]*

Top Tips for Higher Students
✓ Use a wide range of vocab, including some Higher-tier words.
✓ Include a variety of tenses.

Try expressing your own opinions about food...

Almost everyone has opinions on food. In French, tell a friend or family member about what you had for dinner last night, and give your opinion on what you ate and drank. Make sure you use full sentences.

Speaking Questions

Have a crack at these questions to see how healthy your exam skills are. If you're struggling, have another read through the vocabulary in this section and then have a second go.

Candidate's Material

Scenario:

- You are at a sports centre in France, and you are talking to the fitness instructor.
- Find a friend to play the part of the fitness instructor. They will speak first.
- Your friend will ask questions **in French** and you must answer **in French**.
- You are expected to say a few words or a short phrase / sentence in response to each prompt. One-word answers will not be sufficient to gain full marks.

Task:

1. Say what sports you enjoy.
2. Say why you want to join an exercise class.
3. Say what type of exercise class you would like to try.
4. Tell the instructor about any health problems you have.
5. Ask a question about opening times.

Teacher's Material

- Begin the role play with the following introduction:
  'You are in the local sports centre, and you are talking to the fitness instructor. I will play the part of the fitness instructor and speak first.'

1	*Bonjour. Quels sports aimez-vous ?* Allow the candidate to talk about the sports they enjoy.
2	*C'est génial. Pourquoi voulez-vous participer à un cours de sport ?* Allow the candidate to say why they want to join a sports class.
3	*D'accord. Et vous voulez essayer quel activité ?* Allow the candidate to say what exercise class they want to join.
4	*Parfait! Est-ce que vous avez des problèmes de santé ?* Allow the candidate to tell you about their health problems.
5	*Je comprends. Vous avez une question ?* Allow the candidate to ask a question about opening times. *Give an appropriate brief response.*

Listening Questions

1 Listen to this radio phone-in programme about healthy living.
What is mentioned?
Listen to the recording and put a cross in each one of the **three** correct boxes.

Listening Track 12

	A healthy eating
	B losing weight
	C exercise
	D relaxation
	E medication
	F sleep

[3 marks]

2 Myriam, Fatima and Jules are interviewed about drugs.
What do they say?
Listen to the recording and complete the following tables **in English**.
You do not need to write in full sentences.

Listening Track 13

2 a

	Why people shouldn't take drugs
Myriam	....

[1 mark]

Higher

2 b

	One thing that helps people stop using drugs
Fatima	....

[1 mark]

2 c

	One consequence of taking drugs
Jules	....

[1 mark]

Reading Questions

Foundation

1 Read what these French students say about food and drink.

Ana: Je mange toujours des frites, mais je déteste les pâtes et le riz.
Rachid: Moi, je suis végétarien. Je n'aime pas le fromage, mais j'adore boire du thé.
Manon: Au petit-déjeuner, je prends du pain ou des fruits frais et je bois du café au lait.

Who says what? Choose the correct answers.
Put a cross in the correct column for each question.

	Who...	Ana	Rachid	Manon
a)	... eats bread?			
b)	... doesn't like cheese?			
c)	... hates rice?			
d)	... doesn't eat meat?			
e)	... eats fresh products?			
f)	... drinks coffee?			

[6 marks]

Higher

2 Read Jade's blog post about an upcoming football match.

Demain, il y aura un match important pour mon équipe de football. Cependant, je m'inquiète parce que les joueurs ont eu beaucoup de problèmes de santé. Chloé s'est blessé le bras donc elle ne sera pas disponible pour le match. Zoé a mal à l'oreille et donc je lui ai conseillé d'aller chez le médecin et de ne pas jouer demain.

Complete the sentences below. Put a cross in the correct box for each question.

2 a Jade feels...

	A excited about the football match.
	B worried about the football match.
	C disappointed about the football match.

[1 mark]

2 b Chloé can't play because she has...

	A injured her arm.
	B broken her finger.
	C got a sore ear.

[1 mark]

2 c Jade told Zoé to...

	A take Chloé's place in the team.
	B get medical help.
	C get some advice.

[1 mark]

Writing Questions

Foundation

1 Translate the following five sentences **into French**.

1 a I like sport.

.... *[2 marks]*

1 b I am a member of a basketball team.

.... *[2 marks]*

1 c Yesterday, I went to a medical appointment.

.... *[2 marks]*

1 d The doctor works at the local hospital.

.... *[2 marks]*

1 e I have to rest now but I can start doing exercise next week.

.... *[2 marks]*

2 Write to your friend about the role of food in your life.
You **must** include the following points:

- what you do and don't like to eat
- your opinion of restaurants in your town with reasons
- your favourite food when you were a child
- what foods you would like to try in the future.

Write your answer **in French**. You should aim to write between 80 and 90 words. *[18 marks]*

Higher

3 Write a magazine article encouraging teenagers to lead a healthy lifestyle.
You **must** include the following points:

- what makes a healthy lifestyle
- the pros and cons of team sports
- what exercise you did last week
- what you would like to do to become healthier in the future

Write your answer **in French**. You should aim to write between 130 and 150 words. *[22 marks]*

Healthy Living and Lifestyle — Vocabulary

You don't just need a healthy lifestyle — for the exam, you'll also need a healthy knowledge of the words on these pages.

Habits and Lifestyle

la santé	*health*
sain(e)	*healthy*
malsain(e)	*unhealthy*
bon(ne)	*good*
mauvais(e)	*bad*
rester	*to stay*
dormir	*to sleep*
lever	*to lift, raise*
se lever	*to get up*
tôt	*early*
le lit	*bed*
la fois	*time*
la drogue	*drug(s)*
le danger	*danger*
dangereux / dangereuse	*dangerous*
fatigant(e)	*tiring, exhausting*
causer	*to cause*
la cause	*cause*
essayer (de)	*to try*
arrêter (de)	*to stop (doing something), to arrest*
difficile	*difficult*
se reposer	*to rest*
dépendre (de)	*to depend (on)*
le risque	*risk*

Higher:

prévenir	*to warn*
empêcher (de)	*to prevent (someone from)*
risquer (de)	*to risk (doing something)*
refuser (de)	*to refuse (to)*
la menace	*threat*
éviter (de)	*to avoid (doing something)*
cesser	*to stop*
maintenir	*to maintain*
nuire (à)	*to harm (someone)*

Sport and Exercise

l'exercice (m)	*exercise*
l'activité (f)	*activity*
actif / active	*active*
physique	*physical*
le sport	*sport*
sportif / sportive	*sporty, sports*
jouer (à un sport)	*to play (a sport)*
faire (de)	*to do, play*
le foot(ball)	*football*
courir	*to run*
marcher	*to walk*
danser	*to dance*
la natation	*swimming*
le mouvement	*movement*
l'effort (m)	*effort*
la forme	*shape*
en forme	*in shape, fit, healthy*
la vie	*life*
fort(e)	*strong*
faible	*weak*
l'équipe (f)	*team*
bouger	*to move*
la piscine	*swimming pool*
le terrain	*pitch (sports)*
le centre sportif	*sports centre*

Higher:

l'esprit (m)	*spirit*
mener	*to lead*
s'entraîner	*to train*
le poids	*weight*
le gymnase	*gym*

Mental Wellbeing

triste	*sad*
heureux / heureuse	*happy*
mental(e)	*mental*
pleurer	*to cry*
stressé(e)	*stressed*

Higher:

le souci	*worry*
l'inquiétude (f)	*worry, anxiety*
inquiétant(e)	*worrying*
le soutien	*support*

Isobel's fear of heights meant her yoga session was less relaxing than she'd hoped.

Illnesses and Treatments

la maladie	*illness*
malade	*ill*
le virus	*virus*
tomber	*to fall*
avoir mal (à)	*to ache, hurt*
l'accident (m)	*accident*
mort(e)	*dead*
lutter	*to fight, struggle, battle*
la tête	*head*
les yeux (m)	*eyes*
l'oreille (f)	*ear*
la bouche	*mouth*
le nez	*nose*
la langue	*tongue*
la gorge	*throat*
le corps	*body*
le cœur	*heart*
le ventre	*belly, stomach*
le dos	*back*
le bras	*arm*
la main	*hand*
le doigt	*finger*
la jambe	*leg*

le pied	*foot*
médical(e)	*medical*
l'hôpital (m)	*hospital*
la pharmacie	*pharmacy, chemist*
le / la médecin	*doctor*
le rendez-vous	*appointment*
le médicament	*medicine, pill*
qu'est-ce qui ne va pas ?	*what's wrong?*
allergique	*allergic*
améliorer	*to improve*
sauver	*to save, rescue*
traiter	*to treat, handle, deal with*
le traitement	*treatment*
prendre	*to take, have*
la science	*science*
l'être (m)	*being*

Higher

humain(e)	*human*
la fièvre	*fever, temperature*
se blesser	*to hurt oneself, injure oneself*

Higher

se brûler	*to burn oneself*
souffrir	*to suffer, be in pain*
conscient(e)	*conscious, aware*
grave	*serious, grave*
se sentir	*to feel*
la peau	*skin*
le sang	*blood*
conseiller (à... de)	*to advise, (someone to do something)*
le conseil	*advice*
efficace	*efficient*
l'urgence (f)	*emergency*
le soin	*care*
le secours	*help, aid, assistance (in an emergency)*

'To feel' is a reflexive verb in French, so if you're talking about how you're feeling remember to use a reflexive pronoun, e.g. 'je me sens malade' (*I feel ill*).

Food

manger	*to eat*
le pain	*bread*
la baguette	*baguette, French stick*
l'œuf (m)	*egg*
le poisson	*fish*
la viande	*meat*
le légume	*vegetable*
le fruit	*fruit*
le fromage	*cheese*
les pâtes (f)	*pasta*
le riz	*rice*
les frites (f)	*chips*
la glace	*ice cream, ice*
le chocolat	*chocolate*
le fastfood	*fast food, fast food restaurant*
la pâtisserie	*patisserie, cake shop*
le sucre	*sugar*
boire	*to drink*
l'eau (f)	*water*
le café	*coffee, café, coffee house*

le thé	*tea*
le lait	*milk*
la cuisine	*cooking, kitchen*
le goût	*taste*
végan(e)	*vegan*
végétarien(ne)	*vegetarian*
préparer	*to prepare*
couper	*to cut*
se couper	*to cut oneself*
la recette	*recipe*
délicieux / délicieuse	*delicious*
la faim	*hunger*
la soif	*thirst*
le repas	*meal*
le petit-déjeuner	*breakfast*
le déjeuner	*lunch*
l'entrée (f)	*starter*
le dessert	*dessert*
recommander	*to recommend*
les restes	*leftovers*
conserver	*to keep, preserve*
bon appétit !	*enjoy your meal!*
l'énergie (f)	*energy*

Higher

la nourriture	*food*
la boisson	*drink*
le produit	*product*
sentir	*to smell*
goûter	*to taste, try*
contenir	*to contain*
le régime	*diet, regime*
frais / fraîche	*fresh, cool*
aigre	*sour*
sucré(e)	*sweet, sugary*
savoureux / savoureuse	*tasty*
le plat	*dish, course*
l'assiette (f)	*plate*
le verre	*glass*
le couteau	*knife*
la fourchette	*fork*
la cuillère	*spoon*
la bouteille	*bottle*
supplémentaire	*extra, additional*

Revision Summary Test for Section Three

Before you run off to try another section, here's a healthy dose of summary questions for you.

- These questions are **really tricky**, but they'll help you see **how well you know your stuff**.
- Tackle the **revision summary test** below, or scan the QR code to do it **online**.
  You can **keep track of your progress** online and see **which areas need more work**.
- There are **sample answers** here: www.cgpbooks.co.uk/MerciExtras

Summary Test

Physical and Mental Wellbeing

1) 'Je me lève à 6h le matin, donc je dois aller au lit tôt.' What is Camille saying? Answer in English.
2) In French, talk about your evening routine.
3) Translate the following verbs into English: a) jouer b) courir c) marcher d) danser e) faire
4) What are the opposites of these words in French? a) faible b) commencer c) facile
5) Translate this sentence into English: 'J'essaie de faire du sport deux fois par semaine car je veux rester en bonne santé. C'est important pour ma santé mentale d'avoir un style de vie actif.'
6) In French, give 3 things you do to lead a healthy lifestyle, and explain why you do them.
7) What is the French for these phrases? a) in shape b) physical activity c) to rest
8) 'Selon toi, pourquoi la drogue est-elle un problème pour les jeunes ?' Answer in French.
9) [H] What is the French for these verbs? a) to warn b) to prevent c) to harm d) to train
10) [H] What does the word 'souci' mean? Give another French word that means a similar thing.

Illnesses and Treatments

11) How many body parts can you write down in French? There are at least 15 you need to know.
12) Your friend has had a serious accident in France. In French, tell a passer-by: 'My friend has had an accident. He must go to the hospital to receive medical treatment.'
13) Write down the English for these words: a) lutter b) tomber c) mort(e) d) la maladie
14) The pharmacist says, 'Il faut prendre ce médicament pour améliorer votre santé.' What is he saying?
15) Imagine you're visiting the doctor with a medical problem. In French, explain your problem and then say what the doctor might do or advise.
16) What is the French for these phrases?
    a) appointment b) to struggle c) to fall ill d) allergic e) to treat f) to save
17) [Higher] Translate into English: 'Hier, ma copine s'est brûlée, et aujourd'hui elle a de la fièvre et elle a mal. Je lui ai conseillé d'aller voir un médecin.'
18) [Higher] Give the French for these words: a) to hurt oneself b) advice c) to feel d) skin e) blood f) conscious g) a serious illness h) medical emergency

Food

19) How many different foods can you list in French? There are at least 15 you need to know.
20) How many different drinks can you name in French? There are 4 you need to know.
21) Your friend asks you 'Est-ce que tu aimes préparer des repas végétariens ou végans ?' What are they asking you? Answer their question in French.
22) In French, explain why it is important to eat a healthy diet.
23) Write down the French for these words:
    a) recipe b) breakfast c) lunch d) starter e) dessert f) to recommend g) leftovers
24) What does this sentence mean in English? 'J'ai faim, donc je vais manger quelque chose.'
25) Rewrite the French sentence from Q24 so that it is about drinking rather than eating.
26) [H] Translate this sentence into French: 'This cake smells nice, but it's not fresh and it's too sweet.'
27) [H] How many different types of kitchenware can you name? There are at least 7 you need to know.

Music

Quick Quiz

There's a good chance you'll need to talk about free-time activities in the exam. Music's a good one and there's lots of vocab to get your head around, so take your time learning it.

La musique — Music

Head to the CGP RevisionHub for all your online content: www.cgpbooks.co.uk/Merci

Vocabulary

jouer (de)	*to play (an instrument)*	le membre	*member*
l'instrument (m)	*instrument*	le groupe	*group, band*
apprendre (à)	*to learn (to)*	classique	*classic, classical*
chanter	*to sing*	populaire	*popular*
la chanson	*song*	le rythme	*rhythm*
écouter	*to listen (to)*	télécharger	*to download*
le concert	*concert, gig*	H le genre	*genre, type, sort*
		H les paroles (f)	*lyrics*

Grammar — 'jouer de'

'Jouer' is followed by 'de l'', 'du', 'de la' or 'des' when you're talking about playing a musical instrument.

Je joue du violon et de la flûte.
I play the violin and the flute.

Q&A Audio

Question

Est-ce que tu joues d'un instrument de musique ?

Do you play a musical instrument?

Simple Answer

Oui, je joue de la guitare et je chante.

Yes, I play the guitar and I sing.

Extended Answer

Oui, je joue du piano depuis cinq ans et j'apprends à jouer de la trompette. Je suis aussi membre d'un groupe de jazz.

Yes, I have been playing the piano for five years and I'm learning to play the trumpet. I am also a member of a jazz group.

Écouter de la musique — Listening to music

La musique est ma passion et je vais souvent à des concerts avec mes copains.	*Music is my passion and I often go to concerts with my friends.*
Je préfère chanter, mais parfois c'est difficile de me souvenir des paroles.	*I prefer singing, but sometimes it's difficult to remember the lyrics.*
Ma sœur écoute la radio tout le temps et elle télécharge beaucoup de musique populaire.	*My sister always listens to the radio and she downloads lots of popular music.*

rock — rock
techno — techno
classical — classique

Practice Question

Q1 *Listen to three people talk about their attitudes to music and answer the questions below.* LISTENING

a) What does Camille regularly do? *[1 mark]*
b) i) How did Inès find learning an instrument at first? *[1 mark]*
ii) How does she feel about learning an instrument now? *[1 mark]*
H c) i) How long has Dorian been singing for? *[1 mark]*
ii) What has Dorian started doing this year? *[1 mark]*

Listening Track 14

Make sure to remember 'jouer' + 'de'...

Using a range of verbs will help boost your marks — remember that 'jouer' is followed by 'de l'' / 'du' / 'de la' / 'des' when you're talking about musical instruments and 'à' when you're talking about sports.

Quick Quiz

Sport

Ah, sport... Whether you're sporty or not, you need to learn to talk about what sports you do and give your opinion about them. The next two pages should guide you through nicely.

Faire du sport — To do sport

Vocabulary

le sport	*sport*	sportif / sportive	*sporty, sports*	le terrain	*(sports) pitch, ground*
l'exercice (m)	*exercise*	le vélo	*bike, bicycle, cycling*	le Tour de France	*Tour de France*
faire	*to do (a sport)*	la natation	*swimming*	H l'athlétisme (m)	*athletics*
pratiquer	*to practise*	danser	*to dance*		
marcher	*to walk*	la danse	*dance*		
courir	*to run*	le stade	*stadium*		
monter	*to go up*	le centre sportif	*sports centre*		
participer (à)	*to take part (in), participate (in)*	la piscine	*swimming pool*		
la santé	*health*				
actif / active	*active*				

Moi, je suis assez actif / active. Je fais du vélo cinq fois par semaine. À l'avenir, c'est mon rêve de participer à des courses comme le Tour de France.

I'm quite active. I go cycling five times a week. In the future, it's my dream to participate in races like the Tour de France.

sailing — de la voile
skiing — du ski
horse riding — de l'équitation

Je ne suis pas très sportif / sportive mais cet été j'ai beaucoup marché dans la campagne.

I am not very sporty but this summer I walked a lot in the countryside.

I went to the gym every day — je suis allé(e) à la salle du sport chaque jour

Je suis sportif / sportive — I am sporty

Q&A Audio

Question

Est-ce que tu fais du sport souvent ?

Do you do sport often?

Simple Answer

Oui, je danse le lundi, et je cours le mercredi. Je fais aussi partie d'un club de natation.

Yes, I dance on Mondays and I run on Wednesdays. I'm also part of a swimming club.

Grammar — adverbs of time

Use the definite article '<u>le</u>' + the name of a <u>day</u> to say you do something on the <u>same day each week</u>.

Je joue au tennis <u>le jeudi</u>.
I play tennis <u>on Thursdays</u>.

Extended Answer

Oui, j'aime être actif / active. En hiver, je fais du ski — c'est ma passion. Le paysage est beau, mais le ski peut être un sport dangereux. L'année dernière, je suis tombé(e) et je me suis blessé(e).

Yes, I like to be active. In the winter, I go skiing — it's my passion. The landscape is beautiful, but skiing can be a dangerous sport. Last year, I fell and was injured.

Je travaille dans un centre sportif. Pour moi, il est important que tout le monde participe.

I work at a sports centre. For me, it's important that everyone participates.

Cette semaine, la nouvelle piscine ouvrira dans ma ville. Je vais prendre des cours de natation.

This week, the new swimming pool will open in my town. I am going to take swimming lessons.

Les sports (m) d'équipe — Team sports

Vocabulary

le foot(ball)	*football, soccer*	l'équipe (f)	*team*
le tennis	*tennis*	gagner	*to win, earn*
le basket	*basketball*	perdre	*to lose*
le handball	*handball*	dangereux / dangereuse	*dangerous*
le match	*match*	Higher: le concours	*competition*
l'événement (m)	*event*	Higher: blesser	*to hurt, injure*
le jeu	*game*	Higher: se blesser	*to hurt oneself, injure oneself*
le joueur / la joueuse	*player*		

Normalement, je joue au rugby avec mes copains après l'école. — *Normally, I play rugby with my friends after school.*

Je préfère la natation mais mes copains aiment jouer au hockey et ils sont membres d'une équipe locale. — *I prefer swimming but my friends like to play hockey and they are members of a local team.*

J'adore assister aux événements sportifs au stade national à Paris. — *I love to attend sports events at the national stadium in Paris.*

Le week-end dernier, je me suis blessé(e) pendant un concours. — *Last weekend, I got injured during a competition.*

badminton — au badminton
basketball — au basket
netball — au netball
golf — au golf

tournaments — aux tournois

a football match — un match de foot
a game of tennis — une partie de tennis

Practice Questions

Q1 *Translate the following sentences into French.* (WRITING)

a) In my opinion, exercise is essential for your health. *[2 marks]*

b) I am active and I try to do sport every day. *[2 marks]*

c) Yesterday, my sister danced with her friends. *[2 marks]*

d) This summer, I am going to play tennis with my dad. *[2 marks]*

Higher

Q2 *Read what Lola has to say about trying a new sport and answer the questions below.* (READING)

Moi, je cours pour rester en bonne santé. C'est un sport qu'on peut faire seul ou dans une équipe. On peut courir dans un centre sportif, sur une piste d'athlétisme, ou même au parc, et ça ne coûte rien. Chaque semaine je sors avec une amie qui est très sportive. Elle participe à des concours et gagne souvent. Elle m'a beaucoup aidée, parce qu'au début c'était vraiment difficile. Alors, je suis en train d'améliorer mes compétences, et maintenant, quand je fais du sport, je ne me blesse plus.

a) What sport does Lola do? *[1 mark]*

b) According to the text, which three places can you do this sport? *[3 marks]*

c) Give two things Lola has improved on since training with her friend. *[2 marks]*

You don't just have to talk about the sports you currently do...

This topic gives you a good opportunity to use the imperfect tense (see p.170) — you can mention sports that you used to do. Don't forget that 'faire', 'jouer' and 'participer' will still need 'de' or 'à' in the imperfect.

Quick Quiz

Cinema, Theatre and TV

Everyone loves a good film or TV show — and they're great to talk about in the exam. These pages cover some useful vocab you can use to discuss films, plays and TV, so it's time to get reading.

Regarder un film — Watching a film

Vocabulary

le cinéma	*cinema*
regarder	*to watch*
voir	*to see*
le film	*film*
le billet	*ticket*
l'action (f)	*action*

le film d'action	*action film*
le film d'horreur	*horror film*
l'histoire d'amour (f)	*romance*
l'acteur / l'actrice	*actor / actress*
le personnage	*character*
H la séance	*film screening, session*

Q&A Audio

Question	Simple Answer	Extended Answer
Est-ce que tu aimes aller au cinéma ? *Do you like to go to the cinema?*	Non, je préfère regarder des films chez moi. *No, I prefer to watch films at home.*	Oui, je suis membre d'un club de cinéma. J'y vais une fois par semaine, parce que les billets sont moins chers. J'adore discuter des nouveaux films avec les autres membres. *Yes, I am a member of a cinema club. I go once a week because the tickets are less expensive. I love discussing new films with the other members.*

J'adore voir des films d'action au cinéma. Les effets spéciaux sont étonnants sur grand écran.
I love seeing action films at the cinema. The special effects are amazing on the big screen.

horror films — des films d'horreur
romantic films — des histoires d'amour
comedies — des films comiques

Mon frère aime les mêmes films que moi, donc nous les regardons ensemble.
My brother likes the same films as me, so we watch them together.

Je dois acheter deux billets de cinéma pour le nouveau film ce week-end.
I need to buy two cinema tickets for the new film this weekend.

Aller au théâtre — Going to the theatre

Vocabulary

le théâtre	*theatre, drama*
la tragédie	*drama (tragedy)*
la comédie	*comedy*
rire	*to laugh*
passionnant(e)	*exciting*
H la scène	*stage, scene*
H la pièce	*play*

Ce soir, je vais au théâtre pour voir une nouvelle pièce.
Tonight, I'm going to the theatre to see a new play.

a musical — une comédie musicale

Je n'ai pas aimé la scène d'ouverture car la musique était trop forte.
I didn't like the opening scene because the music was too loud.

the plot — l'intrigue

Cependant, la pièce était intéressante et moderne, et les acteurs étaient drôles.
However, the play was interesting and modern, and the actors were funny.

Qu'est-ce qu'il y a à la télé ? — What's on TV?

Vocabulary

la télé(vision)	*television, TV*
l'émission (f)	*TV programme, broadcast*
le programme	*programme*
les informations	*news, information*
la série	*series*
les effets spéciaux (m)	*special effects*
la célébrité	*celebrity*
le / la fan	*fan, supporter*
H l'écran (m)	*screen*
H le documentaire	*documentary*

'On' is usually translated as 'sur' in French, but remember, it's 'à la télé'.

Grammar — 'qui'

'Qui' means 'who' or 'which'. It refers to the subject of the sentence.

La personne qui regarde la télévision.
The person who watches television.

Le personnage qui est mort à la fin.
The character who died at the end.

Mon passe-temps préféré, c'est regarder la télévision — c'est amusant.	*My favourite hobby is watching television — it's fun.*
J'adore les émissions qui me font rire.	*I love programmes that make me laugh.*
La télé-réalité est intéressante car on peut suivre la vie quotidienne des célébrités.	*Reality TV is interesting because you can follow celebrities' daily lives.*
Elle aime les documentaires.	*She likes documentaries.*

relaxing — relaxant
entertaining — divertissant

the news — les informations
soap operas — les feuilletons
crime series — les séries policières

Practice Questions

Q1 Pierre is talking about television. Read the text, then answer the question below. READING

> *Je regarde la télévision presque tous les jours après le collège. Mon père pense que je ne fais jamais mes devoirs parce que je passe trop de temps devant la télé. Il croit que faire du sport va être meilleur pour ma santé, et que je ne bouge pas assez. Moi, je pense que je dois regarder la télé pour me reposer après une longue journée de cours.*

Choose the two correct statements from the list below.

A. Pierre watches TV almost every day after school.
B. Pierre only watches TV after doing his homework.
C. Pierre likes watching sport on TV.
D. Pierre watches TV to rest after a long day at school. *[2 marks]*

Q2 You are writing a blog post about the films and TV shows you like to watch. Write about 80-90 words in French. Describe: WRITING

- *what kinds of films and TV shows you like watching and why*
- *your opinion of theatre with reasons*
- *what types of films you enjoyed as a child*
- *what kind of film you will watch the next time you go to the cinema.*

[18 marks]

Top Tip for Higher Students
✓ Include conjunctions to help you express different opinions, e.g. 'cependant' / 'pourtant'.

Boost your answers by adding comparisons...

If you're running out of things to say about TV shows you like, you could compare your own tastes to your siblings' or parents' tastes. This will extend your answers and increase the amount of vocab you use.

Quick Quiz

Hobbies and Going Out

We've all got different activities we prefer — from computer games to cooking. These pages cover plenty of vocab that will be useful when you're talking about all the fun stuff you get up to.

Mes loisirs (m) — My hobbies

Vocabulary

le loisir	*leisure, leisure activity, hobby*
l'activité (f)	*activity*
la passion	*passion*
l'association (f)	*organisation, club*
libre	*free, available*
le temps	*time, weather*
le temps libre	*free time*
s'intéresser (à)	*to be interested in*
s'amuser	*to enjoy oneself*
plaire (à)	*to please (someone)*
essayer (de)	*to try (to)*
former	*to form*
lire	*to read*
le livre	*book*
la lecture	*reading*
la photo	*photo*
la création	*creation*
le tableau	*painting, picture*
l'ordinateur portable (m)	*laptop*
le jeu vidéo	*video game*

Higher

observer	*to observe, watch*
tenter (de)	*to try (attempt)*
le roman	*novel*
l'œuvre (f)	*work*
le don	*gift, talent*
s'ennuyer	*to be bored, get bored*

Q&A Audio

Question

Qu'est ce-que tu aimes faire dans ton temps libre ?

What do you like to do in your free time?

Simple Answer

Mon loisir préféré, c'est la lecture. Je pense que les livres historiques sont les plus intéressants.

My favourite hobby is reading. I think that historical books are the most interesting.

Extended Answer

J'ai une passion pour l'art et je prends des photos presque tous les jours. Au lycée, il y a un club photo où tout le monde peut partager ses créations — c'est extraordinaire d'observer le travail des autres.

I have a passion for art and I take photos almost every day. At college, there is a photography club where everyone can share their creations — it's extraordinary to observe other people's work.

Je vais sortir — I'm going to go out...

Vocabulary

sortir	*to go out*
aller	*to go*
le centre commercial	*shopping centre*
la valeur	*value*
gratuit(e)	*free*
le parc	*park*
la fête	*party*
le festival	*festival*
le restaurant	*restaurant*
le soleil	*sun*
l'ami(e)	*friend*
le copain	*friend, mate*
la copine	*friend, mate*
la tendance	*trend, tendency*
habituel(le)	*usual*
occupé(e)	*busy*

Je préfère aller au cinéma plutôt que jouer sur mon ordinateur portable.

I prefer going to the cinema to playing on my laptop.

Pendant mon temps libre, j'adore être dehors. Quand il y a du soleil, je vais au parc avec mes amis.

In my free time, I love being outside. When it's sunny, I go to the park with my friends.

Grammar — giving opinions

Use '<u>j'aime</u>' (*I like*), '<u>je préfère</u>' (*I prefer*) and '<u>je déteste</u>' (*I hate*) to give a <u>range</u> of opinions.

<u>Je préfère</u> la lecture au sport.
<u>I prefer</u> reading to sport.
<u>Je déteste</u> les jeux vidéo.
<u>I hate</u> video games.

Manger au restaurant — Eating at the restaurant

Vocabulary

manger	*to eat*	(à) emporter	*to take away, take, remove*
la cuisine	*cooking*	réserver	*to reserve, book*
le repas	*meal*	ouvert(e)	*open, opened*
l'entrée (f)	*starter*	la nourriture (Higher)	*food*
la carte	*menu, credit card*	le plat (Higher)	*dish, course*
la table	*table*	l'addition (f) (Higher)	*bill*
commander	*to order*		

Hier soir, j'ai réservé une table au restaurant que tu aimes. La nourriture est super et les serveurs sont très sympathiques.
Last night, I reserved a table at the restaurant that you like. The food is great and the waiters are very nice.

Je voudrais payer le repas parce que c'est ton anniversaire.
I would like to pay for the meal because it's your birthday.

the drinks — les boissons
the desserts — les desserts

Est-ce qu'on peut voir la carte, s'il vous plaît ? Je pense qu'on va acheter des plats à emporter.
Can we see the menu, please? I think we will buy food to take away.

Comme entrée, je vais prendre le poisson et un peu de pain, s'il vous plaît.
As a starter, I'll take the fish and a bit of bread, please.

For the main course — Comme plat principal

Practice Questions

Q1 *Choose one of the photos below. Talk in French about what is in the photo. You should talk for about a minute and describe who is in the photo, where it takes place, and what is happening.* SPEAKING

Top Tip for Higher Students
✓ Use time expressions such as 'être en train de' or 'venir de'.

[8 marks]

Higher

Q2 *Listen to Anaïs, Izzie, Enzo and Paul talking about activities they do in their free time. Then answer the questions below.* LISTENING

a) Why does Anaïs spend a lot of time on her laptop? *[1 mark]*
b) How does Izzie escape from reality? *[1 mark]*
c) What does Enzo prefer to do? *[1 mark]*
d) Why does Paul dislike parties? Give two reasons. *[2 marks]*

Listening Track 15

Vary your language — don't just use 'j'aime' all the time...

It can be easy to get stuck using the same phrases all the time, so try practising different ways of expressing your opinions. Using verbs like 'préférer' and 's'intéresser à' will make you sound much more sophisticated.

Speaking Questions

Time to have a go at these exam-style questions. Once you're finished, you may need to use up a bit of your own free time to revisit the vocab in this section before having another try.

Candidate's Material

- Choose **one** of the pictures below to describe. Make notes on it to use during the test.
- Your teacher will ask you to describe the picture. You should talk for approximately **one and a half to two minutes**. Your description must cover the **people, location and activity** shown in the picture.
- After you have spoken about the content of the picture, your teacher will ask you two questions about your chosen picture. Then, they will ask you some questions related to any of the topics within the theme of **Lifestyle and Wellbeing**.

Picture 1:

Picture 2:

Teacher's Material

- Begin by asking the candidate which picture they have chosen, then say 'Describe the picture'. Candidates should talk about the picture for approximately **one and a half to two minutes**. They may use any notes they have made during the preparation time.
- When the candidate has finished, ask the questions below that relate to their chosen picture.

Picture 1:

- [F] Est-ce que tu aimes aller au cinéma ?
- Quelles sont les activités pour les jeunes dans ta ville ?
- [H] Qu'est-ce que tu as fait le week-end dernier ?

Picture 2:

- [F] Est-ce que tu aimes les sports d'équipe ?
- Est-ce que tu préfères faire du sport seul(e) ou avec d'autres ?
- [H] Quel sport as-tu fait récemment ?

- Now ask the candidate the following unprepared conversation questions on the theme of **Lifestyle and Wellbeing**:

- Quel est ton loisir préféré ?
- Est-ce que tu vas regarder la télé cette semaine ? Pourquoi ? / Pourquoi pas ?
- Est-ce que tu as mangé dans un restaurant récemment ? C'était comment ?

Listening Questions

1 You are going to hear two people talking about cinema and theatre.

Sentences 1 and 3: Write down the missing words in the gaps provided. In each gap, you will write one word **in French**.

Sentences 2 and 4: Write down the full sentences that you hear in the spaces provided, **in French**.

Listening Track 16

F

1 a Sentence 1

Le .... cinéma est .... *[2 marks]*

1 b Sentence 2

....

.... *[2 marks]*

Higher

1 c Sentence 3

Je préfère .... des .... de

théâtre — c'est plus .... *[2 marks]*

1 d Sentence 4

....

.... *[2 marks]*

2 Léa and Rachid are talking about a new restaurant.
What do they say? Complete the following tables **in English**.

Listening Track 17

2 a

	Why he had a bad experience
Rachid	....

[1 mark]

2 b

	Why she won't return to the restaurant
Léa	....

[1 mark]

Reading Questions

1 Read Charlie's response to an online questionnaire about TV.

> Je suis très sportif et j'adore regarder les émissions de sport. Je regarde un match de football tous les soirs, même si ce n'est pas mon équipe préférée. Je préfère les émissions sportives aux informations que je trouve ennuyeuses. Ce qui se passe dans le monde ne m'intéresse pas, mais ma sœur adore suivre les événements réels.

Complete the gap in each sentence using a word from the box below.
There are more words than gaps.

the weather	football	the news	comedy
follows	dislikes	reads	

1 a Charlie watches .... every night. *[1 mark]*

1 b He thinks .... is boring. *[1 mark]*

1 c His sister .... real events. *[1 mark]*

Higher

2 Read Mehdi's email to his friend. Answer the questions below **in English**.

> Bonjour Camille,
> La musique est ma passion. J'écoute divers genres de musique et c'est mon rêve d'apprendre à jouer d'un instrument. Cet été, je vais à un festival de musique en Angleterre avec mon frère. On a acheté nos billets pour le festival, mais on doit encore organiser le transport et le logement. Si j'ai le temps, j'irai à Londres* pour passer quelques jours chez toi. Je voudrais aller voir un match de foot au stade de Wembley et manger dans le restaurant d'un chef célèbre.
> À bientôt !
>
> *Londres = London

2 a What is Mehdi's dream?

.... *[1 mark]*

2 b Name **one thing** Mehdi and his brother still need to organise.

.... *[1 mark]*

2 c Name **one thing** Mehdi wants to do in London.

.... *[1 mark]*

Writing Questions

Foundation

1 Translate the following five sentences **into French**.

1 a I play basketball.

.... *[2 marks]*

1 b I often practise on the sports pitch.

.... *[2 marks]*

1 c Sport is good for your health.

.... *[2 marks]*

1 d I used to take part in tennis matches.

.... *[2 marks]*

1 e I like to watch the Tour de France with my mum.

.... *[2 marks]*

2 Write to your friend about music.
You must include the following points:

- musical instruments you play or want to play
- your opinion of popular music
- a song you heard recently
- a concert you would like to go to

Write your answer **in French**. You should aim to write between 80 and 90 words. *[18 marks]*

Higher

3 Translate the paragraph **into French**.

> My favourite hobby is reading. I particularly like love stories or historical novels. Every night I try to read for half an hour. Last weekend I went to the library and I found a new series that I want to read. This summer, I am going to a book festival in France.

[10 marks]

Free-time Activities — Vocabulary

Learning all of this vocab about your hobbies will only make your free time more fun — I promise.

Music

la musique	*music*
jouer (de)	*to play (an instrument)*
l'instrument (m)	*instrument*
apprendre (à)	*to learn (to)*
le chanteur / la chanteuse	*singer*
chanter	*to sing*
la chanson	*song*
écouter	*to listen (to)*
le concert	*concert, gig*
le membre	*member*
le groupe	*group, band*
classique	*classic, classical*
populaire	*popular*
le rythme	*rhythm*
Internet (m)	*internet, web*
télécharger	*to download*

Higher

le genre	*genre, type, sort*
les paroles (f)	*lyrics*

Sport

le sport	*sport*
l'exercice (m)	*exercise*
faire	*to do (a sport)*
pratiquer	*to practise*
marcher	*to walk*
courir	*to run*
monter	*to go up*
participer (à)	*to take part (in), participate (in)*
la santé	*health*
actif / active	*active*
sportif / sportive	*sporty, sports*
le vélo	*bike, bicycle, cycling*
la natation	*swimming*
danser	*to dance*
la danse	*dance*
le stade	*stadium*
le centre	*centre*
le centre sportif	*sports centre*
la piscine	*swimming pool*
le terrain	*(sports) pitch, ground*
le Tour de France	*the Tour de France*
le foot(ball)	*football*
le tennis	*tennis*
le basket	*basketball*
le handball	*handball*
le match	*match*
l'événement (m)	*event*
le jeu	*game*
le joueur / la joueuse	*player*
l'équipe (f)	*team*
gagner	*to win, earn*
perdre	*to lose*
dangereux / dangereuse	*dangerous*

Higher

l'athlétisme (m)	*athletics*
la piste	*track, trail*
le concours	*competition*
blesser	*to hurt, injure*
se blesser	*to hurt oneself, injure oneself*

Cinema and Theatre

le cinéma	*cinema*
montrer	*to show*
regarder	*to watch, look at*
voir	*to see*
le film	*film, movie*
le billet	*ticket*
l'action (f)	*action*
l'horreur (f)	*horror*
le film d'action	*action film*
l'histoire d'amour (f)	*romance*
l'acteur / l'actrice	*actor / actress*
le personnage	*character*
le théâtre	*theatre, drama*
la tragédie	*drama (tragedy)*
la comédie	*comedy*
rire	*to laugh*
passionnant(e)	*exciting*

Higher

la séance	*film screening, session*
la scène	*stage, scene*
la pièce	*play*

Television

la télé(vision)	*television, TV*
l'émission (f)	*TV programme, broadcast*
le programme	*programme*
les informations (f)	*news, information*
la réalité	*reality*
la série	*series, soap opera*
la chaîne	*channel, chain*
l'effet (m)	*effect*
les effets spéciaux (m)	*special effects*
le titre	*title*
célèbre	*famous*
la célébrité	*celebrity*
le fan	*fan, supporter*
l'écran (m) (H)	*screen*
le documentaire (H)	*documentary*

Hobbies

le loisir	*leisure, leisure activity, hobby*
l'activité (f)	*activity*
la passion	*passion*
l'association (f)	*organisation, club*
libre	*free, available*
le temps	*time, weather*
le temps libre	*free time*
s'intéresser (à)	*to be interested in*
s'amuser	*to enjoy oneself*
plaire (à)	*to please (someone)*
essayer (de)	*to try (to)*
former	*to form*
lire	*to read*
le livre	*book*
la lecture	*reading*
la photo	*photo*
la création	*creation*
le tableau	*painting, picture*
l'ordinateur portable (m)	*laptop*
le jeu vidéo	*video game*
observer (Higher)	*to observe, watch*
tenter (de) (Higher)	*to try, attempt*
le roman (Higher)	*novel*
l'œuvre (f) (Higher)	*work*
le don (Higher)	*gift, talent*
s'ennuyer (Higher)	*to be bored, get bored*

Going Out

sortir	*to go out*
aller	*to go*
le centre commercial	*shopping centre*
la valeur	*value*
gratuit(e)	*free*
le parc	*park*
la fête	*party*
le festival	*festival*
le restaurant	*restaurant*
le soleil	*sun*
l'ami(e)	*friend*
le copain	*friend, mate*
la copine	*friend, mate*
la tendance	*trend, tendency*
habituel(le)	*usual*
occupé(e)	*busy*
manger	*to eat*
la cuisine	*cooking*
le repas	*meal*
l'entrée (f)	*starter*
la carte	*menu, credit card*
la table	*table*
commander	*to order*
(à) emporter	*to take away, take, remove*
réserver	*to reserve, book*
ouvert(e)	*open, opened*
la nourriture (Higher)	*food*
le plat (Higher)	*dish, course*
l'addition (f) (Higher)	*bill*

Revision Summary Test for Section Four

You've almost made it to the end of the section — now it's time to check your knowledge.

- These questions are **really tricky**, but they'll help you see **how well you know your stuff**.
- Tackle the **revision summary test** below, or scan the QR code to do it **online**.
  You can **keep track of your progress** online and see **which areas need more work**.
- There are **sample answers** here: www.cgpbooks.co.uk/MerciExtras

Summary Test

Music

1) 'Est-ce que tu joues d'un instrument de musique ?' Translate this question, then answer it in French.
2) Imagine you recently went to a music festival. Write two sentences about it in French.
3) Translate into French: 'I used to listen to classical music but now I download popular songs from the internet.'
4) A French musician has given an interview: 'Je suis membre d'un groupe. J'écris les chansons et je chante. Nous participons à beaucoup de concerts.' What's he saying?

Sport

5) Write three sentences about your favourite sport. Why do you like it and when do you play it?
6) Translate Hugo's sentence into English: 'Je fais souvent du vélo et je participe à un événement sportif la semaine prochaine. Si je gagne, je vais devenir membre de l'équipe nationale française.'
7) 'Do you enjoy team sports? Why? / Why not?' Answer in French.
8) Write this sentence in French: 'I am quite active because it's good for your health to exercise.'
9) Translate these words into French: a) sports centre b) football match c) swimming d) stadium e) sports pitch f) swimming pool g) basketball h) game
10) [H] 'Je pratique la natation régulièrement mais récemment je me suis blessée pendant un concours, donc je ne peux pas faire de sport pendant cinq semaines.' What's Nadia saying?

Cinema, Theatre and TV

11) What do these words mean in English?
    a) l'acteur b) le personnage c) le film d'action d) l'émission e) le billet f) rire
12) 'Est-ce que tu aimes aller au cinéma ? Pourquoi ? / Pourquoi pas ?' Respond in French.
13) In French, describe the last film or TV show you watched. Did you enjoy it? Why? / Why not?
14) Translate what Sylvie says about her job: 'J'adore travailler pour le théâtre — c'est ma passion. Je préfère les tragédies aux comédies parce que les personnages sont plus intéressants.'
15) [Higher] 'Cette série est ennuyeuse et elle donne aux jeunes une fausse image de la vie normale.' Translate this statement into English and then give your opinion on reality TV.
16) [Higher] Translate these phrases into French:
    a) to watch a documentary b) screen c) stage d) play e) film screening

Hobbies and Going Out

17) What do these words mean in English? a) la tendance b) le repas c) la fête d) le tableau
18) 'Pendant mon temps libre, je lis un livre ou, s'il y a du soleil, je vais au parc avec un ami.' Translate Lola's sentence into English, then describe what you do in your own free time in French.
19) In French, how would you say 'I would like to reserve a table but the restaurant isn't open yet'?
20) Translate these phrases into French: a) He's interested in reading. b) I play video games. c) They go out often. d) She will try a new hobby. e) I hate festivals.
21) You're at a restaurant in France. Say that you'd like to see the menu and order food to take away.
22) [H] Translate these words into English:
    a) s'ennuyer b) le don c) le roman d) l'addition e) la nourriture f) le plat

Where You Live

Quick Quiz

Whether you love the rural lifestyle or you're more suited to living in urban areas, you'll need to know how to talk about where you live. Reading this page should do the trick.

Don't forget you can access your online content here: www.cgpbooks.co.uk/Merci

Tu habites où ? — Where do you live?

Vocabulary

habiter	*to live*	le coin	*corner*	l'habitant(e)	*resident*
l'adresse (f)	*address*	le bord	*edge, side*	situer	*to situate, locate*
le / la voisin(e)	*neighbour*	la côte	*coast*	se situer	*to be situated, be located*
le village	*village*	la montagne	*mountain*		
la ville	*town, city*	la forêt	*forest*	vivre	*to live*
la capitale	*capital city*	la campagne	*countryside*	la banlieue	*suburbs*
la région	*region*	la ferme	*farm*	la cité	*(council) estate*
la province	*province*	le lac	*lake*	le chemin	*way, path*
la rue	*street*	où	*where*	le champ	*field*
la route	*road, way, route*	sûr(e)	*safe*	le paysage	*landscape*

(Higher: l'habitant(e) to le paysage)

Ma mère habite près d'une vieille ferme dans un petit village à la campagne. — *My mother lives near an old farm in a small village in the countryside.*

by a lake — au bord d'un lac
in the mountains — à la montagne

Moi, je préfère vivre dans la banlieue d'une grande ville où il y a plus de transports publics. — *I prefer to live on the outskirts of a large town where there is more public transport.*

Dans ma cité, tous les voisins s'entendent bien et c'est toujours calme. — *On my council estate, all the neighbours get on well and it's always quiet.*

Grammar — using prepositions for location

Some prepositions are used to describe the location of something or someone. See p.150 for more on prepositions.

La maison se situe entre deux forêts.
The house is situated between two forests.

Il y a une montagne près de la maison.
There is a mountain near the house.

Practice Question

Q1 *Read the following text about where Élodie lives and answer the questions below in English.*

READING

J'habite dans une petite ville sur la côte nord-ouest de la France. Ma ville est belle, avec beaucoup de grandes plages. Malheureusement, il n'y a pas beaucoup à faire ici en hiver. Alors, habiter dans cette ville est quelquefois ennuyeux. Un jour, je voudrais habiter dans le sud-ouest du pays car il fait plus chaud là-bas et j'adore la cuisine de la région.

a) Where in France is Élodie's town situated? *[1 mark]*

b) What is her town like? Give **two** details. *[2 marks]*

c) Why is it sometimes boring to live there? *[1 mark]*

d) Why does Élodie want to live in the south-west? Give **two** reasons. *[2 marks]*

Back up your opinions to reach for those higher marks...

You might love the area you live in, or maybe you wish you lived somewhere else entirely. Either way, tell the examiner and expand on your opinions by giving reasons — 'parce que...' or 'car...' will be useful.

Quick Quiz

The Home

Big, small, clean, dirty, well-built... However your home looks, these pages will help you learn how to describe it in French. Remember to use your opinion toolkit to score those higher marks.

La maison — The home

Vocabulary

la maison	*house, home*	la porte	*door*	le foyer (Higher)	*home*
l'appartement (m)	*apartment, flat*	la fenêtre	*window*	l'étage (m) (Higher)	*floor (of a building)*
l'immeuble (m)	*building, block of flats*	la clé	*key*	l'escalier (m) (Higher)	*stairs*
chez	*at (the house of), to (the house of), with*	le sol	*floor, ground*	l'ascenseur (m) (Higher)	*lift*
		le jardin	*garden*		
		l'animal (m)	*animal, pet*		

Je suis propriétaire d'une grande maison. — *I am the owner of a large house.*

Dans l'appartement où j'habite, les portes et les fenêtres sont énormes. — *In the flat where I live, the doors and the windows are enormous.*

Je prends toujours l'ascenseur parce qu'il y a plusieurs étages dans mon immeuble. — *I always take the lift because there are several floors in my building.*

a detached house — une maison individuelle
a terraced house — une maison mitoyenne

Les pièces (f) de la maison — The rooms in the house

Vocabulary

la salle	*room*	la table	*table*
le mur	*wall*	la boîte	*box*
la chambre	*bedroom*	les toilettes	*toilet*
le lit	*bed*	la pièce (H)	*room*
la cuisine	*kitchen, cooking*	la couverture (H)	*blanket*

On a mis un nouveau lit dans ma chambre. — *We put a new bed in my bedroom.*

Nous avons une grande table dans la cuisine pour dîner ensemble en famille. — *We have a big table in the kitchen to eat dinner together as a family.*

Il y a des photos anciennes sur les murs du salon. — *There are old photos on the walls of the living room.*

a gigantic wardrobe — une armoire gigantesque
bathroom — de la salle du bain

Q&A Audio

Question

Décris ta maison.
Describe your home.

Simple Answer

Chez moi, il y a deux chambres, un bureau et une cuisine.
In my home, there are two bedrooms, an office and a kitchen.

Extended Answer

Moi, j'habite dans un appartement au troisième étage. C'est assez petit et il n'y a que deux chambres. Un jour, je voudrais habiter dans une belle maison avec un grand jardin.
I live in an apartment on the third floor. It's quite small and there are only two bedrooms. One day, I would like to live in a beautiful home with a big garden.

C'est comment chez toi ? — What's it like at your place?

Vocabulary

idéal(e)	*ideal*
propre	*clean, proper, own*
énorme	*enormous, big*
moderne	*modern*
H construire	*to build, construct*
H posséder	*to own, have*

Some adjectives have a different meaning depending on whether they go before or after a noun. See p.156 for more.

Currently under construction. Please come back later.

Ma maison est toujours propre car je la nettoie tous les jours. — *My house is always clean because I clean it every day.*

Devant chez nous, une entreprise construit beaucoup de nouveaux bâtiments, ce qui n'est pas idéal. — *Outside our place, a company is building lots of new buildings, which isn't ideal.*

Chez moi, c'est calme parce que je n'ai qu'un voisin et qu'il habite tout seul. — *At my place, it's quiet because I only have one neighbour and he lives alone.*

messy — en désordre

I hate tidying up — je déteste ranger

annoys me — m'énerve

Grammar (Higher only) — 'ne...que'

You can use the negative form 'ne...que' to say 'only'. See p.175 for more on negative forms.

Il n'y a que deux appartements au premier étage. ***There are only two flats on the first floor.***

Practice Questions

Q1 Translate the following sentences into French. WRITING

a) I live in a modern block of flats.
b) It's always very pleasant at my place.
c) I want to buy a house with a garden.
d) I used to have an enormous bedroom.
H **e)** I wouldn't like to build my own home.
H **f)** My flat is situated on the fourth floor. *[12 marks]*

Higher

Q2 You receive a phone call from a French estate agent about a new home on the market. Listen to the call and choose the correct option for each question below. LISTENING

Listening Track 18

a) Where is the house situated?
A. In the mountains
B. In the countryside
C. On the coast *[1 mark]*

b) Who is the house ideal for?
A. A young couple
B. A single person
C. A family *[1 mark]*

c) Which room is the agent's favourite?
A. The bathroom
B. The bedroom
C. The kitchen *[1 mark]*

d) What else is great about this house?
A. The garden is ideal for a dog.
B. The neighbours are nice.
C. The shops are nearby. *[1 mark]*

Use adjectives to make your descriptions more detailed...

Sure, you could just tell the examiner you have a kitchen with a table in it. But if you want to cook up a more interesting sentence, try telling them you have a big, beautiful, red kitchen with a new table in it.

Quick Quiz

The Local Area

Your local area could be a hot topic of discussion in the exams, so it's important you know how to talk about it. Luckily for you, these pages have plenty of useful vocab to help you do just that.

Les lieux (m) d'intérêt — Places of interest

Vocabulary

visiter	*to visit*	le parc	*park*	le café	*café*
le quartier	*neighbourhood*	le centre	*centre*	le restaurant	*restaurant*
la place	*square, place*	la plage	*beach*	le marché	*market*
l'endroit (m)	*place, spot*	la piscine	*swimming pool*	la boulangerie	*bakery*
l'espace (m)	*space*	la poste	*post office*	central(e)	*central*
le pont	*bridge*	la banque	*bank*	ancien(ne)	*former, ancient, old*
la tour	*tower*	l'hôpital (m)	*hospital*	H le lieu	*place*
le château	*castle*	le cinéma	*cinema*	H la bibliothèque	*library*
le musée	*museum*				

J'allais à la boulangerie le matin.	*I used to go to the bakery in the morning.*
Le week-end, mes amis et moi aimons aller au parc où il y a un café génial.	*At the weekend, my friends and I like going to the park where there's a great café.*
Cette ville a une tour énorme au centre et un stade de l'autre côté du pont.	*This town has an enormous tower in the centre and a stadium on the other side of the bridge.*
Il y a un nouveau musée d'art moderne sur la place — il ouvrira demain.	*There is a new modern art museum in the square — it will open tomorrow.*

cake shop — la pâtisserie

three hospitals — trois hôpitaux

Dans ma ville... — In my town...

Q&A Audio

Question

Tu aimes aller où dans ta ville ?

Where do you like to go in your town / city?

Simple Answer

J'aime faire de la natation à la piscine au centre-ville.

I like to go swimming at the pool in the town centre.

Extended Answer

J'adore aller dans le vieux quartier. Là-bas, il y a une belle place avec un super restaurant qui sert des plats délicieux. Il y a aussi un pont très ancien — je ne l'ai découvert que la semaine dernière. Il vaut la peine de le visiter.

I love going to the old quarter. There's a beautiful square with a great restaurant that serves delicious dishes. There is also a very old bridge — I only discovered it last week. It's worth visiting.

Grammar (Higher only) — 'il vaut la peine'

Use 'il vaut la peine de' when you're talking about something that is worth doing. It's always followed by an infinitive.

Il vaut la peine d'aller.

It's worth going.

Améliorer la ville — Improving the town

Vocabulary

l'organisation (f)	*organisation*
la station	*(tube) station*
la gare	*station*
le port	*port, harbour*
comparer	*to compare*
social(e)	*social*
public / publique	*public*
local(e)	*local*
vert(e)	*green*

divers(e)	*various, diverse*

Higher

le siège	*seat*
le véhicule	*vehicle*
l'arrêt (m)	*stop*
l'avantage (m)	*advantage, pro*
le besoin	*need*
le manque	*lack*
efficace	*efficient*

Les habitants de cette ville bénéficient d'espaces verts et d'un bon réseau de transports.	*The residents of this town benefit from green spaces and a good transport network.*
La région a besoin de nouvelles routes et un hôpital plus moderne.	*The region needs new roads and a more modern hospital.*
Les organisations locales font beaucoup pour améliorer la réputation de la ville.	*Local organisations do a lot to improve the reputation of the town.*

new housing — nouveaux logements
more funding — plus de financement

Local politicians — Les élus locaux
Local charities — Les organisations caritatives locales

Practice Questions

Q1 Choose one of the photos below. Talk in French about what is in the photo. You should talk for about a minute and describe who is in the photo, where it takes place, and what is happening.

SPEAKING

[8 marks]

Q2 You are writing an email to your French uncle about your local area. Write about 80-90 words in French. Describe:

WRITING

- *the places of interest in your local area*
- *your opinion of the town centre with reasons*
- *something you did recently in your town*
- *where you will take your uncle when he visits.* *[18 marks]*

Top Tips for Higher Students
✓ Use irregular verbs in the proper future, e.g. 'On ira...' (We will go...).
✓ Add interesting adjectives to nouns, e.g. 'un musée historique' (a historical museum).

Remember to use 'à' with 'aller' when you're going somewhere...

Maybe you've heard it before, but I'll say it again — when you're talking about going to the different places in your local area, make sure you use 'aller + à + place'. For example, 'Je vais au centre commercial'.

Quick Quiz

Shopping

Right, off to the shops. You might moan and groan now, but it'll come in handy if you're in France and spill beans on your jeans. Which, no offence, are so 1990s. Have a little browse...

Tu aimes aller aux magasins ? — Do you like to go shopping?

Vocabulary

le magasin	*shop, shopping*	s'habiller	*to get dressed*	la différence	*difference*
le centre commercial(e)	*shopping centre*	essayer	*to try*	gratuit(e)	*free (of charge)*
les vêtements (m)	*clothes*	la caisse	*checkout, till*	dépenser (Higher)	*to spend (money)*
la mode	*fashion*	la vente	*sale*	l'achat (m) (Higher)	*purchase*
à la mode	*fashionable, trendy*	le prix	*price*	la consommation (Higher)	*consumption*
la marque	*brand, mark*	payer	*to pay for*	l'envie (f) (Higher)	*wish, desire, want*
habiller	*to dress*	coûter	*to cost*	les espèces (f) (Higher)	*cash*
		acheter	*to buy*		
		vendre	*to sell*		

Au marché, on m'a vendu ce pull à prix réduit. — *At the market, they sold me this jumper at a discounted price.*

I bought a shirt — j'ai acheté une chemise
they were selling jumpers — on vendait des pulls

Mon copain a fait beaucoup d'achats parce qu'il adore la mode. — *My mate made lots of purchases because he loves fashion.*

Dans le centre commercial en ville, on vend toutes sortes de produits. — *In the shopping centre in town, they sell all kinds of products.*

there are sales — il y a des soldes

J'adore aller dans les magasins. Je fais souvent du shopping avec mes amis et on achète de nouveaux vêtements. Cependant, c'est une activité qui coûte cher. — *I love to go to the shops. I often go shopping with my friends and we buy new clothes. However, it's an expensive hobby.*

Je voudrais acheter... — I would like to buy...

Vocabulary

la chemise	*shirt*	la chaussette	*sock*
la cravate	*tie*	les baskets (f)	*trainers*
le pull	*jumper*	les lunettes (f)	*glasses*
la jupe	*skirt*	confortable	*comfortable*
la robe	*dress*	ça va bien	*it fits*
le pantalon	*trousers*	la veste (H)	*jacket*
la chaussure	*shoe*	moulant(e) (H)	*tight*

Grammar — indirect object pronouns

Indirect objects are things that are affected by the action being done, but not directly. They often have 'to' or 'for' before them in English.

Je <u>lui</u> ai montré mon nouveau pantalon.
I showed my new trousers <u>to him</u>.

See p.146 for more on indirect object pronouns.

Ces baskets coûtent combien ? Est-ce que je peux payer en espèces ? — *How much do these trainers cost? Can I pay in cash?*

by card — par carte

Pour mon anniversaire, mon ami m'a acheté une belle robe rouge et des chaussures noires. — *For my birthday, my friend bought me a beautiful red dress and some black shoes.*

J'aime porter... — I like to wear...

J'ai essayé le pantalon et il me va bien, mais la veste est trop moulante.	I tried on the trousers and they fit, but the jacket is too tight.	too loose — trop ample
J'ai envie d'acheter ces jupes et cette chemise en ligne, mais je ne veux pas dépenser beaucoup d'argent.	I want to buy these skirts and this jumper online, but I don't want to spend a lot of money.	these dungarees — cette salopette these sandals — ces sandales
Hier, j'ai trouvé un T-shirt et un pull à la friperie.	Yesterday, I found a T-shirt and jumper at the second hand clothes shop.	

Q&A Audio

Question

Qu'est ce que tu portes normalement ?

What do you normally wear?

Simple Answer

J'adore acheter des vêtements confortables et je porte toujours des robes.

I love to buy comfortable clothes and I always wear dresses.

This is Sandra. Sandra likes hats. Like, *really* likes hats.

Extended Answer

Quand je travaille, je dois porter un pantalon gris, une chemise blanche, une veste bleue et des chaussures noires. J'aime bien mon uniforme — je semble très professionnel(le).

When I'm working, I have to wear grey trousers, a white shirt, a blue jacket and black shoes. I really like my uniform — I seem very professional.

Practice Questions

Foundation

Q1 Ana is talking about shopping. What does she say? Choose the correct option to finish each sentence. LISTENING

Listening Track 19

a) Ana often...
A. buys clothes.
B. sells clothes.
C. goes shopping. *[1 mark]*

b) She likes to be...
A. comfortable.
B. trendy.
C. unique. *[1 mark]*

c) She's going to buy...
A. a skirt.
B. a dress.
C. a jumper. *[1 mark]*

d) For his birthday, Ana's friend wants...
A. trainers.
B. trousers.
C. socks. *[1 mark]*

Q2 Translate the following sentences into French. WRITING

a) I like to wear comfortable clothes.
b) This weekend, I am going to go to the shopping centre.
c) At work, I sold several dresses.
H **d)** I spent a lot of money and made a lot of purchases last week. *[8 marks]*

Sometimes plural nouns in English become singular in French...

... and singular nouns in English become plural in French. For example, 'trousers' is plural in English but 'le pantalon' is singular. 'Cash' is the opposite — it's singular in English whilst 'les espèces' is plural in French.

Quick Quiz

Directions and Weather

Exams can be unfamiliar territory and it's easy to feel lost. Learn the vocab on this page to get the directions you need to reach greener pastures, bluer skies and, yep, those higher marks...

Où est... ? — Where is...?

Vocabulary

la direction	*direction*	dessous	*underneath, below*
le feu	*traffic light*	entre	*between*
la droite	*the right*	la face	*front, face, side*
la gauche	*the left*	le fond	*bottom, back*
à droite	*on the right*	dehors	*outside, outdoors*
à gauche	*on the left*	voici	*here is*
droit(e)	*right, straight (adj.)*	autour (Higher)	*around*
devant	*in front of*	partout (Higher)	*everywhere*
derrière	*behind, at the back*	le signe (Higher)	*sign*
dessus	*on top, above*	envers (Higher)	*towards*

Pour arriver à la gare, tourne à droite et suis le chemin jusqu'au coin. — *To arrive at the railway station, turn right and follow the path to the corner.*

Voilà le parc du quartier, qui se trouve devant la plage. — *Here is the local park, which is located in front of the beach.*

Excusez-moi, je suis perdu(e). Vous pouvez m'indiquer comment aller au centre-ville ? — *Excuse me, I'm lost. Can you direct me to the town centre?*

to the tourist information office — à l'office de tourisme
to the art gallery — au musée d'art

C'est loin d'ici ? — Is it far from here?

Vocabulary

la distance	*distance*	tourner	*to turn, go round*
ici	*here*	décrire	*to describe*
là	*there*	donner	*to give*
là-bas	*over there*	le mètre	*metre*
près (de)	*nearby, close by, near*	le kilomètre	*kilometre*
		le nord	*north*
proche	*nearby*	le sud	*south*
loin (de)	*far (from)*	l'est (m)	*east*
bas(se)	*low*	l'ouest (m)	*west*
traverser	*to cross*		

Grammar — using the imperative

You can use the imperative form to give directions or instructions:

Suivez le chemin de droite.
Follow the right-hand path.

Traverse la rue !
Cross the street!

See p.176 for more on the imperative.

La distance entre ici et le pont est d'environ dix kilomètres. — *The distance between here and the bridge is around ten kilometres.*

my house and my school — chez moi et mon école

Dites-moi, le véhicule est allé dans quelle direction ? — *Tell me, in which direction did the vehicle go?*

where exactly — où exactement

Quel temps fait-il ? — What's the weather like?

Vocabulary

le temps	*weather, climate*	il y a du brouillard	*it's foggy*	le vent	*wind*
le soleil	*sun*			sec / sèche (Higher)	*dry*
chaud(e)	*hot*	la neige	*snow*	pleuvoir (Higher)	*to rain*
froid(e)	*cold*	il neige	*it snows, it's snowing*	il a plu (Higher)	*it rained*
il fait (beau)	*it is, it's (nice)*	il pleut	*it rains, it's raining*	humide (Higher)	*wet, humid, moist*

Le temps est génial aujourd'hui — il fait vraiment chaud et il y a du soleil. — *The weather is great today — it's really hot and sunny.*

breezy — il y a du vent
cloudless — il n'y a pas de nuages

Là-bas, le climat est froid et il y a toujours de la neige partout. — *The climate there is cold and there's always snow everywhere.*

dry — sec
damp — humide

Selon la météo, il va pleuvoir demain. — *According to the weather forecast, it's going to rain tomorrow.*

it's going to snow — il va neiger
it'll be icy — il y aura du gel

Q&A Audio

Question

Quel temps fait-il généralement dans ta région ?
What's the weather generally like in your area?

Simple Answer

Il fait froid et il pleut tout le temps.
It's cold and it rains all the time.

Extended Answer

Normalement, il fait assez chaud et sec, mais récemment il a plu pendant des semaines. Je n'aime pas ça et j'espère que le soleil va revenir bientôt.
Usually it's quite hot and dry, but recently it rained for weeks. I don't like it and I hope the sun will return soon.

Practice Questions

Q1 Read the following text about the weather in Réunion and answer the questions below in English.

READING

> *La Réunion est une petite île de près d'un million de gens. Sur l'île, il y a beaucoup de montagnes qui sont toutes énormes et un climat tropical avec seulement deux saisons. L'été dure de novembre à avril. Pendant ces six mois, il fait chaud mais il pleut beaucoup dans le sud de l'île. De mai à octobre, c'est l'hiver et il fait généralement beau mais plus froid dans le nord et l'ouest.*

a) According to the text, how many people live in Réunion? *[1 mark]*
b) What is the island's landscape like? *[1 mark]*
c) What is the weather like in the summer? Give **two** details. *[2 marks]*
d) What is the weather like in the winter? Give **two** details. *[2 marks]*

Higher

Q2 Listen to this message your friend left on your voicemail. Complete the sentences in English.

LISTENING

Listening Track 20

a) Cross the street and you will see... *[1 mark]*
b) Get off at the post office and... *[1 mark]*
c) Next, get off at the church, then turn right and... *[1 mark]*
d) After about 100 metres the café will be... *[1 mark]*

You'll be using 'il' a lot when you're talking about the weather...

In French, some verbs can be used in an impersonal way, and they take the pronoun 'il' as their subject. Most of the verbs you'll use to talk about weather are impersonal, so they'll follow this rule (e.g. 'il pleut').

Speaking Questions

Now you've navigated your way to the end of another section, have a go at the questions on these pages. You can always revisit the other pages in this topic and try again if you're feeling a little off-track.

Candidate's Material

Scenario:

- You are visiting a town in France, and you are talking to a local resident.
- Find a friend to play the part of your teacher. They will speak first.
- Your friend will ask questions **in French** and you must answer **in French**.
- You are expected to say a few words or a short phrase / sentence in response to each prompt. One-word answers will not be sufficient to gain full marks.

Task:

1. Say what you want to visit in the town.
2. Say how long you are visiting for.
3. Ask for directions to a local landmark.
4. Tell the resident what you think about the transport options in the town.
5. Ask a question about shops in the area.

Teacher's Material

- Begin the role play with the following introduction:
  'You are in town, and you are talking to a local resident.
  I will play the part of the local resident and speak first.'

1	*Bonjour. Qu'est-ce que vous voulez visiter dans notre ville ?* Allow the candidate to talk about what they want to visit in town.
2	*C'est génial. Vous voulez rester ici pendant combien de temps ?* Allow the candidate to say how long they are visiting for.
3	*D'accord. Vous avez une question ?* Allow the candidate to ask for directions to a local landmark. *Give an appropriate brief response.*
4	*Que pensez-vous des transports dans la région ?* Allow the candidate to give their opinion of local transport options.
5	*Je comprends. Vous avez une autre question ?* Allow the candidate to ask a question about shopping. *Give an appropriate brief response.*

Listening Questions

1 Hugo is talking about his local area. What does he say?
Complete the gap in each sentence using a word or phrase from the box below.
There are more words than gaps.

Listening Track 21

green spaces	museums	transport options	clothes shops
train station	harbour	tower	bridge

1 a There are not a lot of .... *[1 mark]*

1 b In the town centre there are lots of .... *[1 mark]*

1 c The new .... is perfect. *[1 mark]*

2 a Ahmed is talking about the shopping centre. What does he say?
Listen to the recording, then answer the questions **in English**.

Listening Track 22

(i) Why did Ahmed come to the shopping centre?

.... *[1 mark]*

(ii) Why does Ahmed like to go there?

.... *[1 mark]*

2 b Nadia and Dorian are also talking about the shopping centre.
What do they like and dislike? Complete the following tables in **English**.

(i) Nadia ...

likes ...	....
dislikes ...	....

[1 mark]

[1 mark]

(ii) Dorian ...

likes ...	....
dislikes ...	....

[1 mark]

[1 mark]

Reading Questions

Foundation

1 Read these comments from your friends online.

Rachid: Dans ma région, il fait généralement beau — il ne fait pas trop froid et il ne neige jamais.
Myriam: Ma ville est au bord de la mer. Il fait chaud presque toute l'année, mais il y a du vent.
Clément: J'habite à la montagne — les vues sont géniales mais il y a souvent du brouillard.

Who says what? Choose the correct answers.
Put a cross in the correct column for each question.

	Who...	Rachid	Myriam	Clément	
a)	... gets lovely views?				*[1 mark]*
b)	... lives in a moderate climate?				*[1 mark]*
c)	... lives in a windy area?				*[1 mark]*
d)	... never gets snow?				*[1 mark]*
e)	... lives in a foggy area?				*[1 mark]*
f)	... lives by the sea?				*[1 mark]*

2 Read this post on an online community page for a French town.
Yasmina is discussing how to improve her town.

Yasmina
Notre ville est à la campagne, alors les espaces naturels sont excellents. Par contre, il faut améliorer notre réseau de bus — les arrêts actuels sont inutiles.

Il n'y a qu'un centre sportif en ville. L'exercice est essentiel pour la santé, et il faut donc ouvrir plus de centres.

À mon avis, il n'y a pas assez de musées et d'hôtels dans la région.

Put a cross in each one of the **three** correct boxes.
The town needs...

	A more green spaces.
	B a better bus system.
	C to build sports facilities.
	D better housing for locals.
	E more tourist attractions.
	F less visitor accommodation.

[3 marks]

Writing Questions

Foundation

1 Translate the following five sentences **into French**.

1 a I love my town.

.... *[2 marks]*

1 b I like to go to the castle.

.... *[2 marks]*

1 c There's a small café on the square.

.... *[2 marks]*

1 d Last week, I went to a new cake shop.

.... *[2 marks]*

1 e There's always a lot of people at the restaurant on Saturdays.

.... *[2 marks]*

2 Write to your friend about your home.
You must include the following points:

- the rooms in your current house
- your opinion of where you live with reasons
- what you have done recently in your local area
- where you would like to live in the future.

Write your answer **in French**. You should aim to write between 80 and 90 words. *[18 marks]*

Higher

3 Translate the paragraph **into French**.

> I live in the suburbs of a big city. My house is situated next to a supermarket. Our neighbourhood is ideal because it is close to the city centre but it is also quiet and very safe. Last year, the residents created a new public garden. I would like to stay here for several years.

[10 marks]

Places in Town — Vocabulary

Learn the vocab on this page so you can talk confidently in the exam about your home and the surrounding area.

Where You Live

habiter	*to live*
l'adresse (f)	*address*
le / la voisin(e)	*neighbour*
le village	*village*
la ville	*town, city*
la capitale	*capital city*
le pays	*country*
la région	*region*
régional(e)	*regional*
la province	*province*
la rue	*street*
la route	*road, way, route*
le coin	*corner*
le bord	*edge, side*
le bâtiment	*building*
le terrain	*ground*
la côte	*coast*
la montagne	*mountain*
la forêt	*forest*
la campagne	*countryside*
la ferme	*farm*
le lac	*lake*
où	*where*
sûr(e)	*safe*
calme	*quiet*
le trafic	*traffic*
national(e)	*national*
international(e)	*international*
global(e)	*global*

Higher

l'habitant(e)	*inhabitant, resident*
situer	*to situate, locate*
se situer	*to be situated, be located*
exister	*to exist*
vivre	*to live*
la banlieue	*suburbs*
la cité	*(council) estate*
le chemin	*way, path*
le champ	*field*
la rivière	*river*
le paysage	*landscape*
vaste	*huge, vast, enormous*

The Home

la maison	*house, home*
l'appartement (m)	*apartment, flat*
l'immeuble (m)	*building, block of flats*
chez	*at (the house of), to (the house of), with*
la porte	*door*
la fenêtre	*window*
la clé	*key*
le sol	*floor, ground*
le jardin	*garden*
l'animal (m)	*animal, pet*
les animaux (m)	*animals, pets*
la salle	*room*
le mur	*wall*
la chambre	*bedroom*
le lit	*bed*
la cuisine	*kitchen, cooking*
la table	*table*
la boîte	*box*
les toilettes	*toilets*
idéal(e)	*ideal*
propre	*clean, proper, own*
énorme	*enormous, big*
historique	*historical*
moderne	*modern*

Higher

le foyer	*home*
l'étage (m)	*floor (of a building)*
l'escalier (m)	*stairs*
l'ascenseur (m)	*lift*
la pièce	*room, coin*
la couverture	*blanket*
construire	*to build, construct*
posséder	*to own, have, possess*

The Local Area — Places of Interest

visiter	*to visit*
aller	*to go*
le quartier	*neighbourhood*
la place	*square, place*
l'endroit (m)	*place, spot*
la zone	*zone*
l'espace (m)	*space*
le pont	*bridge*
la tour	*tower*
le stade	*stadium*
l'hôtel (m)	*hotel*
le château	*castle*
le musée	*museum*
le parc	*park*
le centre	*centre*
la plage	*beach*
la piscine	*swimming pool*
la poste	*post office*
la banque	*bank*
l'hôpital (m)	*hospital*
le cinéma	*cinema*
le café	*café, coffee house*
le restaurant	*restaurant*
le marché	*market*
le supermarché	*supermarket*
la boulangerie	*bakery*
la pâtisserie	*patisserie, cake shop*
la sortie	*exit, outing*
central(e)	*central*
ancien(ne)	*former, ancient, old*
neuf / neuve	*new*
nouveau / nouvel / nouvelle	*new*

H

le lieu	*place*
la bibliothèque	*library*

The Local Area — Improving the Town

l'organisation (f)	*organisation*
la station	*(bus) stop, (tube) station*
la gare	*station*
le port	*port, harbour*
public / publique	*public*
social(e)	*social*
local(e)	*local*
vert(e)	*green*
divers(e)	*various, diverse*
H le siège	*seat*
H le véhicule	*vehicle*
H l'arrêt (m)	*stop*
Higher l'avantage (m)	*advantage, pro*
Higher le besoin	*need*
Higher le manque	*lack*
Higher efficace	*efficient*

Shopping

le magasin	*shop, shopping*
le centre commercial	*shopping centre*
les courses (f)	*shopping*
les vêtements (m)	*clothes*
la mode	*fashion*
à la mode	*fashionable, trendy*
tendance	*fashionable, trendy*
la marque	*brand, mark*
habiller	*to dress*
s'habiller	*to get dressed*
porter	*to wear*
essayer	*to try*
la caisse	*checkout, till*
la vente	*sale*
le prix	*price*
payer	*to pay for*
coûter	*to cost*
acheter	*to buy*
vendre	*to sell*
l'euro (m)	*euro*
comparer	*to compare*
la différence	*difference*
cher / chère	*expensive, dear*
gratuit(e)	*free*
la chemise	*shirt*
la cravate	*tie*
le pull	*jumper*
la jupe	*skirt*
la robe	*dress*
le pantalon	*trousers*
la chaussure	*shoe*
la chaussette	*sock*
les baskets (m)	*trainers*
les lunettes (f)	*glasses*
confortable	*comfortable*
ça va bien	*it fits*
Higher dépenser	*to spend (money)*
Higher l'achat (m)	*purchase*
Higher la consommation	*consumption*
Higher l'envie (f)	*wish, desire, want*
Higher les espèces (f)	*cash*
Higher la veste	*jacket*
Higher moulant(e)	*tight*

Directions and Weather

la direction	*direction*
la distance	*distance*
le plan	*map*
le feu	*traffic light*
la droite	*the right*
la gauche	*the left*
droit(e)	*right, straight (adj.)*
devant	*in front of*
derrière	*behind, at the back*
dessus	*on top, above*
dessous	*underneath, below*
entre	*between*
la face	*front, face, side*
le fond	*bottom, back*
dehors	*outside, outdoors*
voici	*here is*
ici	*here*
là	*there*
là-bas	*over there*
près (de)	*nearby, close by, near*
proche	*near*
loin (de)	*far*
bas(se)	*low*
traverser	*to cross*
tourner	*to turn, go round*
décrire	*to describe*
donner	*to give*
le mètre	*metre*
le kilomètre	*kilometre*
le nord	*north*
le sud	*south*
l'est (m)	*east*
l'ouest (m)	*west*
le temps	*weather, climate*
climatique (adj.)	*climate*
le soleil	*sun*
chaud(e)	*hot*
froid(e)	*cold*
il fait (beau)	*it is / it's (nice)*
il y a du brouillard	*it's foggy*
la neige	*snow*
il neige	*it snows, it's snowing*
il pleut	*it rains, it's raining*
le vent	*wind*
Higher autour	*around*
Higher partout	*everywhere*
Higher le signe	*sign*
Higher envers	*towards*
Higher sec / sèche	*dry*
Higher pleuvoir	*to rain*
Higher il a plu	*it rained*
Higher humide	*wet, humid, moist*

Revision Summary Test for Section Five

That's another section under your belt — time to put your knowledge to the test.

- Yep, these questions are **hard** — they'll really help you see **how well you know your stuff**.
- Tackle the **revision summary test** below, or scan the QR code to do it **online**. Use the CGP RevisionHub to **track your progress** and see **which areas need more work**.
- You can find **sample answers** here: www.cgpbooks.co.uk/MerciExtras

Summary Test

Where You Live

1) How do you say the words below in French?
a) forest b) farm c) coast d) edge e) road f) ground g) neighbour
2) 'Moi, j'ai deux adresses. La première est une maison dans un petit village à la campagne, et l'autre est un appartement à la montagne.' What's Xavier saying? Answer in English.
3) 'I live in the capital city of my country, and it's very international. For example, the people on my street come from the four corners of the world.' Translate Marianne's sentences into French.

Higher

4) How do you say the words below in English? a) la banlieue b) la cité c) le paysage d) le champ
5) 'Ma femme et moi habitions dans un vieux bâtiment qui se situait entre un grand lac et une belle rivière. J'aimais y vivre, parce que c'était très calme.' Where did Marc used to live and why did he like living there? Answer in English.

The Home

6) 'Qu'est-ce que tu penses de ta maison ou de ton appartement ?' Answer in French, then describe one room in detail.
7) How do you say the words below in French?
a) window b) box c) room d) door e) wall f) key g) bed h) bedroom i) floor

Higher

8) 'Je possède une maison avec un jardin énorme car j'ai beaucoup d'animaux.' Translate Rémie's sentence into English.
9) How do you say the following words in English? a) l'étage b) l'escalier c) l'ascenseur

The Local Area

10) How many buildings in the local area can you name in French? There are at least 14 in this section (plus 1 extra for Higher tier).
11) How do you say the words below in English?
a) le quartier b) le parc c) la plage d) la place e) l'endroit f) le pont g) la gare

Higher

12) 'Quels sont les avantages et les inconvénients d'habiter dans ta région ?' Answer in French.
13) 'Ici, on a besoin de divers espaces verts. Il faut réduire le trafic et réserver les zones centrales pour les transports publics.' Translate these sentences into English.

Shopping

14) In French, list things you can wear. There are 10 in this section (plus 1 extra for Higher tier).
15) Describe a recent trip to the shopping centre. Mention what you bought and how much it cost.

Directions and Weather

16) How do you say the words below in French?
a) the left b) the right c) outside d) over there e) far f) behind g) in front of h) near
17) How many words and expressions related to weather can you write down in French? There are at least 11 you need to know (plus 4 extra for Higher tier).
18) Name the compass points in French. There are 4 you need to know.

H

19) 'The distance between the two towns is quite small — it's only twenty kilometres.' Translate Simon's sentence into French.

The Natural World

Quick Quiz

That's right — it's time to start thinking about all things green, natural and... polluted. These pages cover many of the problems poor old Mother Nature is facing, so get learning.

Head to the CGP RevisionHub for all your online content: www.cgpbooks.co.uk/Merci

La nature — Nature

Vocabulary

le monde	*world*	l'air (m)	*air*	la science	*science*
naturel(le)	*natural*	la mer	*sea*	la recherche	*research*
la planète	*planet*	l'eau (f)	*water*	l'information (f)	*information*
la terre	*earth, ground*	sauver	*to rescue, save*	l'effort (m)	*effort*
la forêt	*forest*	protéger	*to protect*	améliorer	*to improve*
la montagne	*mountain*	la protection	*protection*	H l'arbre (m)	*tree*
le ciel	*sky*	le progrès	*progress*	H l'espèce (f)	*species, type, kind*

Q&A Audio

Question

Est-ce que la nature est importante pour toi ?

Is nature important to you?

Simple Answer

Je m'intéresse à la nature et j'adore découvrir les parcs nationaux.

I'm interested in nature and I love discovering national parks.

Extended Answer

Oui, je m'intéresse à la nature, surtout à la mer et aux espèces d'animaux qui y habitent. Il faut faire plus de recherche pour savoir les aider. C'est à nous de protéger la planète.

Yes, I am interested in nature, especially the sea and the species of animal that live there. We must do more research to know how to help them. It's up to us to protect the planet.

Grammar — 'on doit' / 'il faut'

Use 'on doit...' or 'il faut...' to say 'we must'. The verb which follows is in the infinitive.

On doit visiter les montagnes.
We must visit the mountains.

Il faut sauver les mers.
We must save the seas.

J'adore la nature — je voudrais habiter près de la mer. — *I love nature — I'd like to live near the sea.*

in the hills — dans les collines
in the woods — dans les bois

Je me détends en marchant dans la forêt près de chez moi. J'aime voir tous les beaux oiseaux. — *I relax by walking in the forest close to my house. I like seeing all the beautiful birds.*

by the pond — au bord de l'étang
on the cliffs — sur les falaises

Practice Question

Q1 *Listen to this extract from a podcast about nature.*
Which two locations does each person mention?
Choose the correct options from each list.

LISTENING — Listening Track 23

a) **A.** the sea
B. forests
C. mountains
D. the countryside *[2 marks]*

b) **A.** lakes
B. parks
C. farms
D. beaches *[2 marks]*

You've got the green light to get to grips with this vocab...

The more vocab you know the better — it will allow you to give more detailed answers. Show the examiners you really know your stuff by using the 'on doit' and 'il faut' structures too. Impressive.

Environmental Problems

Quick Quiz

You might prefer hiding away in a darkened room to roaming the hills and basking in the glories of nature, but you still need to have an opinion about environmental problems, so listen up...

La planète en crise — The planet in crisis

Vocabulary

l'environnement (m)	*environment*		climatique	*climate (adj.)*		brûler	*to burn*	
le changement	*change*		mondial(e)	*global, world*	Higher	ignorer	*to ignore*	Higher
la destruction	*destruction*	Higher	menacer (de)	*to threaten (to)*		risquer	*to risk*	
la catastrophe	*catastrophe*		la menace	*threat*		grave	*serious, important, grave*	
dangereux / dangereuse	*dangerous*		disparaître	*to disappear*				
			détruire	*to destroy*				

Beaucoup d'espèces sont menacées par le réchauffement de la planète. Si les êtres humains ne prennent pas soin de la nature, certaines espèces vont disparaître.

Many species are threatened by global warming. If human beings don't take care of nature, certain species will disappear.

by extinction — d'extinction

L'énergie renouvelable cause des débats.

Renewable energy causes debates.

Nuclear — nucléaire

Les grandes entreprises sont responsables de la pollution de l'eau des rivières.

Large companies are responsible for water pollution in rivers.

for deforestation — du déboisement
for the environmental crisis — de la crise écologique

Grammar — adjective position

In French, adjectives usually come after the noun. However, this isn't always the case, e.g.

Il y a une grande usine. ***There is a big factory.***

Adjectives such as beau (*beautiful*), jeune (*young*), grand (*big*) and petit (*small*) usually come before the noun. See p.156 for more.

Ce beau paysage est en danger.
This beautiful landscape is in danger.

Les petites actions ont un grand effet.
Small actions have a big effect.

Les causes (f) de la pollution — Causes of pollution

Vocabulary

causer	*to cause*	la voiture	*car*		la conséquence	*consequence*
la cause	*cause*	le trafic	*traffic*		contribuer	*to contribute*
jeter	*to throw (away / out)*	le bruit	*noise*	Higher	augmenter	*to increase*
le plastique	*plastic*	sérieux / sérieuse	*serious, responsible*		baisser	*to lower*
conduire	*to drive, lead*	remplir	*to fill (up / in)*		les déchets (m)	*rubbish, waste*
					la circulation	*traffic*

Dans les grandes villes, le niveau de pollution causée par les voitures peut être dangereux.

In big cities, the level of pollution caused by cars can be dangerous.

large companies — les grandes entreprises

La population augmente, donc on utilise plus d'énergie.

The population is increasing, so we use more energy.

Réduire, réutiliser et recycler — Reduce, reuse and recycle

Vocabulary

la population	*population*	le recyclage	*recycling*	conscient(e) (Higher)	*conscious, aware*
l'action (f)	*action*	zéro	*zero*	durable (Higher)	*durable, sustainable*
la ressource	*resource*	prévenir (H)	*to warn*	renouvelable (Higher)	*renewable*
l'énergie (f)	*energy*	agir (H)	*to act*		

Q&A Audio

Question

Qu'est-ce que tu fais pour protéger la planète ?

What do you do to protect the planet?

Simple Answer

Je recycle tout ce que je peux et j'utilise les transports publics.

I recycle everything that I can and I use public transport.

Extended Answer

Bien sûr, protéger l'environnement est très important. J'essaie de recycler tous mes déchets — le verre, le plastique et même mes vieux vêtements. À mon avis, chaque personne doit faire un effort pour prendre soin de l'environnement.

Of course, protecting the environment is very important. I try to recycle all my rubbish — glass, plastic and even my old clothes. In my opinion, everyone must make an effort to take care of the environment.

On peut réduire la quantité de déchets plastiques dans la mer si les gens jettent leurs déchets dans la poubelle.

We can reduce the quantity of plastic waste in the sea if people throw their rubbish in the bin.

packaging — les emballages

Tout le monde doit faire un effort pour acheter des vêtements durables.

Everybody must make an effort to buy sustainable clothing.

eco-friendly — écologiques

Je réutilise les sacs en plastique quand je vais au supermarché. J'essaie toujours de ne rien gaspiller.

I reuse plastic bags when I go to the supermarket. I always try not to waste anything.

Practice Questions

Q1 *Answer these questions out loud in French.* SPEAKING

- *Quelles sont les causes de la pollution ?*
- *Est-ce que tu recycles souvent ? Pourquoi ?* *[4 marks]*

Higher

Q2 *Read this passage written by Hugo and answer the questions below.* READING

La pollution cause de graves problèmes pour l'environnement. Chaque jour, la situation semble être pire — je veux protéger la planète pour la prochaine génération. Dans mon pays, on peut voir les effets de la crise climatique. Cet été, il y a eu des feux qui ont détruit plusieurs forêts et de nombreux arbres. C'était une grave menace pour les animaux, et il y a aussi moins de touristes qui visitent le pays. Je m'inquiète pour l'été prochain.

a) Why is protecting the planet important to Hugo? *[1 mark]*

b) What does he say happened during summer? *[1 mark]*

c) Give two consequences of the event that happened in summer. *[2 marks]*

d) How does he feel about next summer? *[1 mark]*

It's 'un grand problème', not 'un problème grand'...

Remember that not all adjectives come after the noun — some come before. Make a list and learn the few that come before the noun so they don't catch you out, especially in the Writing and Speaking exams.

Quick Quiz

Equality and Social Issues

Social problems, protests, prison — the themes in this section are pretty heavy hitters. It's enough to make you want to pull the duvet over your head and stay there. Here's something to pass the time...

L'égalité (f) — Equality

Vocabulary

égal(e)	*equal*	gay	*gay*	humain(e) (Higher)	*human (adj.)*
l'identité (f)	*identity*	lesbien(ne)	*lesbian*	la représentation (Higher)	*representation*
le handicap	*disability*	hétéro, hétérosexuel(le)	*straight*	la communauté (Higher)	*community*
handicapé(e)	*disabled*	non-binaire	*non-binary*	multiculturel(le) (Higher)	*multicultural*
le fauteuil roulant	*wheelchair*	transgenre	*transgender*	s'intégrer (Higher)	*to fit in*
le respect	*respect*	l'être (m)	*being*	tolérer (Higher)	*to tolerate*
respecter	*to respect*			la fierté (Higher)	*pride*
bisexuel(le)	*bisexual*			la paix (Higher)	*peace*

Le respect est essentiel dans une société multiculturelle.	*Respect is essential in a multicultural society.*
Il faut respecter et tolérer les autres pour vivre en paix.	*We must respect and tolerate others in order to live in peace.*
Il est plus difficile pour certaines personnes de s'intégrer dans la société à cause de la discrimination.	*It is more difficult for certain people to fit into society because of discrimination.*

to create a more inclusive world — pour créer un monde plus inclusif

due to social prejudices — à cause des préjugés sociaux

Les problèmes sociaux — Social problems

Vocabulary

le crime	*crime*	le vol (Higher)	*robbery*	le souci (Higher)	*worry*
arrêter	*to stop, arrest*	voler (Higher)	*to steal*	moral(e) (Higher)	*moral*
la prison	*prison*	la lutte (Higher)	*fight*	la honte (Higher)	*shame*
le choc	*shock, clash*	le conflit (Higher)	*conflict*	l'avantage (m) (Higher)	*advantage, pro*
la violence	*violence*	combattre (Higher)	*to fight*	l'inconvénient (m) (Higher)	*disadvantage, con, inconvenience*
pauvre	*poor*	le chômage (Higher)	*unemployment*	actuel(le) (Higher)	*current*
la faim	*hunger*	l'écart (m) (Higher)	*gap*		
l'attitude (f)	*attitude*	l'inquiétude (f) (Higher)	*worry, anxiety*		

L'inégalité sociale entre les riches et les pauvres peut mener au conflit.	*Social inequality between the rich and the poor can lead to conflict.*
La police a arrêté les deux hommes responsables du vol.	*Police have arrested the two men responsible for the robbery.*
Dans la société actuelle, le chômage est un problème inquiétant.	*In today's society, unemployment is a worrying problem.*

to political instability — à l'instabilité politique

for acts of violence — d'actes violents

the crime rate — le taux de criminalité

Aider la société — Helping society

Vocabulary

la société	*society*	considérer (Higher)	*to consider*	l'état (m) (Higher)	*state, condition*
l'association (f)	*organisation, charity, association*	défendre (Higher)	*to defend*	le gouvernement (Higher)	*government*
commun(e)	*common*	la manifestation (Higher)	*demonstration, protest*	le / la citoyen(ne) (Higher)	*citizen*
l'enquête (f) (H)	*survey*	convaincre (Higher)	*to convince*	l'économie (f) (Higher)	*economy*
le don (H)	*donation*	résoudre (Higher)	*to solve, resolve*	la loi (Higher)	*law*
		voter (Higher)	*to vote*	l'accord (m) (Higher)	*agreement*

Q&A Audio

Question

Est-ce que tu aimes aider les autres ?

Do you like helping others?

Simple Answer

Oui, j'aime passer du temps à aider les personnes qui ont des problèmes.

Yes, I like spending time helping people who have problems.

Extended Answer

Oui. Chaque mois, je fais un don à une association qui aide les personnes qui n'ont pas de maison. Je voudrais faire plus pour aider, mais c'est difficile — on a besoin de plus de soutien. Si les personnes sont au chômage, elles n'ont pas les moyens de payer un logement, et il est difficile de trouver un emploi quand on n'a pas d'adresse.

Yes. Every month, I make a donation to a charity that helps people who don't have a home. I would like to do more to help, but it's difficult— we need more support. If people are unemployed, they don't have the means of paying for accommodation, and it's difficult to find a job when you don't have an address.

Grammar (Higher only) — 'avoir besoin de...'

'Avoir besoin de' means 'to need' something.

Nous avons besoin d'emplois.
We need jobs.

You can also use 'avoir besoin de' with a verb, to say you need to do something.

Le gouvernement a besoin de prendre des mesures pour aider les citoyens.
The government needs to take action to help citizens.

What do we want? New pens!
When do we want them? Now!

Practice Questions

Q1 *Translate the following sentences into French.* (WRITING)

a) Hunger is a serious problem in society. *[2 marks]*

b) Every person's identity deserves respect. *[2 marks]*

c) It was a shock to see violence in the streets. *[2 marks]*

d) I spend my free time helping others. *[2 marks]*

Higher

Q2 *Listen to Lucy talk about issues in society. Complete the following sentences in English.* (LISTENING)

Listening Track 24

a) The government recently introduced ....

b) The new agreement about crime will improve ....

c) According to a survey, people have negative attitudes towards ....

d) Though the conflict is over, the effects of the violence will last .... *[4 marks]*

Use the vocab on these pages to really elevate your answers...

There's been a lot of new (and sometimes tricky) vocab in this section. It's useful to read sentences aloud or write out any words that you find challenging. Then give the exam-style questions on the next few pages a go.

Speaking Questions

Here are four pages of exam-style practice for you. See how much you can do without looking anything up.

Candidate's Material

- Choose **one** of the pictures below to describe. Make notes on it to use during the test.
- Your teacher will ask you to describe the picture. You should talk for approximately **one and a half to two minutes**. Your description must cover the **people, location and activity** shown in the picture.
- After you have spoken about the content of the picture, your teacher will ask you two questions about your chosen picture. Then, they will ask you some questions related to any of the topics within the theme of **My Neighbourhood**.

Picture 1:

Picture 2:

Teacher's Material

- Begin by asking the candidate which picture they have chosen, then say 'Describe the picture'. Candidates should talk about the picture for approximately **one and a half to two minutes**. They may use any notes they have made during the preparation time.
- When the candidate has finished, ask the questions below that relate to their chosen picture.

Picture 1:

- F Quel est ton espace naturel préféré ?
- Qu'est-ce que tu fais pour protéger la nature ?
- H Qu'est-ce que tu as recyclé cette semaine ?

Picture 2:

- F Qu'est-ce que tu fais pour réduire la pollution ?
- Quelle est ton opinion sur l'énergie verte ?
- H Qu'est-ce qui a contribué au changement climatique ?

- Now ask the candidate the following unprepared conversation questions on the theme of **My Neighbourhood**:

  - Quels sont les problèmes sociaux dans ta région ?
  - Qu'est-ce que tu as fait cette semaine pour aider les autres ?
  - Est-ce que tu vas donner de l'argent à une association cette année ?

Listening Questions

Foundation

1 Toni is talking about recycling. What does she say?
Complete the gap in each sentence using a word or phrase from the box below.
There are more words / phrases than gaps.

Listening Track 25

seas	forests	animals	
products	paper	boxes	plastic bags

1 a Toni says we need to protect our .... *[1 mark]*

1 b The .... are in danger. *[1 mark]*

1 c Toni always reuses .... *[1 mark]*

Higher

2 Enzo is giving a news report on environmental and social issues in France.
Listen to the recordings and complete the sentences by putting a cross in the correct box for each question.

Listening Track 26

2 a In Lyon, it took three hours to...

	A stop the violence.
	B break up the protest.
	C find all the injured victims.

[1 mark]

2 b The goal of the charity event in Paris was...

	A to encourage people to do sport.
	B to raise money for associations.
	C to support poor families in need.

[1 mark]

2 c The weather event in the south of France caused...

	A rainfall to stop for five days.
	B serious flooding in the area.
	C over five serious road accidents.

[1 mark]

Reading Questions

Foundation

1 Read these comments from a social media site.

> **Hugo**: Il faut faire plus pour lutter contre la faim — c'est un gros problème.
> **Axel**: On doit accepter toutes les identités différentes dans la société.
> **Jade**: Il faut réduire le nombre de voitures à cause de la pollution.

Who says what? Choose the correct answers.
Put a cross in the correct column for each question.

	Who ...	**Hugo**	**Axel**	**Jade**
a)	... accepts different identities?			
b)	... cares about pollution?			
c)	... wants to fight hunger?			
d)	... thinks there are too many cars?			

[1 mark]
[1 mark]
[1 mark]
[1 mark]

2 Translate these sentences into **English**:

2 a La présidente va continuer à lutter contre le crime.

.... *[2 marks]*

2 b L'égalité des sexes est essentielle pour une société plus juste.

.... *[2 marks]*

Higher

3 Read Sofiane's blog post about traffic in Nice.

> *À Nice, il y a beaucoup de pollution à cause de la circulation. Il y a toujours trop de voitures et c'est mauvais pour la santé. Selon moi, le gouvernement a une responsabilité — il doit réduire le niveau de pollution en créant des espaces verts au centre-ville. Mais c'est à nous aussi de changer notre façon de vivre. Par exemple, hier je suis allé au travail à pied, et quelquefois je prend le bus. S'il est vraiment nécessaire de conduire pour aller au travail, on peut partager une voiture avec des collègues.*

What does Sofiane say?

Put a cross next to each one of the **two** correct statements.

	A He wants to ban cars in the city centre.
	B The city needs more outdoor areas.
	C Public transport needs to be quicker.
	D He encourages people to lift share.

[2 marks]

Writing Questions

Foundation

1 Write an article about issues in your neighbourhood.
You **must** include the following points:

- problems in your local area
- your opinion of crime in your area
- what you will do to help people in your neighbourhood.

Write your answer **in French**. You should aim to write between 40 and 50 words. *[14 marks]*

2 Describe the photo.

Write **four** short sentences **in French**.

2 a .... *[2 marks]*

2 b .... *[2 marks]*

2 c .... *[2 marks]*

2 d .... *[2 marks]*

3 Write to your friend about the environment.
You **must** include the following points:

- natural spaces in your area
- your opinion of recycling with reasons
- how you travelled around last week
- what you will do to help save the planet.

Write your answer **in French**. You should aim to write between 80 and 90 words. *[18 marks]*

Higher

4 Translate the paragraph **into French**.

> It's important to give people clear information about forest fires. It's a very serious problem. Last week, I gave money to an international organisation that rescues animals in danger. I want to help protect the woods and the trees. We must do more research to learn how to take care of nature.

[10 marks]

Environmental and Social Issues — Vocabulary

Some of the vocab in this section might seem a little heavy, but learning it all will show you really know your stuff.

The Natural World

la nature	*nature*
le monde	*world*
naturel(le)	*natural*
la planète	*planet*
la terre	*earth, ground*
la forêt	*forest*
la montagne	*mountain*
le ciel	*sky*
l'air (m)	*air*
la mer	*sea*
l'eau (f)	*water*
sauver	*to rescue, save*
protéger	*to protect*
la protection	*protection*
le progrès	*progress*
la science	*science*
rechercher	*to look for, search, collect*
la recherche	*research*
l'information (f)	*information*
l'effort (m)	*effort*
améliorer	*to improve*
important(e)	*important*

H

l'arbre (m)	*tree*
l'espèce (f)	*species, type, kind*
la lumière	*light*

Environmental Problems

l'environnement (m)	*environment*
le changement	*change*
la destruction	*destruction*
la catastrophe	*catastrophe*
la crise	*crisis*
le danger	*danger*
dangereux / dangereuse	*dangerous*
la nécessité	*necessity*
causer	*to cause*
la cause	*cause*
jeter	*to throw (away / out)*
le plastique	*plastic*
le bois	*wood, woods*
le papier	*paper*
l'or (m)	*gold*
conduire	*to drive, lead*
le transport	*transportation*
la voiture	*car*
le trafic	*traffic*
la pollution	*pollution*
le bruit	*noise*
sérieux / sérieuse	*serious, responsible*
remplir	*to fill (up / in)*
vide	*empty*
la qualité	*quality*
la quantité	*quantity*
la population	*population*
l'action (f)	*action*
la ressource	*resource*
l'énergie (f)	*energy*
réduire	*to reduce*
recycler	*to recycle*
le recyclage	*recycling*
zéro	*zero*

Higher

climatique	*climate (adj.)*
mondial(e)	*global, world*
l'inondation (f)	*flood*
menacer (de)	*to threaten (to)*
la menace	*threat*
le dommage	*damage*
disparaître	*to disappear*
détruire	*to destroy*
brûler	*to burn*
ignorer	*to ignore, not know*
risquer	*to risk*
le taux	*rate*
grave	*serious, important, grave*
sérieusement	*seriously*
l'explication (f)	*explanation*
se souvenir de	*to remember*
remplacer	*to replace, swap*
sombre	*dark*
le pire	*the worst*
la conséquence	*consequence*
contribuer	*to contribute*
augmenter	*to increase*
baisser	*to lower, turn down*
les déchets (m)	*rubbish, waste*
la circulation	*traffic*
réutiliser	*to reuse*
prévenir	*to warn*
agir	*to act*
adapter	*to adapt*
limiter	*to limit*
l'acte (m)	*act, gesture*
conscient(e)	*conscious, aware*
durable	*durable, sustainable*
renouvelable	*renewable*

Equality

l'égalité (f)	*equality*
égal(e)	*equal*
l'identité (f)	*identity*
le sexisme	*sexism*
le racisme	*racism*
le handicap	*disability*
handicapé(e)	*disabled*
le fauteuil roulant	*wheelchair*
le respect	*respect*
respecter	*to respect*
bisexuel(le)	*bisexual*
gay	*gay*
lesbien(ne)	*lesbian*
hétéro, hétérosexuel(le)	*straight*
le mariage du même sexe	*same-sex marriage*
non-binaire	*non-binary*
transgenre	*transgender*
différent(e)	*different*
l'être (m)	*being*

Higher

humain(e)	*human (adj.)*
la liberté	*freedom*
libérer	*to free, set free, release*
la représentation	*representation*
la discrimination	*discrimination*
la minorité	*minority*
l'individu (m)	*individual*
civil(e)	*civil*
la communauté	*community*
multiculturel(le)	*multicultural*
intégrer	*to integrate*
s'intégrer	*to fit in*
tolérer	*to tolerate*
l'allié(e)	*ally*
fier / fière	*proud*
la fierté	*pride*
la paix	*peace*
la volonté	*will, desire*
profond(e)	*deep, profound*
développer	*to develop*

Social Issues

le problème	*problem, issue*
le crime	*crime*
arrêter	*to stop, arrest*
juste	*fair, just, only*
la justice	*justice*
la cour	*court*
la prison	*prison*
le choc	*shock, clash*
la solution	*solution*
lutter	*to struggle, fight, battle*
la violence	*violence*
extrême	*extreme*
pauvre	*poor*
la faim	*hunger*
l'attitude (f)	*attitude*
la victoire	*victory, winning*
la société	*society*
l'unité (f)	*unity*
l'association (f)	*organisation, charity, association*
commun(e)	*common*

Higher

le vol	*robbery*
voler	*to steal*
la lutte	*fight*
le conflit	*conflict*
combattre	*to fight*
le chômage	*unemployment*
l'écart (m)	*gap*
inquiet / inquiète	*worried, anxious*
l'inquiétude (f)	*worry, anxiety*
le souci	*worry*
se soucier (de)	*to show concern for*
moral(e)	*moral*

Higher

la honte	*shame*
l'avantage (m)	*advantage, pro*
l'inconvénient (m)	*disadvantage, con, inconvenience*
cacher	*to hide*
se cacher	*to hide (oneself)*
échapper (à)	*to escape (from)*
s'échapper (de)	*to escape (from)*
actuel(le)	*current, present*
immédiat(e)	*immediate*
l'enquête (f)	*survey*
le don	*donation*
considérer	*to consider*
défendre	*to defend*
défendre de	*to forbid, ban*
juger	*to judge*
imposer	*to impose*
manifester	*to demonstrate, show*
la manifestation	*demonstration, protest*
convaincre	*to convince*
résoudre	*to solve, resolve*
voter	*to vote*
l'état (m)	*state, condition*
le gouvernement	*government*
le / la citoyen(ne)	*citizen*
l'économie (f)	*economy*
la loi	*law*
le jugement	*judgement*
l'accord (m)	*agreement*
permanent(e)	*permanent*
contrôler	*to check, control*
la frontière	*border*

Revision Summary Test for Section Six

Don't let all this vocab go to landfill — re-use and recycle it with these summary questions...

Summary Test

- These questions are **really tricky**, but they'll help you see **how well you know your stuff**.
- Tackle the **revision summary test** below, or scan the QR code to do it **online**. You can **keep track of your progress** online and see **which areas need more work**.
- There are **sample answers** here: www.cgpbooks.co.uk/MerciExtras

The Natural World

1) What do these words mean in English?
   a) la terre b) la montagne c) le ciel d) la mer e) rechercher f) améliorer
2) 'If I use less water, I am helping to protect the environment.' Translate this sentence into French.
3) 'Je recherche des informations sur la protection de la nature dans cette forêt.'
   Translate this sentence into English.

H 4) Translate these words into English: a) l'arbre b) la lumière c) l'espèce

Environmental Problems

5) Translate the words below into French:
   a) necessity b) wood c) paper d) gold e) noise f) to fill (up / in) g) empty h) quality
6) In French, describe two ways you can protect the environment. Give as much detail as you can.
7) 'Many animals are in danger because of plastic.' Translate this sentence into French.
8) An environmental leaflet advises: 'Pour réduire la pollution de l'air, il faut moins utiliser la voiture. On peut prendre les transports publics ou faire du vélo.' What's it saying?
9) 'Dans ta région, quels sont les problèmes qui ont un effet négatif sur la nature ?' Respond in French.
10) 'On utilise trop de ressources et on ne recycle pas assez souvent.' Translate this sentence into English.

Higher

11) 'The climate crisis has many serious consequences — for example, it threatens nature. Species are disappearing and forests are burning.' Translate this passage into French.
12) 'Qu'est-ce que tu penses de l'énergie renouvelable ?' Translate the question, then respond in French.
13) 'Do environmental problems worry you?' Respond in French and explain your answer.

Equality and Social Issues

14) Translate the words below into English:
    a) l'égalité b) juste c) bisexuel(le) d) hétérosexuel(le) e) non-binaire f) transgenre
15) Aïda says: 'My aunt is lesbian and she is disabled. She has a really good wheelchair that helps her to be more independent.' Translate what she says into French.
16) 'Dans une société juste, tout le monde doit respecter les différences entre les gens.'
    Translate this sentence into French, then write a sentence of your own about equality in society.
17) How would you say the words below in French?
    a) hunger b) poor c) to struggle d) victory e) justice f) clash
18) 'En général, la violence n'est pas un problème dans ma région.' Translate this sentence into English.
19) 'Qu'est-ce qu'on peut faire pour aider les personnes qui habitent dans la rue ?'
    Translate the question, then respond in French.

Higher

20) Translate these verbs into French, then try conjugating them in the first person singular:
    a) to set free b) to fit in c) to tolerate d) to develop e) to hide f) to escape (from)
21) In French, explain one of the main worries you have about today's society.
22) Translate the words below into French:
    a) citizen b) border c) survey d) to convince e) pro f) con g) agreement
23) Your friend tells you: 'La représentation de différentes communautés dans les médias est importante. Il faut être un allié des minorités.' Translate this passage into English.

Technology

Quick Quiz

Technology is a hot topic these days — it's difficult to imagine life without it. It's quite likely you'll get asked about its advantages and disadvantages, so go over this section carefully.

Remember there's also lots of online content here: www.cgpbooks.co.uk/Merci

La technologie moderne — Modern technology

Vocabulary

la technologie	*technology*	répondre (à)	*to answer, reply (to)*	électrique	*electric*
l'ordinateur portable (m)	*laptop*	écouter	*to listen to*	l'appareil (m) (Higher)	*device, apparatus*
le portable	*mobile phone*	téléphoner	*to phone*	l'écran (m) (Higher)	*screen*
l'e-mail (m)	*e-mail*	marcher	*to function*	la lumière (Higher)	*light*
le message	*message*	fonctionner	*to function, work*	enregistrer (Higher)	*to record*
envoyer	*to send*			communiquer (Higher)	*to communicate*
recevoir	*to receive*	charger	*to load, charge*		

Q&A Audio

Question

Est-ce que tu utilises souvent la technologie ?

Do you often use technology?

Simple Answer

Oui, je dois utiliser ma tablette tous les jours. J'envoie et je reçois beaucoup de messages.

Yes, I have to use my tablet everyday. I send and receive lots of messages.

Extended Answer

Oui, j'utilise beaucoup d'applis très utiles, mais je pense qu'on passe trop de temps sur nos portables. Les messages ont remplacé la conversation.

Yes, I use a lot of very useful apps, but I think that we spend too much time on our phones. Messages have replaced conversation.

Grammar — 'pouvoir' / 'vouloir' / 'devoir' / 'il faut' + infinitive

Some verbs can be followed directly by an infinitive (see p.167).

- **Il ne peut pas vivre sans son téléphone.**
  He can't live without his telephone.
- **Je veux acheter des écouteurs.**
  I want to buy some headphones.
- **Tu dois faire une vidéo.**
  You have to make a video.
- **Il faut charger ton portable.**
  You must charge your phone.

Practice Question

Q1 Read Hugo's article about technology and decide if the statements below are true or false.

READING

Ma mère m'a acheté un nouveau téléphone portable pour mon anniversaire. C'est très utile parce que je peux répondre à mes amis tout le temps. Je peux aussi télécharger des chansons sur Internet et les écouter tous les jours. Si je ne rentre pas à la maison après l'école, ma mère peut m'envoyer un message. Elle aime savoir que je suis en sécurité.

a) Hugo bought a new phone. *[1 mark]*

b) Hugo downloads music from the internet. *[1 mark]*

c) Hugo's mum is glad that he has a phone. *[1 mark]*

d) Hugo doesn't bring his phone to school. *[1 mark]*

Translating 'il faut' is easier than you'd think...

'Il faut' means 'it is necessary' or 'you must'. It's common in French and is often followed by an infinitive. For example, 'Il faut faire les exercises' means 'You must do the exercises'. Not at all threatening...

Quick Quiz

The Internet and Gaming

Of course, technology isn't just about phones — the internet practically runs the world, so it probably deserves a mention. It's likely to be a popular topic in the exam, so learn this vocab well.

Parler d'Internet — Talking about the internet

Vocabulary

Internet (m)	*internet, web*	la protection	*protection*
en ligne	*online*	le danger	*danger*
le site	*site*	dangereux / dangereuse	*dangerous*
le mot	*word*	la victime	*victim*
sûr(e)	*safe, sure, certain*	le risque	*risk*
la sécurité	*security, safety*	la santé	*health*
protéger	*to protect*	l'action (f)	*action*
		prendre	*to take*
		le mot de passe	*password*

Higher:

voler (à...)	*to steal (from someone)*
le vol	*theft*
vérifier	*to check*
l'accès (m)	*access*
les données (f)	*data*

Unlike other nouns in French, the word 'Internet' doesn't need the article 'l''.

L'accès à Internet est essentiel de nos jours.	*Internet access is essential nowadays.*
Il faut faire attention quand tu donnes tes informations personnelles en ligne.	*You should be careful when you give out your personal information online.*
L'année dernière, j'ai été victime d'un vol — quelqu'un a volé mes coordonnées bancaires.	*Last year, I was the victim of a theft — someone stole my bank details.*

your telephone number — ton numéro de téléphone

of fraud — de fraude

Le streaming — Streaming

Vocabulary

la télé(vision)	*television / TV*	la série	*series*	direct(e)	*direct*
l'émission (f)	*TV programme, broadcast*	regarder	*to watch, look at*	directement	*directly, straight away*
le film	*film, movie*	facile	*easy*	H découvrir	*to discover*
		rapide	*fast, quick*		

J'ai découvert des sites de streaming qui proposent des séries — je les utilise souvent.	*I discovered some streaming sites which offer series — I often use them.*
Le streaming est très utile car on peut regarder des émissions en ligne quand on veut.	*Streaming is very useful because you can watch TV programmes online whenever you want.*

Grammar — direct object pronouns ('me', 'te', 'le', 'la', 'nous', 'vous', 'les')

A direct object is the person or thing (noun) that an action is being done to.

Elle regarde un film en ligne. ***She's watching a film online.***

Direct object pronouns (see p.146) replace that noun.

In French, they come before the verb and are used to avoid repetition.

Elle le regarde en ligne. ***She's watching it online.***

The final letter of 'me', 'te', 'le' and 'la' is dropped and replaced with an apostrophe when they come directly before a word beginning with a vowel.

Les jeux (m) vidéo — Video games

Vocabulary

la console	*console*	le jeu vidéo	*video game*	télécharger	*to download*
jouer (à)	*to play (something)*	couper	*to cut, switch off*	voir	*to see*
le jeu	*game*			H l'abonnement (m)	*subscription*

Selon moi, les jeux vidéo sont une perte de temps, et j'estime qu'ils exposent les enfants à la violence.

In my opinion, video games are a waste of time, and I think that they expose children to violence.

to inappropriate content — à des contenus inappropriés

Q&A Audio

Question

Est-ce que tu aimes les jeux vidéo ?

Do you like video games?

Simple Answer

Oui, j'adore jouer aux jeux vidéo. C'est amusant et intéressant.

Yes, I love playing video games. They're fun and interesting.

Extended Answer

Non, j'essaie d'éviter les jeux vidéos, mais mon petit frère les adore. Il essaie d'agir comme les personnages qu'il voit à l'écran, mais à mon avis ces personnages ne sont pas toujours de bons modèles.

No, I try to avoid video games, but my little brother loves them. He tries to act like the characters he sees on screen, but in my opinion these characters are not always good role models.

"If it's not a CGP book, I'm not interested."

Practice Questions

Q1 *Answer these questions out loud in French.* SPEAKING

a) Qu'est-ce que tu penses du streaming ?

b) Quels sont les dangers d'Internet ?

c) Quel est ton avis sur les jeux vidéo ? *[6 marks]*

Top Tip for Higher Students

✓ Use interesting adverbs like 'tellement', 'évidemment' and 'entièrement'.

Q2 *In this extract from a podcast, Maxine is being interviewed about how her family uses technology. In each list below, there is one true statement. Choose the true statement from each list.* LISTENING

Listening Track 27

a) **A.** Maxine's mum doesn't like gaming.
B. Her mum plays video games regularly.
C. Her mum thinks video games can be boring. *[1 mark]*

b) **A.** Maxine's dad uses the internet too much.
B. Her dad thinks the internet is bad for your health.
C. Her dad doesn't use the internet at work. *[1 mark]*

c) **A.** Maxine is helping her brother write an email about streaming sites.
B. Her brother uses the internet to study.
C. Her brother uses the internet to watch programmes. *[1 mark]*

Not everything you talk about has to be true...

You might have lots of opinions about the internet that you're just dying to share with the examiners, but if you don't, remember that it's fine to make something up — just make sure you use lots of interesting vocab.

Quick Quiz

Social Media

Chances are you already know a fair bit about the pros and cons of social media. All you need to do is learn how to talk about those pros and cons in French, and off you go...

La vie en ligne — Life online

Vocabulary

social(e)	*social*	l'appli(cation) (f)	*app*	l'influence (f)	*influence*
les médias (m)	*media*	la conversation	*conversation*	l'influenceur / l'influenceuse	*influencer*
le réseau	*network*	la communication	*communication*	populaire	*popular*
utiliser	*to use*	le contact	*contact*	disponible (Higher)	*available*
suivre	*to follow*	le commentaire	*comment, remark*	la communauté (Higher)	*community*
partager	*to share*			la génération (Higher)	*generation*
la photo	*photo*	l'ado (m/f), l'adolescent(e)	*teenager*	la jeunesse (Higher)	*youth*
la vidéo	*video*			virtuel(le) (Higher)	*virtual*
l'image (f)	*picture, image*	jeune	*young*		
		le / la jeune	*young person*		

J'aime bien partager des photos en ligne pour informer mes amis de ce que je fais. — *I really like sharing photos online to inform my friends about what I'm doing.*

Il n'est jamais disponible parce qu'il passe trop de temps en ligne. — *He is never available because he spends too much time online.*

Les réseaux sociaux — Social networks

Q&A Audio

Question

Est-ce que tu utilises souvent les réseaux sociaux ?

Do you often use social networks?

Simple Answer

Oui, j'utilise les réseaux sociaux chaque jour. J'aime suivre mes amis.

Yes, I use social networks every day. I like to follow my friends.

Extended Answer

Oui, j'adore les réseaux sociaux. Je partage des vidéos une fois par jour. Normalement, je passe une heure par jour en ligne à discuter avec d'autres jeunes.

Yes, I love social networks. I share videos once a day. Normally, I spend an hour a day online chatting with other young people.

J'utilise les réseaux sociaux pour suivre les influenceurs qui mettent des vidéos en ligne. — *I use social networks to follow influencers who put videos online.* (*companies* — les entreprises)

Les réseaux sociaux me permettent d'être en contact avec d'autres jeunes qui partagent les mêmes intérêts que moi. Je trouve la communauté en ligne très sympathique. — *Social networks allow me to be in contact with other young people who share the same interests as me. I find the online community very nice.* (*close-knit* — très unie)

Il y a beaucoup de débats autour des réseaux sociaux — il est difficile de décider si c'est une bonne chose pour les ados ou pas. — *There are lots of debates around social networks — it's hard to decide if they're a good thing for teenagers or not.* (*of worries* — d'inquiétudes)

Les dangers (m) — Dangers

Vocabulary

négatif / négative	*negative*
inconnu(e)	*unknown*
la cybercriminalité	*cybercrime, online crime*
souffrir	*to suffer, be in pain*
inquiétant(e)	*worrying*
l'inquiétude (f)	*worry, anxiety*
le souci	*worry*

Higher

Grammar — 'de' (preposition)

Many set phrases like 'à cause de' and 'faire de' use the preposition 'de'. Don't forget that if 'de' is followed by 'le' or 'les', the two words are combined:

'de' + 'le' = 'du' **'de' + 'les' = 'des'**

À cause des réseaux sociaux...
As a result of social networks...

Il fait du shopping pour trouver une console neuve...
He is shopping for a brand new console...

Hier soir, j'ai un peu perdu confiance en moi à cause des commentaires négatifs sur mon post.	*Last night, I lost a little self-confidence because of negative comments on my post.*
Je sais que beaucoup de jeunes souffrent à cause des gens qui les harcèlent en ligne.	*I know that lots of young people suffer because of people who bully them online.*
J'ai reçu beaucoup de critiques au sujet d'une image que j'ai partagée avec mes amis.	*I received a lot of criticism about an image that I shared with my friends.*
Il y a des personnes très méchantes qui écrivent des choses complètement fausses sur les réseaux sociaux.	*There are really nasty people who write completely false things on social networks.*

of internet users — d'internautes

insult — insultent

anonymous — anonymes

on forums — dans les forums

Practice Questions

Q1 *Write a short speech that you will present to your class about social media. You should aim to write 80-90 words. Write about:*

- *the benefits of social media*
- *your opinion of influencers with reasons*
- *the last time you used social media*
- *how you will use social media in the next few weeks.* *[18 marks]*

WRITING

Top Tips for Higher Students
✓ Use superlatives when giving your opinion.
✓ Include more than one detail for each bullet point.

Higher

Q2 *In this interview for a local newspaper, Michael talks about how he uses social media. Listen to what Michael says and answer the questions below in English.*

a) How much time does Michael spend on social media each day? *[1 mark]*
b) What does Michael do whilst he is doing his homework? *[1 mark]*
c) What does Michael think of social media? *[1 mark]*
d) How does social media help Michael stay connected to his family? *[1 mark]*

LISTENING

Listening Track 28

Giving a balanced opinion will really impress the examiner...

Giving both sides of an argument allows you to expand on the range of vocab you use and also gives you a chance to use conjunctions like 'par contre' (*however*) and 'donc' (*therefore*). Very fancy.

Speaking Questions

Technology may have its flaws, but these practice questions will have your French flawless in no time.

Candidate's Material

Raphaël has contributed to a blog about the internet.
Read out the text below to your teacher.

Foundation

Il y a beaucoup de dangers en ligne.

Internet est utile, mais aussi dangereux.

Certaines personnes écrivent des choses négatives.

Passer trop de temps sur son portable est mauvais pour la santé.

Il faut travailler ensemble pour réduire ces risques.

Higher

Je viens de découvrir que la cybercriminalité est une vraie menace sur Internet.

Actuellement, quelqu'un essaie de voler mon identité et mon argent en ligne.

C'est mauvais pour ma santé mentale, et je m'inquiète parce que la personne responsable est encore inconnue.

Il faut toujours vérifier que nos données sont en sécurité.

- Once you have read the text, you will then be asked two questions related to what you have read.
- You are expected to say a few words or a short phrase/sentence in response to each question. One-word answers will not be sufficient to gain full marks.

Teacher's Material

- Start by asking the candidate to read the text by saying '*Please read the text*'.
- Allow the candidate to read the text aloud, then ask the following two questions for their tier.
- Allow the student to develop their answers as much as possible.

F

- Est-ce que tu aimes utiliser Internet ?
- Qu'est-ce que tu penses des enfants qui utilisent Internet ?

H

- Est-ce que tu aimes avoir une vie virtuelle ?
- Quel est ton avis sur la cybercriminalité ?

Listening Questions

1 Listen to these interviews about social media.
For each person, tick the correct statement.

Listening Track 29

1 a Clara uses social media to...

	A talk to her best friend in person.
	B share photos with her friends online.
	C speak to her best friend every day.

[1 mark]

1 b When using social media, Jules...

	A prefers to keep his pictures and videos private.
	B likes to show people what he's been doing.
	C doesn't follow many influencers.

[1 mark]

Higher

1 c When asked about her online life, Chloé says that...

	A she never uses social media.
	B her school gave students tips on staying safe online.
	C she believes the internet isn't dangerous.

[1 mark]

2 You hear this radio debate about technology. Answer the questions **in English**.

Listening Track 30

2 a What does Diane use her phone for?

.... *[1 mark]*

2 b Why does Fatima like technology?

.... *[1 mark]*

2 c What does Fatima use an app for?

.... *[1 mark]*

Higher

2 d What does Mohamed think about young people?

.... *[1 mark]*

2 e According to Mohamed, what can't you avoid online?

.... *[1 mark]*

Reading Questions

Foundation

1 Read these comments from a forum about technology.

> **Jade**: J'ai téléchargé beaucoup d'applications utiles sur ma tablette.
>
> **Toni**: Mon portable ne marche pas en ce moment. Je ne peux plus recevoir de messages.
>
> **Sarah**: Je vais acheter un nouvel ordinateur portable pour faire mes devoirs.

Who says what? Choose the correct answers.
Put a cross in the correct column for each question.

	Who...	Jade	Toni	Sarah	
a)	... wants to buy a new laptop?				*[1 mark]*
b)	... has downloaded useful apps?				*[1 mark]*
c)	... has a broken phone?				*[1 mark]*
d)	... has a tablet?				*[1 mark]*
e)	... can't receive messages?				*[1 mark]*

Higher

2 Read Manon's forum post about how she uses the internet.

> *Je passe des heures devant l'écran à parler à mes amis. En ligne, c'est plus facile de communiquer. C'est très agréable parce qu'on ne se sent jamais seul.*
>
> *Cependant, je ne mets jamais d'informations personnelles sur les réseaux sociaux. On doit lutter contre la cybercriminalité parce que les gens peuvent voler vos informations.*
>
> *J'ai été victime de harcèlement en ligne l'année dernière. Maintenant, je suis inquiète pour d'autres jeunes qui utilisent les réseaux sociaux parce que les commentaires négatifs ont eu un effet sur ma confiance en soi.*

What does Manon say about how she uses the internet?
Complete the tables **in English**. You do not need to write in full sentences.

2 a

The positives of social media (1 detail)
....

[1 mark]

2 b

The risk of putting personal details online (1 detail)
....

[1 mark]

2 c

How negative comments affected her (1 detail)
....

[1 mark]

Writing Questions

Foundation

1 Translate the following three sentences **into French**.

1 a My sister doesn't use the internet.

.... *[2 marks]*

1 b I follow influencers on social media.

.... *[2 marks]*

1 c You can download free TV shows.

.... *[2 marks]*

2 Write a blog post on how you use technology.
You must include the following points:

- what you use technology for
- your opinion of mobile phones
- what technology you will use tomorrow.

Write your answer **in French**. You should aim to write between 40 and 50 words. *[14 marks]*

Higher

3 Translate the paragraph **into French**.

> Today's young people are the online generation. They have lots of devices, lead a virtual life on social networks, and their online skills are excellent. However, they also have access to a lot of information on the internet. I started using technology when I was three years old, and I discovered that the internet is dangerous.

[10 marks]

4 Write an article for the school newsletter on the dangers of social media.
You **must** include the following points:

- how you use social media
- the pros and cons of online communication
- a recent negative experience you had online
- how you will avoid the dangers of social media in the future.

Write your answer **in French**. You should aim to write between 130 and 150 words. *[22 marks]*

Social Media and Technology — Vocabulary

The digital world is a challenge at the best of times, but learning this vocab will make your life easier in the exam.

Technology

la technologie	*technology*
l'ordinateur portable (m)	*laptop*
neuf / neuve	*(brand) new*
nouveau, nouvelle, nouvel	*new*
le portable	*mobile phone*
le téléphone	*telephone*
la tablette	*tablet*
le numéro	*number*
l'e-mail (m)	*e-mail*
le message	*message*
envoyer	*to send*
recevoir	*to receive*
répondre (à)	*to answer, reply (to)*
écouter	*to listen to*
téléphoner	*to phone*
marcher	*to function*
fonctionner	*to function, work*

'Neuf' is used to describe something <u>brand new</u> and comes after the noun. 'Nouveau' is used to describe something new to the speaker, and comes before the noun. See p.## for more on adjectives.

charger	*to load, charge*
la version	*version*
le volume	*volume*
électrique	*electric*
la science-fiction	*sci-fi*

Higher

l'appareil (m)	*device, apparatus*
les écouteurs (m)	*headphones, earbuds*
l'écran (m)	*screen*
l'objet (m)	*object, subject line*
le code	*code*
la lumière	*light*
enregistrer	*to record*
communiquer	*to communicate*

The Internet

Internet (m)	*internet, web*
en ligne	*online*
le site	*site*
le mot	*word*
sûr(e)	*safe, sure, certain*
la sécurité	*security, safety*
le danger	*danger*
dangereux / dangereuse	*dangerous*
protéger	*to protect*
la protection	*protection*
la victime	*victim*
le risque	*risk*
la santé	*health*
l'action (f)	*action*
prendre	*to take*
le mot de passe	*password*

Higher

voler (à...)	*to steal (from someone)*
le vol	*theft*
vérifier	*to check*
l'accès (m)	*access*
les données (f)	*data*

No computer virus was getting past Linda.

Streaming and Gaming

le streaming	*streaming*
la télé(vision)	*television / TV*
l'émission (f)	*TV programme, broadcast*
le film	*film, movie*
la série	*series*
regarder	*to watch, look at*
facile	*easy*
rapide	*fast, quick*
direct(e)	*direct*
directement	*directly, straight away*
la console	*console*
jouer (à)	*to play (something)*

le jeu	*game*
le jeu vidéo	*video game*
couper	*to cut, switch off*
télécharger	*to download*
voir	*to see*
H l'abonnement (m)	*subscription*
H découvrir	*to discover*

You can add 'ment' to the feminine form of an adjective to make an adverb.

Social Media

les médias (m)	*media*
le réseau	*network*
social(e)	*social*
utiliser	*to use*
suivre	*to follow*
partager	*to share*
la photo	*photo*
la vidéo	*video*
l'image (f)	*picture, image*
l'appli(cation) (f)	*app*
la conversation	*conversation*
la communication	*communication*
le contact	*contact*
le commentaire	*comment, remark*
l'ado (m/f), l'adolescent(e)	*teenager*
jeune	*young*
le / la jeune	*young person*
l'influence (f)	*influence*
l'influenceur / l'influenceuse	*influencer*

'La fois' is used to describe how many times something happens, but you'll need to use 'le temps' to talk about time more generally.

la fois	*time*
moderne	*modern*
populaire	*popular*
négatif / négative	*negative*
informer	*to inform*
Higher disponible	*available*
Higher la communauté	*community*
Higher la génération	*generation*
Higher la jeunesse	*youth*
Higher virtuel(le)	*virtual*
Higher inconnu(e)	*unknown*
Higher la cybercriminalité	*cybercrime, online crime*
Higher souffrir	*to suffer, be in pain*
Higher inquiétant(e)	*worrying*
Higher l'inquiétude (f)	*worry, anxiety*
Higher le souci	*worry*

Revision Summary Test for Section Seven

Once you've recharged those brain cells, test your tech knowledge with these summary questions.

- These questions are **hard**, but they'll really help you see **how well you know your stuff**.
- Tackle the **revision summary test** below, or scan the QR code to do it **online**. You can **track your progress** online and see **which areas need more work**.
- There are **sample answers** for the test here: www.cgpbooks.co.uk/MerciExtras

Summary Test

Technology

1) How do you say the following words in French?
   a) volume b) to receive c) to listen d) version e) new technologies f) to function
2) Yanis says: 'Maintenant, les jeunes préfèrent les portables aux ordinateurs portables.' What does this mean in English?
3) 'I want to reply to an e-mail, but my tablet isn't working.' How would you say this in French?
4) Sylvie says: 'Il ne faut pas avoir de portable avant l'âge de onze ans.' What does this mean in English? Do you agree with her statement? Answer in French.
5) Your friend explains: 'Mon numéro de téléphone a changé, donc je dois envoyer un message à tout le monde.' Translate this into English.

Higher

6) 'Quels appareils utilises-tu chaque jour ?' Respond in French using complete sentences.
7) Translate the sentence below into French: 'This morning, I recorded a song, then I listened to music on my brand-new headphones.'

The Internet and Gaming

8) 'Qu'est-ce que tu fais sur Internet en général ?' Respond in French.
9) You're reading a leaflet about internet safety: 'Pour rester en sécurité sur Internet, il ne faut pas partager ton mot de passe sur les sites publics, car c'est dangereux.' What advice is the leaflet giving? Answer in English.
10) In French, explain one more action you can take to stay safe online.
11) 'En ligne, tu peux lire des choses intéressantes, regarder des films et des émissions sur des sites de streaming et télécharger des jeux.' Translate this into English.
12) Translate these words into French:
    a) health b) risk c) easy d) victim e) protection f) to protect

Higher

13) In French, write down two advantages and two disadvantages of the internet.
14) 'Lola has a subscription to a streaming site because she likes discovering new series.' How would you say this in French?
15) Translate these words into French: a) access b) theft c) to steal d) to check e) data

Social Media

16) 'Do you use social media? Why / Why not?' Answer in French.
17) 'Quels sont les dangers des réseaux sociaux ?' Respond in French.
18) Translate these words and phrases into French: a) contact b) online communication c) comment d) teenager e) to inform f) modern g) popular h) to follow influencers
19) How many things can you name that you might share on social media? There are at least 3 you need to know.

Higher

20) 'Théo uses social networks from time to time, but he thinks the influence of some new apps is worrying for his generation.' How would you say this in French?
21) Translate these words into French: a) youth b) to suffer c) available d) unknown e) virtual f) cybercrime g) anxiety

School Subjects

Quick Quiz

Talking about subjects is fairly simple. You're probably bursting to say that you adore all things French-related. Explaining your opinion will get you more marks, so use this page to prepare properly.

Les matières (f) — Subjects

Remember there's also lots of online content here: www.cgpbooks.co.uk/Merci

Vocabulary

la matière	*subject*	le français	*French*
le sujet	*subject, topic*	le théâtre	*drama*
l'anglais (m)	*English*	la musique	*music*
les maths (f)	*maths*		
les sciences (f)	*science*		
la technologie	*technology*		
l'histoire (f)	*history*		
la religion	*religion*		
les langues modernes (f)	*modern languages*		

Grammar (Higher only) — 'depuis'

To say you've been doing something since a certain age, use the present tense with 'depuis' (*since*). See p.167 for more on this.

J'étudie le français depuis l'âge de six ans.
I've been studying French since the age of six.

Moi, j'adore l'histoire parce que j'aime étudier le passé. — *I love history because I like studying the past.*

À mon avis, la physique est une matière bien trop difficile. — *In my opinion, physics is a far too difficult subject.*

chemistry — la chimie
biology — la biologie

Je trouve la géographie très intéressante. — *I find geography very interesting.*

stimulating — stimulante

Ma matière préférée, c'est... — My favourite subject is...

Q&A Audio

Question

Quelle est ta matière préférée ?
What's your favourite subject?

Simple Answer

J'aime bien les maths. Les réponses sont toujours claires.
I like maths. The answers are always clear.

Extended Answer

J'aime les maths car c'est facile, mais je préfère l'anglais parce que j'aime lire des romans passionnants.
I like maths because it's easy, but I prefer English because I like to read exciting novels.

Practice Question

WRITING

Q1 *Write to your friend about school subjects. You should write about 80-90 words* ***in French****. You must include the following points:*

- *the subjects taught at your school*
- *your opinion of one subject with reasons*
- *the lessons you had last week*
- *what you would like to study in the future.* *[18 marks]*

Top Tips for Higher Students
✓ Use superlatives, e.g. 'le pire', 'le meilleur'.
✓ Link phrases together with conjunctions.

Always explain your opinions — it'll gain you marks...

Everyone has subjects they love and subjects they just can't stand — whatever they are for you, make sure you can say them in French and fully explain why that's the case. Have a go now — you'll thank me later.

Quick Quiz

School Life

You probably already know everything there is to know about life at your school. Well, now's your opportunity to learn how to speak about it in French. It's thrilling stuff, so time to get cracking.

Aller à l'école — Going to school

Vocabulary

l'école (f)	*school*	la quatrième	*Year 9*	la classe	*class, classroom*
le collège	*secondary school*	la troisième	*Year 10*	la journée	*day*
l'éducation (f)	*education*	la seconde	*Year 11*	la semaine	*week*
scolaire	*school (adj.)*	la première	*Year 12*	l'année (f)	*year*
l'élève (m/f)	*pupil, student*	les études (f)	*studies*	la rentrée	*start of school year*
le / la jeune	*young person*	le cours	*course, lesson*	H l'emploi du temps (m)	*timetable*
l'adolescent(e)	*teenager*	la leçon	*lesson*		

Ma première leçon commence à 8h30. — *My first lesson starts at 8:30 am.*

J'assiste à cinq cours chaque jour. — *I attend five lessons every day.*

Nous travaillons jusqu'à la pause. — *We work until breaktime.* (*study* — étudions)

Cette année, je rentre en seconde. — *This year, I'm going into Year 11.* (*I'm leaving school* — je quitte l'école)

Grammar — feminine nouns starting with a vowel

Feminine nouns beginning with vowels always take masculine possessive adjectives — it's easier to say.

- **Mon école** → ***My school***
- **Son éducation** → ***His/her education***

En classe — In class

Vocabulary

le / la prof(esseur)	*teacher*	l'information (f)	*information*	enseigner (à)	*to teach*
apprendre (à)	*to learn (to)*	lire	*to read*	la compétence	*competence, skill, ability*
demander	*to ask*	comprendre	*to understand*	la connaissance	*knowledge*
écrire	*to write*	utile	*useful*	se concentrer	*to concentrate*
pratiquer	*to practise*	inutile	*useless*	expliquer	*to explain*
discuter	*to discuss*	difficile	*difficult*	l'explication (f)	*explanation*
les devoirs (m)	*homework*	facile	*easy*		

(Higher: enseigner (à), la compétence, la connaissance, se concentrer, expliquer, l'explication (f))

En cours d'anglais, nous avons discuté des thèmes du roman. — *In the English lesson, we discussed the themes of the novel.* (*the message of the poem* — du message du poème)

Je trouve l'enseignement trop simple et je sais toutes les réponses. — *I find the teaching too simple and I know all the answers.* (*hard* — dur; *I find it boring* — je trouve cela ennuyeux)

À mon école, il y a... — At my school, there is...

Vocabulary

la salle	*room*	le club	*club*	la bibliothèque	*library*
la cour	*playground*	le football	*football*	la scène	*stage*
les toilettes (f)	*toilet(s)*	l'activité (f)	*activity*	l'écran (m)	*screen*
l'équipement (m)	*equipment*	l'équipe (f)	*team*	prêter	*to lend*
le tableau	*board, picture, painting*	organiser	*to organise*	emprunter (à)	*to borrow (from)*

(Higher: la bibliothèque, la scène, l'écran (m), prêter, emprunter (à))

La récré dure quinze minutes — nous aimons jouer au football en équipe. — *Break lasts fifteen minutes — we like to play football in teams.*

Je peux emprunter ton stylo et ta règle ? — *Can I borrow your pen and ruler?*

your pencil — ton crayon

La bibliothèque prête des livres et organise un club de lecture. — *The library lends books and organises a book club.*

bookshop — la librairie

Q&A Audio

Question

Il est comment, ton collège ?
What is your school like?

Simple Answer

C'est une grande école avec beaucoup d'espace.
It's a big school with a lot of space.

Extended Answer

C'est un petit collège, mais nous avons tout ce qu'il faut. Par exemple, nous avons une bibliothèque géniale et une grande cour où nous passons la pause.
It's a little school, but we have everything we need. For example, we have a great library and a big playground where we spend breaktime.

Practice Questions

Q1 Read the passages and answer the question below. READING

> **Morgane :** *Je vais au lycée et je suis en seconde. J'adore les cours de sciences parce que je m'intéresse au monde naturel et j'aime faire des expériences.*

> **Sacha :** *Dans mon collège, tout le monde doit étudier l'anglais. Je déteste ça : le prof est vraiment ennuyeux, donc je n'arrive pas à m'intéresser aux cours.*

*Answer the following questions **in English**.*

a) What year is Morgane in? *[1 mark]*

b) Why does Morgane love science? *[1 mark]*

c) Why isn't Sacha interested in English lessons? *[1 mark]*

Higher

*Q2 Listen to Mehdi speak about his time at school. Complete the following sentences **in English**.* LISTENING

Listening Track 31

a) i) Mehdi thinks that maths will be very ....

ii) Mehdi arrives late to school because ....

b) i) As well as English, Mehdi also studies ....

ii) After lunch, Mehdi .... *[4 marks]*

Make sure you're ready to describe your school life...

Examiners may well ask questions about your school and what you think of it, so if you've got all this vocab learnt and some opinions stored up and ready to go, you'll be well on your way to acing the exam. Nice.

Quick Quiz

School Pressures and Difficulties

School can be pretty stressful — you're trying to study and get the grades you need whilst maintaining a social life and doing your hobbies. Here's how to talk about it in French — let all that stress out...

Les examens (m) — Exams

Vocabulary

l'examen (m)	*exam, test*	l'erreur (f)	*mistake, error*	la pression (Higher)	*pressure*
passer	*to take (an exam)*	essayer (de)	*to try*	stressé(e) (Higher)	*stressed*
préparer	*to prepare*	la chance	*luck*	l'épreuve (f) (Higher)	*test*
améliorer	*to improve*	sérieux, sérieuse	*serious, important*	le courage (Higher)	*courage, bravery*
l'effort (m)	*effort*				

Q&A Audio

Question

Qu'est-ce que tu penses des examens ?

What do you think of exams?

Simple Answer

Je trouve les examens difficiles, et donc je dois travailler dur.

I find exams hard, so I have to work hard.

Extended Answer

Les examens sont très difficiles, mais à mon avis, le pire, c'est de devoir attendre les résultats ! Il y a trop de pression et il faut être patient.

Exams are very difficult, but in my opinion, what's worse is having to wait for results! There is too much pressure and you have to patient.

J'ai obtenu de bons résultats — I got good results

Vocabulary

réussir (à)	*to succeed (in), pass*	nul(le)	*rubbish*	répéter	*to repeat*
le succès	*success*	faible	*weak*	l'échec (m) (Higher)	*failure*
le résultat	*result*	fort(e)	*strong*	la réussite (Higher)	*success*
la note	*mark, grade*	le but	*goal, aim, purpose*	obtenir (Higher)	*to get, obtain, get hold of*
gagner	*to earn*				

J'ai réussi l'examen de maths, donc je vais fêter mon succès !	*I passed the maths exam, so I'm going to celebrate my success!*
Le prof a corrigé mon contrôle et m'a donné une bonne note.	*The teacher marked my test and gave me a good grade.*
Quel candidat n'a fait qu'une erreur ?	*Which candidate only made one mistake?*
Fatou a échoué à l'épreuve de français et doit la repasser.	*Fatou failed the French paper and has to resit it.*

sat / took — passé

'ne...que' means 'only'. See p.175 for more.

didn't prepare for — ne s'est pas préparée pour

Grammar — 'quel'

'Quel', meaning 'which' or 'what', agrees in number and gender with the noun following it.

- **Quels élèves ont réussi ?** — ***Which students passed?***
- **Quelle chance !** — ***What luck!***

"What an amazing piece of paper!"

Les règles (f) scolaires — School rules

Vocabulary

devoir	*to have to, must*	le respect	*respect*
attendre	*to wait*	l'égalité (f)	*equality*
la règle	*rule*	égal(e)	*equal*
interdire (de)	*to forbid, ban*	le comportement (Higher)	*behaviour*
l'uniforme (m)	*uniform*	se comporter (Higher)	*to behave*
strict(e)	*strict*	le principe (Higher)	*principle*
respecter	*to respect, follow*		

Le collège nous oblige à porter des vêtements qui nous donnent un air très professionnel. — *The school makes us wear professional-looking clothes.*

very ugly — très laids
very smart — très chic / élégants

L'objectif de l'école est de réduire le nombre d'absences et d'améliorer le comportement des élèves. — *The school's objective is to reduce the number of absences and improve the behaviour of pupils.*

equality among pupils — l'égalité entre les élèves

Les problèmes (m) à l'école — Problems at school

Vocabulary

aider	*to help*	surveiller (Higher)	*to watch, keep an eye on*	la confiance (Higher)	*trust*
l'aide (f)	*help*	le harcèlement (Higher)	*bullying, harassment*	le soutien (Higher)	*support*
se taire (H)	*to be quiet, keep quiet*	régler (Higher)	to settle, set	le souci (Higher)	worry
				l'inquiétude (f) (Higher)	*worry, anxiety*

Sékou est très intelligent, mais il est aussi paresseux. — *Sékou is very intelligent, but he is also lazy.*

doesn't have much confidence — n'a pas beaucoup de confiance en lui

L'école offre son soutien aux élèves inquiets. — *The school offers support to worried students.*

Practice Questions

Q1 *You are talking to your pen pal about school. Respond to their questions **in French**.* (SPEAKING)

a) Quelle est ton opinion sur les repas scolaires ?

b) Que penses-tu de ton uniforme scolaire ?

c) Dans ton opinion, quel est le plus grand problème dans ton école ?

d) Quel est ton avis sur les repas scolaires ? *[8 marks]*

Q2 *Listen to these four sentences and write down **in French** exactly what you hear. Use your knowledge of French to make sure that what you have written is accurate.* *[8 marks]* (LISTENING)

Listening Track 32

Keep learning this vocab if you want to get great 'résultats'...

You might have to talk about your exams in the exams. Get yourself ready by learning all these words and making sure you know how to pronounce them — it'll help you pick up marks in the speaking exam.

Speaking Questions

It's time to put what you've learnt to the test — have a go at answering these practice questions.

Candidate's Material

Zoé has written a letter about her school life. Read out the text below to your teacher.

Foundation

Je prends le bus pour aller au collège.

La journée commence tôt.

Mon premier cours, c'est histoire.

La technologie est ma matière préférée.

Pendant la pause, je parle avec mes amis.

Higher

Dans mon école, nous avons une grande bibliothèque où on peut emprunter des livres.

Nous l'utilisons pour nos cours de français et d'anglais.

J'aime les langues, mais je préfère la musique parce qu'elle me permet de mieux m'exprimer.

Cependant, quelques élèves ne respectent pas toujours le prof, ce qui est dommage.

- Once you have read the text, you will then be asked two questions related to what you have read.
- You are expected to say a few words or a short phrase/sentence in response to each question. One-word answers will not be sufficient to gain full marks.

Teacher's Material

- Start by asking the candidate to read the text by saying '*Please read the text*'.
- Allow the candidate to read the text aloud, then ask the following two questions for their tier.
- Allow the student to develop their answers as much as possible.

F

- Quelle est ta matière préférée ?
- Que penses-tu des devoirs ?

H

- Qu'est-ce que tu aimes faire pendant la pause ?
- Quel est ton avis sur le comportement des élèves dans ton collège ?

Listening Questions

Foundation

1 Listen to this recording of young people talking about their studies.
Put a cross in the correct box to complete the sentences.

Listening Track 33

1 a Inès thinks that...

	A languages are not easy.
	B science is the hardest subject.
	C it's useful to speak another language.

[1 mark]

1 b Yasmina thinks it's essential to...

	A learn without the help of technology.
	B not waste your time in front of a screen.
	C know how to use technology.

[1 mark]

1 c Théo thinks that...

	A young people use laptops too much.
	B we should use laptops for everything.
	C laptops help you to study maths.

[1 mark]

Higher

2 Listen to these recordings of young people talking about school challenges.
What is mentioned? Put a cross in each of the **three** correct boxes.

Listening Track 34

2 a

	A Exams
	B Pressure
	C Staff
	D Holidays
	E Sports clubs
	F Workload

[3 marks]

2 b

	A Teachers
	B Pupil conduct
	C School uniforms
	D Bullying
	E Independence
	F Regulations

[3 marks]

Reading Questions

1 Read these comments from Lola. Complete the following table **in English**.
You do not need to write in full sentences.

Lola : Moi, j'adore aller à l'école — mes profs sont vraiment sympas. Apprendre de nouvelles choses au collège, c'est vraiment génial. Malheureusement, certains élèves causent des problèmes quand ils disent des choses négatives aux autres élèves.

1 a	One thing she likes about school	....	*[1 mark]*
1 b	One thing she doesn't like about school	....	*[1 mark]*

Higher

2 Read Théo's letter about his school.

Mon collège est assez moderne et très grand. Il propose beaucoup de matières différentes — on nous oblige à étudier les sciences, les maths et le français, mais on peut aussi choisir d'autres matières qui nous intéressent. Moi, j'ai choisi l'histoire, la musique et l'anglais, parce que j'aime comprendre les autres cultures. Il y a aussi beaucoup d'occasions de développer d'autres compétences utiles, comme jouer d'un instrument. Le lundi soir, un des profs organise un club de théâtre et j'aime y aller. Le mercredi, je fais du sport pendant la pause.

Complete the sentences below. Put a cross in the correct box for each question.

2 a Théo's school...

	A doesn't allow students to choose any subjects.
	B allows students to choose some subjects.
	C allows students to choose all their subjects.

[1 mark]

2 b Théo studies English because...

	A he likes word-based subjects.
	B it's a compulsory subject.
	C he likes learning about different cultures.

[1 mark]

2 c On Mondays, Théo...

	A plays sport at break.
	B attends drama club.
	C plays a musical instrument.

[1 mark]

Writing Questions

Foundation

1 Describe the photo.

Write **four** short sentences **in French**.

1 a .... *[2 marks]*

1 b .... *[2 marks]*

1 c .... *[2 marks]*

1 d .... *[2 marks]*

2 Write an article about school dinners.
You must include the following points:

- what you have for school dinners
- your opinion of the food
- what you are having for school dinner next week.

Write your answer **in French**. You should aim to write between 40 and 50 words. *[14 marks]*

3 Write to your friend about your school.
You must include the following points:

- describe the teachers at your school
- your opinion of your school's rules with reasons
- what you did at breaktime yesterday
- what you will do next week at school.

Write your answer **in French**. You should aim to write between 80 and 90 words. *[18 marks]*

Higher

4 Translate the paragraph **into French**.

> Our school timetable is very strict. This morning, we arrived at school at 8am. We spent the whole day in front of a screen. Sometimes school is so tiring that it is difficult to concentrate. I feel stressed and worried because if I don't learn anything, I won't succeed.

[10 marks]

School — Vocabulary

School is all about learning things. And it just so happens there are three whole pages of words for you to learn here...

School Subjects

la matière	*subject*
le sujet	*subject, topic*
l'anglais (m)	*English*
les maths (f)	*maths*
les sciences (f)	*science*
la technologie	*technology*
l'histoire (f)	*history*
la religion	*religion*
les langues modernes (f)	*modern languages*

Use 'matière' when you're talking about a school subject, and 'sujet' when you're talking about a specific topic.

le français	*French*
le théâtre	*drama*
la musique	*music*
l'art (m)	*art*

School Life — Going to School

l'école (f)	*school*
le collège	*secondary school*
le lycée	*college, sixth form*
l'éducation (f)	*education*
scolaire	*school (adj.)*
étudier	*to study*
l'élève (m/f)	*pupil, student*
l'étudiant(e)	*student*
l'ami(e)	*friend*
jeune	*young*
le / la jeune	*young person*
l'adolescent(e)	*teenager*
la quatrième	*Year 9*
la troisième	*Year 10*
la seconde	*Year 11*
la première	*Year 12*
les études (f)	*studies*
le cours	*course, lesson*
la leçon	*lesson*
inclus(e)	*included*
divers(e)	*diverse, various*
travailler	*to work*
la classe	*class, classroom*
la pause	*break(time)*
septembre	*September*
la journée	*day*
la semaine	*week*
l'année (f)	*year*

les vacances (f)	*holidays*
le voyage	*journey*
commencer (à)	*to start, begin (to)*
arriver (à)	*to arrive (at), manage (to)*
quitter	*to leave*
durer	*to last*
la fois	*time*
le retard	*delay*
continuer (de)	*to continue, go on, carry on*
rentrer	*to go back in, return*
la rentrée	*start of school year*
H prêt(e)	*ready*
H l'emploi du temps (m)	*timetable*

The school's new policy of compulsory smiling had done wonders for student attitudes.

School Life — In Class

l'enseignement (m)	*teaching*
le / la prof(esseur)	*teacher*
savoir	*to know (how to), can*
connaître	*to know (a person)*
apprendre (à)	*to learn (to)*
demander	*to ask*
se demander	*to wonder, ask oneself*
la réponse	*answer, response, reply*
écrire	*to write*
pratiquer	*to practise*
mériter (de)	*to deserve (to)*
inspirer	*to inspire*
discuter	*to discuss*
la passion	*passion*
les devoirs (m)	*homework*
le thème	*theme, topic*
la communication	*communication*
l'information (f)	*information*
lire	*to read*
la lecture	*reading*
le livre	*book, textbook*
la page	*page*
le texte	*text*
l'histoire (f)	*story*
l'exercice (m)	*exercise*
l'expérience (f)	*experience, experiment*
le niveau	*level*
comprendre	*to understand*
lever	*to lift, raise*
se lever	*to get up*
assis(e)	*sitting, seated*
utile	*useful*
inutile	*useless*
passionnant(e)	*exciting*
difficile	*difficult*
dur(e)	*hard (adj.)*
dur	*hard (adv.)*
facile	*easy*
simple	*simple, plain*
pratique	*practical, convenient*
idéal(e)	*ideal*

Higher

enseigner (à)	*to teach*
la compétence	*competence, skill, ability*
la connaissance	*knowledge*
la discussion	*discussion*
capable	*capable*
le renseignement	*piece of information*
le roman	*novel*
la scène	*scene*
imaginer	*to imagine*
se concentrer	*to concentrate*
encourager (à)	*to encourage (to)*
expliquer	*to explain*
l'explication (f)	*explanation*
l'objectif (m)	*objective*
le point	*point*
s'asseoir	*to sit*
conscient(e)	*conscious, aware*

School Life — Facilities and Equipment

l'espace (f)	*space, room*
la salle	*room*
la cour	*playground, court*
les toilettes (f)	*toilet(s)*
la piscine	*swimming pool*
le bus	*bus*
l'équipement (m)	*equipment*
le sac	*bag, sack*
le tableau	*board, picture, painting*
l'e-mail (m)	*email*
la lettre	*letter*
le stylo	*pen*
la règle	*ruler*
le cahier	*exercise book*
le club	*club*
le football	*football*
l'activité (f)	*activity*
l'équipe (f)	*team*
organiser	*to organise*

Higher

la bibliothèque	*library*
le gymnase	*gym (sports hall)*
la scène	*stage*
l'écran (m)	*screen*
prêter	*to lend*
emprunter (à)	*to borrow (from)*

School Pressures and Difficulties — Exams

l'examen (m)	*exam, test*
passer	*to take (an exam)*
préparer	*to prepare*
améliorer	*to improve*
l'effort (m)	*effort*
l'erreur (f)	*mistake, error*
essayer (de)	*to try*
la chance	*luck*
sérieux / sérieuse	*serious, important*
réussir (à)	*to succeed (in), pass*
le succès	*success*
le résultat	*result*
la note	*mark, grade, note*
gagner	*to win, earn*
nul(le)	*rubbish, bad*
faible	*weak*
fort(e)	*strong, good at*
le but	*goal, aim, purpose*
répéter	*to repeat*
la présentation	*presentation*
accepter	*to accept*

Higher

la pression	*pressure*
stressé(e)	*stressed*
l'épreuve (f)	*test*
le courage	*courage, bravery*
l'échec (m)	*failure*
la réussite	*success*
obtenir	*to get, obtain, get hold of*

"...heads, shoulders, knees and toes..."

School Pressures and Difficulties — Rules and Behaviour

devoir	*to have to, must*
attendre	*to wait*
la règle	*rule*
le silence	*silence*
interdire (de)	*to forbid, ban*
l'uniforme (m)	*uniform*
porter	*to wear, carry*
les vêtements	*clothes*
la chemise	*shirt*
le pantalon	*trousers*
la poche	*pocket*
se changer	*to get changed*
la mode	*fashion*
terrible	*terrible*
strict(e)	*strict*
ennuyeux / ennuyeuse	*boring*
travailleur / travailleuse	*hard-working*
responsable	*responsible*
respecter	*to respect, follow*
le respect	*respect*
l'égalité (f)	*equality*
égal(e)	*equal*
l'indépendance (f)	*independence*
indépendant(e)	*independent*
aider	*to help*
l'aide (f)	*help*

Higher

le comportement	*behaviour*
se comporter	*to behave*
se taire	*to be quiet, keep quiet*
permettre (à...de)	*to allow (someone to do something)*
surveiller	*to watch, keep an eye on*
le harcèlement	*bullying, harassment*
obliger	*to require, force, oblige*
sévère	*severe, strict, harsh*
régler	*to settle, set*
le principe	*principle*
la responsabilité	*responsibility*
la confiance	*trust*
le soutien	*support*
le souci	*worry*
inquiéter	*to worry*
s'inquiéter (de)	*to worry*
l'inquiétude (f)	*worry, anxiety*
inquiet / inquiète	*worried*

Revision Summary Test for Section Eight

Now you've educated yourself on education, it's time to crack on with these summary questions.

- These questions are **hard**, but they'll really help you see **how well you know your stuff**.
- Tackle the **revision summary test** below, or scan the QR code to do it **online**. You can **track your progress** online and see **which areas need more work**.
- There are **sample answers** for the test here: www.cgpbooks.co.uk/MerciExtras

Summary Test

School Subjects

1) How many school subjects can you name in French? There are at least 11 you need to know.
2) Translate this sentence into English: 'Mes matières préférées, ce sont les langues modernes — ce sont des matières difficiles, mais la communication est importante.'

School Life

3) Your French friend is complaining: 'Je ne sais pas comment faire cet exercice.' What is he saying?
4) Translate these school years into French: a) Year 9 b) Year 10 c) Year 11 d) Year 12
5) 'When does your school day start and finish? How long does it last?' Answer in French.
6) In French, give three adjectives you could use to describe a teacher. Then give three different adjectives you could use to describe a lesson.
7) Write down the English for these words: a) se demander b) quitter c) connaître d) comprendre e) se lever f) lever g) discuter
8) 'Quel équipement y a-t-il dans ta salle de classe ?' Translate the question and respond in French.
9) 'Qu'est-ce que tu fais pendant la pause ?' Answer in French.

Higher

10) Translate the sentence below into English: 'Le prof m'a encouragé à imaginer les scènes du roman. J'ai appris beaucoup pendant ses cours.'
11) Give the English for these words: a) enseigner (à) b) l'objectif c) l'écran d) prêter e) emprunter (à) f) la connaissance

School Pressures and Difficulties

12) In French, describe a rule in your school. Then give your opinion on your school's rules.
13) Your friend tells you: 'Il faut porter un uniforme scolaire à l'école — par exemple, je dois avoir un pantalon noir. Et toi, qu'est-ce que tu portes à l'école ?' Translate her words.
14) Give the English translation of these words: a) l'erreur b) améliorer c) l'effort d) préparer e) gagner f) répéter g) accepter
15) Give the French translation of these words: a) weak b) terrible c) hard-working d) strict e) boring f) strong g) responsible
16) Translate this sentence into English: 'Respectez les règles de l'examen et travaillez en silence. Bonne chance.'
17) Someone tells you: 'The students passed the exam — they worked hard for their success.' Translate his words into French.
18) Write down the adjective forms of these nouns: a) l'égalité b) l'indépendance
19) What do these words mean in English? a) sérieux b) la présentation c) essayer (de) d) se changer e) interdire (de) f) le but
20) 'In your opinion, what are the biggest two problems at your school?' Answer in French.

Higher

21) Translate this sentence into English: 'Les nouvelles règles n'ont ni amélioré le comportement des élèves ni réduit le harcèlement.'
22) Write down the English for these words: a) l'épreuve b) l'échec c) se comporter d) surveiller e) s'inquiéter (de) f) le soutien

Education Post-16

Quick Quiz

You've probably thought lots about the future already — all that's left is to talk about it in French. Here's a little something to help you on your way...

Don't forget you can access your online content here: www.cgpbooks.co.uk/Merci

Après le collège, je veux... — After school, I want to...

Vocabulary

le lycée	*college, sixth form*	rêver (à / de)	*to dream (of / about)*
le résultat	*result*	le rêve	*dream*
la formation	*apprenticeship, training*	la recherche	*research*
le progrès	*progress*	l'occasion (f) (Higher)	*chance, opportunity*
le projet	*plan, project*	le conseil (Higher)	*advice*
choisir	*to choose*	réfléchir (à) (Higher)	*to reflect (on), think (about)*
le choix	*choice*	le chemin (Higher)	*way, path*
décider (de)	*to decide (to)*	l'apprenti(e) (Higher)	*apprentice*

Je veux aller au lycée l'année prochaine pour continuer mes études. — *I want to go to sixth form next year to continue my studies.*

to vocational college — au lycée technique / lycée professionnel

Au besoin, elle peut demander conseil pour décider quoi faire. — *If needed, she can ask for advice to decide what to do.*

Ils rêvent de faire une formation pratique, parce qu'ils veulent apprendre de nouvelles compétences. — *They dream of doing practical training because they want to learn new skills.*

have chosen to do — ont choisi de faire

Faire des choix — Making choices

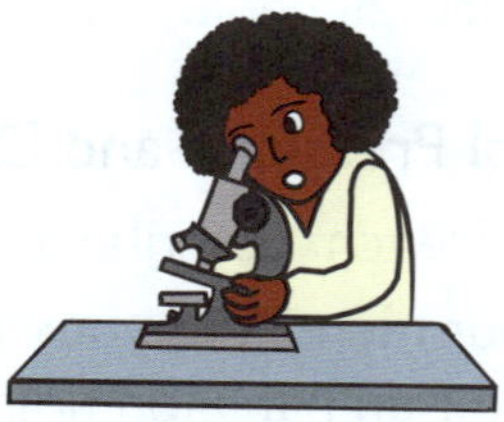

Q&A Audio

Question

Pourquoi as-tu choisi d'aller / ne pas aller au lycée?

Why have you chosen to go / not go to college?

Simple Answers

J'adore les sciences, et je veux continuer à étudier cette matière.

I love science, and I want to continue studying this subject.

J'ai décidé de devenir apprenti(e) car je préfère les formations pratiques.

I decided to become an apprentice because I prefer practical training.

Extended Answers

Je viens de commencer le lycée. Pour faire mon métier idéal, je dois aller à l'université, et pour faire ça, j'ai besoin de bonnes notes au lycée.

I've just started at sixth form. To do my ideal job, I have to go to university, and to do that, I need good grades at college.

J'aimerais trouver un emploi et gagner de l'argent. J'y ai réfléchi et j'ai décidé que la meilleure façon de réaliser ça, c'est de faire une formation pratique.

I would like to find a job and earn money. I've thought about it and I've decided the best way to achieve that is by doing practical training.

Grammar (Higher only) — venir + de + infinitive

'Venir + de + infinitive' means 'to have just done something'. Don't forget that 'venir' (*to come*) is an irregular verb.

Je viens de terminer le collège.
I have just finished secondary school.

Inès vient de décider ses projets pour l'avenir.
Inès has just decided her future plans.

Aller à l'université — Going to university

Vocabulary

l'avenir (m)	*future*	réussir à	*to succeed (in), pass*
le futur	*future*	la condition	*condition*
l'université (f)	*university*	**Higher:** l'entretien (m)	*interview*
étudier	*to study*	le champ	*field*
l'étudiant(e)	*student (university)*	atteindre	*to reach*
la carrière	*career*	poursuivre	*to pursue*
commencer (à)	*to start, begin (to)*	la bourse	*scholarship, grant*
		terminer	*to end, finish*

Avant d'aller à l'université, je voudrais découvrir le monde avec mes amis.
Before going to university, I would like to discover the world with my friends.
← *finding a job* — de trouver un boulot

Claire n'a pas l'intention d'étudier à l'université car ce n'est pas nécessaire pour sa future carrière.
Claire doesn't intend to study at university because it's not necessary for her future career.
← *to get a degree* — d'obtenir une licence

Il faut remplir certaines conditions pour aller à l'université — il y a beaucoup de concours.
You have to fulfil certain conditions to go to university — there are lots of entrance exams.
← *go for an interview* — passer un entretien

Grammar — avoir l'intention de

'Avoir l'intention de' means 'to intend to' do something.
It is followed by an infinitive (see p.167).

Elle a l'intention d'aller à l'université.
She intends to go to university.

Practice Questions

Q1 *Translate the following sentences into French.* (WRITING)

a) In September, I will go to college.
b) I want to go to the university of my dreams.
c) My best friend wants to do an apprenticeship.
H **d)** We have the opportunity to ask for advice about careers. *[8 marks]*

Q2 *Answer the questions below out loud in French. Try to answer as fully as you can.* (SPEAKING)

- *What do you want to do after you leave school? Why?*
- *What are the main differences between doing an apprenticeship and going to college?*
- *Describe a job you have done or would like to do.*
- *In your opinion, is going to university worth it?* *[4 marks]*

Top Tips for Higher Students
✓ Use the conditional and future tenses.
✓ Use subject-specific vocabulary.

They may be future plans, but prepare your answers now...

You'll need to use the future tense to describe your plans, so why not spend some time now brushing up on it? If you're doing Higher, you need to be able to use both forms of the future — see page 172 for more.

Quick Quiz

Career Choices and Ambitions

Planning your future isn't always plain sailing, so don't worry about having to reveal your grand plans to the world in French. If you're uncertain, don't let it stop you — just make something up.

Le monde du travail — The world of work

Vocabulary

travailler	*to work*	vendre	*to sell*
le travail	*work*	le rôle	*role*
les affaires (f)	*business*	le service	*service*
l'entreprise (f)	*business, company*	l'ambition (f)	*ambition*
l'organisation (f)	*organisation*	l'employé(e) (Higher)	*employee, worker*
le salaire	*salary*	le métier (Higher)	*job*
l'argent (m)	*money*	le chômage (Higher)	*unemployment*
le / la client(e)	*customer, client*	l'économie (f) (Higher)	*economy*
la grève	*strike*	la loi (Higher)	*law*
le bureau	*desk, office*		

Ma femme était au chômage, mais elle vient de recevoir une offre de travail du gouvernement.

My wife was unemployed, but she has just received a job offer from the government.

a charity — d'une association caritative

Je suis actuellement en grève parce que notre industrie ne nous traite pas bien.

I am currently on strike because our industry doesn't treat us well.

Ton métier idéal — Your ideal job

Vocabulary

For more jobs, see the vocab list on p.128.

le chef / la cheffe	*boss*	la poste	*post office*
le / la prof(esseur)	*teacher*	la banque	*bank*
le policier / la policière	*police officer*	la boulangerie	*bakery*
l'artiste (m/f)	*artist*	la police	*police, police station*
le / la médecin	*doctor*	le gouvernement (Higher)	*government*
l'acteur / l'actrice	*actor*	le / la patron(ne) (Higher)	*boss*
le chanteur / la chanteuse	*singer*	le directeur / la directrice (Higher)	*headteacher, boss*
l'influenceur / l'influenceuse	*influencer*	le courrier (Higher)	*mail*
le / la président(e)	*president*	professionnel(le) (Higher)	*professional*
		construire (Higher)	*to build*

Mon métier idéal, c'est d'être chanteur / chanteuse car j'aime faire de la musique.

My ideal job is to be a singer because I like making music.

Travailler dans une boulangerie, c'est un rôle idéal pour moi — j'adore parler aux clients.

Working in a bakery is an ideal role for me — I love talking to customers.

at the vet's — chez le vétérinaire

À l'avenir, je veux être... — In the future, I want to be...

Mon frère veut être policier mais moi, je serai directeur / directrice d'école. — *My brother wants to be a police officer but I will be a headteacher.*

Ma mère travaillait dans une banque, mais maintenant elle est artiste. — *My mum used to work in a bank, but now she is an artist.*

Elle va être présidente un jour. — *She is going to be president one day.*

a fireman — pompier
a mechanic — mécanicien(ne)
a hairdresser — coiffeuse

Q&A Audio

Question

Quel est ton métier idéal ? Pourquoi ?
What is your ideal job? Why?

Simple Answer

Je veux être influenceur / influenceuse pour gagner beaucoup d'argent.

I want to be an influencer to earn a lot of money.

Extended Answer

Je crois qu'avoir ma propre entreprise serait idéal pour moi — être son propre patron, ce serait génial !

I believe that having my own business would be ideal for me — being your own boss would be great!

Grammar — articles with jobs / professions

In French, you don't use an indefinite article ('un' / 'une') when you describe someone's job.

Mon père est acteur. — ***My father is an actor.***
Je veux être médecin. — ***I want to be a doctor.***

Practice Questions

Q1 *Read this email that Ismaïl, your Algerian penfriend, has sent you. Then answer the questions below in English.*

READING

Quand j'étais jeune, mon rêve était de travailler dans une boulangerie parce que j'adorais faire du pain. Aujourd'hui, je continue à m'intéresser à la cuisine, et je voudrais avoir mon propre restaurant après l'école. Cet été, je travaille dans la cuisine d'un café. Je ne gagne pas beaucoup d'argent, mais j'espère que l'expérience va être utile.

a) What did Ismaïl want to do when he was younger? *[1 mark]*
b) What does he want to do when he leaves school? *[1 mark]*
c) Where does he currently work? *[1 mark]*
d) Give one positive and one negative of his current job. *[2 marks]*

Higher

Q2 *In this extract from a podcast, Fabienne is being interviewed about her career.*

LISTENING — Listening Track 35

There are two true statements in each list below.
Choose the correct statements from each list.

a)
A. Fabienne works in finance.
B. Fabienne's job lets her travel.
C. Fabienne finds her job easy.

b)
A. Fabienne worked when she was a student.
B. Fabienne used to be a police officer.
C. Fabienne worked abroad as a teacher. *[4 marks]*

Remember — you don't need 'un(e)' to talk about someone's job...

There are lots of job options out there — and so there are lots of things you can say in French. Now, go find a friend and, in French, tell them what job or jobs you want to do in the future and why they appeal to you.

Speaking Questions

Now that you're an expert on your options for the future, have a go at these exam-style questions.

Candidate's Material

- Choose **one** of the pictures below to describe. Make notes on it to use during the test.
- Your teacher will ask you to describe the picture. You should talk for approximately **one and a half to two minutes**. Your description must cover the **people, location and activity** shown in the picture.
- After you have spoken about the content of the picture, your teacher will ask you two questions about your chosen picture. Then, they will ask you some questions related to any of the topics within the theme of **Studying and My Future**.

Picture 1:

Picture 2:

Teacher's Material

- Begin by asking the candidate which picture they have chosen, then say 'Describe the picture'. Candidates should talk about the picture for approximately **one and a half to two minutes**. They may use any notes they have made during the preparation time.
- When the candidate has finished, ask the questions below that relate to their chosen picture.

Picture 1:

- [F] Est-ce que tu veux aller à l'université ? Pourquoi ?
- Qu'est-ce qui fait un(e) bon(ne) étudiant(e) ? Pourquoi ?
- [H] Quand tu étais jeune, qu'est-ce que tu a voulu être ?

Picture 2:

- [F] Est-ce que tu aimes travailler avec le public? Pourquoi ?
- Qu'est-ce qui fait un bon environnement de travail ? Pourquoi ?
- [H] As-tu déjà pensé à faire un travail de bureau ? Pourquoi ?

- Now ask the candidate the following unprepared conversation questions on the theme of **Studying and My Future**:

- Où travaille ton père / ta mère ?
- Est-ce que tu as fait une formation pratique ?
- Qu'est-ce que tu vas faire après l'école ?

Listening Questions

1 You are going to hear someone talking about their job.

Sentences 1 and 3: Write down the missing words in the gaps provided. In each gap, you will write one word **in French**.

Sentences 2 and 4: Write down the full sentences that you hear in the spaces provided, **in French**.

Listening Track 36

F

1 a Sentence 1

Je suis .... pour .... *[2 marks]*

1 b Sentence 2

....

.... *[2 marks]*

Higher

1 c Sentence 3

J'aime offrir du .... C'est .... j'ai décidé de

devenir .... *[2 marks]*

1 d Sentence 4

....

.... *[2 marks]*

2 You hear these job adverts on the radio.
Answer the questions in **English**.

Listening Track 37

2 a Give one attribute that an applicant for this job should have.

.... *[1 mark]*

2 b What age group are the employers looking to recruit?

.... *[1 mark]*

Reading Questions

Foundation

1 Translate these sentences **into English**.

1 a Ma sœur veut être actrice.

.... *[2 marks]*

1 b Elle ne va pas à l'université.

.... *[2 marks]*

1 c Elle rêve d'être célèbre.

.... *[2 marks]*

Higher

2 Translate the following paragraph **into English**.

> Je viens d'obtenir l'emploi de mes rêves. Après avoir poursuivi mes passions, j'ai enfin atteint mon but, et je peux maintenant dire que je suis directrice d'école. Cependant, le chemin n'était pas facile. J'ai travaillé très dur pour réussir dans ce champ, donc je suis très fière de moi.

[10 marks]

3 Read Dorian's email to Mathis. Answer the questions below in **English**.

> Mathis, je suis en crise. Je ne sais pas ce que je veux faire à l'avenir. Il y a simplement trop de choix, et je suis inquiet. Je pourrais devenir médecin comme ma mère ou prof comme mon père, mais avec ces métiers viennent trop de responsabilités. Quand j'étais petit, j'ai voulu être chanteur, mais je n'aime plus l'industrie de la musique. Que faire ?

3 a How does Dorian feel about the future?

.... *[1 mark]*

3 b What does Dorian's mother do for work?

.... *[1 mark]*

3 c What does Dorian's father do for work?

.... *[1 mark]*

3 d Why does Dorian no longer want to be a singer?

.... *[1 mark]*

Writing Questions

Foundation

1 Write a blog post about finishing school.
You must include the following points:

- your plans after school
- your opinion of apprenticeships
- what job you will do in the future.

Write your answer **in French**. You should aim to write between 40 and 50 words. *[14 marks]*

2 Translate the following three sentences **into French**.

2 a My brother is going to university this year.

.... *[2 marks]*

2 b My mum works as a teacher.

.... *[2 marks]*

2 c I want to earn a lot of money in the future.

.... *[2 marks]*

Higher

3 Write a letter to your friend about jobs.
You must include the following points:

- types of jobs in your area
- your opinion of these jobs with reasons
- a job you have researched
- a job you will not do in the future.

Write your answer **in French**. You should aim to write between 80 and 90 words. *[18 marks]*

4 Translate the paragraph **into French**.

> A lot of people think you need to go to university to find a good job, but I think they are wrong. My dad always says that attitude is as important as education, and I agree with him. It depends on what you want to do in your career.

[10 marks]

Future Opportunities — Vocabulary

Deciding what to do after your GCSEs can be difficult — discuss your future plans in French using this vocab.

Education Post-16 — Next Steps

le lycée	*college, sixth form*
le résultat	*result*
la formation	*apprenticeship, training*
le progrès	*progress*
le projet	*plan, project*
le plan	*plan, project*

choisir	*to choose*
le choix	*choice*
décider (de)	*to decide (to)*
rêver (à / de)	*to dream (of / about)*
le rêve	*dream*
la recherche	*research*

Higher

l'occasion (f)	*chance, opportunity*
le conseil	*advice*
réfléchir (à)	*to reflect (on), think (about)*
le chemin	*way, path*
l'apprenti(e)	*apprentice*

Education Post-16 — University

l'avenir (m)	*future*
le futur	*future*
l'université (f)	*university*
étudier	*to study*
l'étudiant(e)	*student (university)*
la carrière	*career*

commencer (à)	*to start, begin (to)*
réussir (à)	*to pass, succeed (in)*
la condition	*condition*

H

l'entretien (m)	*interview*
le champ	*field*

Higher

atteindre	*to reach*
poursuivre	*to pursue*
la bourse	*scholarship, grant*
terminer	*to end, finish*

Career Choices and Ambitions — At Work

travailler	*to work*
le travail	*work*
le poste	*job, position*
l'affaire (f), les affaires (f)	*business*
l'entreprise (f)	*business, company*
l'organisation (f)	*organisation*
le salaire	*salary*
le traitement	*salary, treatment*
l'argent (m)	*money*
le / la client(e)	*customer, client*

la grève	*strike*
riche	*rich*
le bureau	*desk, office*
vendre	*to sell*
traduire	*to translate*
servir	*to serve*
le service	*service*
le rôle	*role*
le contact	*contact*
l'offre (f)	*offer*
l'ambition (f)	*ambition*

H

l'œuvre (f)	*work, task*

Higher

refléter	*to reflect*
l'emploi (m)	*employment*
l'employé(e)	*employee, worker*
le métier	*job*
signer	*to sign*
la compagnie	*company*
l'industrie (f)	*industry*
le chômage	*unemployment*
l'économie (f)	*economy*
inventer	*to invent*
la loi	*law*

Career Choices and Ambitions — Jobs

le chef / la cheffe	*boss*
le / la prof(esseur)	*teacher*
le policier / la policière	*police officer*
l'artiste (m/f)	*artist*
le / la médecin	*doctor*
l'acteur / l'actrice	*actor*
le chanteur / la chanteuse	*singer*

l'influenceur / l'influenceuse	*influencer*
le / la président(e)	*president*
la poste	*post office*
la banque	*bank*
la boulangerie	*bakery*
la police	*police, police station*

Higher

le gouvernement	*government*
le / la patron(ne)	*boss*
le directeur / la directrice	*headteacher, boss*
le courrier	*mail*
professionnel(le)	*professional*
construire	*to build*
le commissariat	*police station*

Revision Summary Test for Section Nine

You've almost made it to the end of the section — now it's time to check your knowledge.

- Yep, these questions are **hard** — they'll really help you see **how well you know your stuff**.
- Tackle the **revision summary test** below, or scan the QR code to do it **online**.
  Use the CGP RevisionHub to **track your progress** and see **which areas need more work**.
- You can find **sample answers** here: www.cgpbooks.co.uk/MerciExtras

Summary Test

Education Post-16

1) You read this message on a university website: 'Are you deciding what to do after school? If you want to go to university, you must have good results.' Translate it into French.
2) 'Do you think practical training is useful?' Explain your answer in French.
3) Write down a French synonym for the following words: a) le salaire b) l'avenir
4) 'Would you like to do an apprenticeship? Why? / Why not?' Answer in French.
5) 'Quels sont tes projets après le collège ?' Translate the question and answer in French.
6) Translate this sentence into French: 'The student did some research and chose a career.'
7) Nicolas's teacher has given him some advice. Translate what they say into English.
   a) 'Tu peux commencer à faire une formation.'
   b) 'Pour aller à l'université, tu dois avoir de bons résultats.'
8) Translate these words into English:
   a) le progrès b) le lycée c) le rêve d) la carrière e) le choix f) la condition

Higher

9) In French, ask your friend for advice about interviews and becoming an apprentice.
10) Give the English for these words:
    a) le chemin b) réfléchir à c) l'occasion d) le champ e) poursuivre f) la bourse

Career Choices and Ambitions

11) Translate this sentence into French: 'I love my role because I like working with rich clients.'
12) How many jobs can you name in French? There are at least 8 you need to know (plus 1 for Higher tier).
13) You read this headline in a newspaper: 'Les jeunes ont de l'ambition mais ils n'ont pas d'offres de travail.' What is it saying?
14) How many different places of work can you name in French? There are at least 4 you need to know (plus 1 for Higher tier).
15) 'Would you like to work in an office? Why? / Why not?' Answer in French.
16) In French, name a job you would like to do and why.
17) Translate these verbs into French: a) to translate b) to serve c) to sell d) to work
18) A friend asks you, 'Comment est-ce que tu vas gagner de l'argent comme adulte ?' Translate the question and respond in French.
19) What do these words mean in English?
    a) le service b) le traitement c) l'entreprise d) la grève e) le contact f) les affaires

Higher

20) What does 'le poste' mean in English? Give a synonym for it in French.
21) Translate this sentence into English: 'Les salaires de nos nouveaux employés doivent refléter leurs métiers.'
22) Translate these words into English:
    a) l'économie b) le gouvernement c) la loi d) l'emploi e) le chômage f) l'œuvre

Quick Quiz

Where to Go

It's no good planning a seaside break to Switzerland. That's why it's important to know where to go...

Head to the CGP RevisionHub for all your online content: www.cgpbooks.co.uk/Merci

Les pays (m) du monde — The countries of the world

Vocabulary

le pays	*country*	le Royaume-Uni	*United Kingdom*	global(e)	*global*
l'Angleterre (f)	*England*	l'Afrique (f)	*Africa*	national(e)	*national*
l'Algérie (f)	*Algeria*	l'Amérique (f)	*America*	international(e)	*international*
le Canada	*Canada*	l'Asie (f)	*Asia*	francophone	*francophone*
la France	*France*	l'Europe (f)	*Europe*	la francophonie	*French-speaking world*
la France d'Outre-mer (f)	*overseas France*	la région	*region*		
Madagascar (m)	*Madagascar*	la province	*province*	H mondial(e)	*global, world (adj.)*
la Martinique	*Martinique*	Paris	*Paris*		
		le monde	*world*		

Je vais au Québec, une province du Canada. — *I'm going to Quebec, a province of Canada.*

Les Pyrénées se trouvent dans le sud de la France. — *The Pyrenees are situated in the south of France.* (*are located* — se situent)

L'Algérie est un pays d'Afrique du nord. — *Algeria is a country in North Africa.* (*a French-speaking country* — un pays francophone)

La Réunion est une région française. — *Reunion is a French region.* (*an overseas department* — un département d'outre-mer)

Grammar — to go to...

To say you're 'going to' a country, you need the correct form of 'aller' (*to go*) and the correct preposition. Use:

- au for masc. sing. countries starting with a consonant.
- aux for plural countries.
- en for masc. sing. countries starting with a vowel and all fem. sing. countries.

If you're going to a town or city, you just need 'à'.

Benoît was the proud owner of the world's first franco-phone.

Le temps à l'étranger — The climate abroad

Vocabulary

le temps	*time, weather, climate*	froid(e)	*cold*	l'été (m)	*summer*
		la saison	*season*	l'automne (m)	*autumn*
le soleil	*sun*	l'hiver (m)	*winter*	H climatique	*climate (adj.)*
chaud(e)	*hot*	le printemps	*spring*	H humide	*wet, humid, moist*

Elle adore le temps du sud de la France — il n'y a pas besoin de regarder la météo parce qu'il fait toujours beau. — *She loves the weather in the south of France — there's no need to look at the forecast because the weather is always nice.* (*warm* — chaud)

Quelle est la meilleure saison pour aller en Suisse ? Je déteste la pluie. — *What is the best season to go to Switzerland? I hate rain.* (*snow* — la neige)

Où vas-tu cet été ? — Where are you going this summer?

Vocabulary

aller	*to go*	pratiquer	*to practise*
à l'étranger	*abroad*	la langue	*language*
les vacances (f)	*holiday(s)*	H étranger / étrangère	*foreign*
l'échange (m)	*exchange*	H annuel(le)	*annual, yearly*
le projet	*plan, project*		
rêver (à / de)	*to dream (about)*		

Cet été, nous allons en Corse, une île de la Méditerranée. — *This summer, we're going to Corsica, an island in the Mediterranean.*

to Cyprus — à Chypre
to Majorca — à Majorque

Je passe mes vacances annuelles à l'étranger. — *I spend my annual holiday abroad.*

annual leave — congés annuels

J'essaie de pratiquer le français avant d'aller en vacances. — *I am trying to practise French before going on holiday.*

Q&A Audio

Question

Quels sont tes projets pour les vacances ?
What are your plans for the holidays?

Simple Answer

Je vais faire un échange à l'étranger, au Canada.
I'm going to do an exchange programme, in Canada.

Extended Answer

À la fin août, j'irai à Madagascar pendant trois semaines avec deux amis. Nous aimons visiter les pays francophones.
At the end of August, I will go to Madagascar for three weeks with two friends. We like visiting francophone countries.

Practice Questions

Q1 *Read this email from Françoise about her holidays and answer the questions below in English.*

READING

Les vacances d'été sont arrivées ! Mais je ne suis pas contente : ma famille n'a pas de projets pour les vacances. Moi, je voudrais aller en France parce que je veux voir les montagnes. Ma sœur voudrait passer les vacances au Canada. Elle veut voir son amie au Québec. Ma mère préfère rester en Angleterre parce qu'elle veut visiter des musées. Par contre, mon père veut aller au sud de l'Europe pour faire du camping.

a) How does Françoise want to spend the holidays? Why? *[2 marks]*
b) Where does her sister want to go? Give **two** details. *[2 marks]*
c) What does her mum want to do? Give **two** details. *[2 marks]*
d) What would her dad like to do? Give **two** details. *[2 marks]*

Q2 *Write to your penfriend about holidays.*
You should write about 80-90 words **in French**. *Describe:*

WRITING

- *your favourite holiday destination*
- *your opinion of hot weather with reasons*
- *a trip you have taken recently*
- *a place you would like to visit.*

[18 marks]

Top Tip for Higher Students
✓ Use complex constructions like 'venir de' (*to have just done*).

Use 'en', 'au' or 'aux' to say which country you're going to...

Remember, 'en' goes with feminine countries and regions, and 'au' goes with most masculine ones. As you learn each country, try putting it in the sentence 'Je suis allé(e)...' — make sure you use the right preposition.

Quick Quiz

Accommodation and Travel

Holidays work best when you know where you're going to stay and how you'll get there. These pages will help you to be as prepared for the exam as you would be for a holiday...

Le logement — Accommodation

Vocabulary

l'hôtel (m)	*hotel*
l'appartement (m)	*apartment, flat*
la place	*room, space*
la chambre	*bedroom*
le camping	*camping, campsite*
la tente	*tent*
propre	*clean*
réserver	*to book*
chercher	*to look for, search*

organiser	*to organise*
rester	*to stay*
dormir	*to sleep*
coûter	*to cost*
le coût	*cost*
la monnaie	*change, currency*
complet / complète	*full, complete*
la vue	*view*
la mer	*sea*
le bord	*edge, side*

la côte	*coast*
la plage	*beach*
l'île (f)	*island*
la campagne	*countryside*
la forêt	*forest*
la montagne	*mountain*
la valise (Higher)	*suitcase*
l'étage (m) (Higher)	*floor (of a building)*
le sable (Higher)	*sand*
se plaindre (Higher)	*to complain*

J'ai pris une chambre dans un hôtel qui n'est pas cher.	*I'm staying at a hotel that isn't expensive.*	*a luxury hotel* — un hôtel de luxe
Ils font du camping au bord de la mer.	*They are camping at the seaside.*	*in Nice* — à Nice
Je voudrais réserver une chambre pour deux personnes au deuxième étage.	*I'd like to reserve a room for two people on the second floor.*	
Ils veulent un grand appartement avec vue sur la forêt.	*They want a big apartment with a view of the forest.*	*the mountains* — les montagnes; *the town centre* — le centre-ville

Le transport — Transportation

Vocabulary

l'avion (m)	*plane*
la voiture	*car*
le bateau	*boat*
le train	*train*
le car	*coach*
le métro	*underground, tube*
l'aéroport (m)	*airport*
la gare	*station*
le vol (H)	*flight*
voler (H)	*to fly*

Q&A Audio

Question

Est-ce que tu aimes voyager en avion ?

Do you like travelling by plane?

Simple Answer

Oui, l'avion est le moyen de transport le plus sûr.

Yes, aeroplanes are the safest mode of transport.

Extended Answer

J'ai peur de prendre l'avion parce que j'imagine toujours le pire. Mais les avions sont si pratiques et si rapides !

I'm scared of flying because I always imagine the worst. But planes are so practical and fast!

Je suis allé(e) à l'aéroport en train, mais j'ai perdu mon billet.	*I went to the airport by train, but I lost my ticket.*	*to the central station* — à la gare centrale
Tu peux emprunter mon vélo.	*You can borrow my bike.*	*their motorhome* — leur camping-car

À quelle heure part le bus ? — What time does the bus leave?

Vocabulary

voyager	*to travel*	manquer	*to miss (public transport)*
le voyage	*journey, trip, travel*	le billet	*ticket*
partir	*to leave*	l'aller (m)	*single ticket*
retourner	*to return, come back*	l'aller-retour (m)	*return ticket*
revenir	*to come back*	le départ	*departure*
arriver	*to arrive*	le retour	*return*
descendre (de)	*to go down*	le retard	*delay*
traverser	*to cross*	l'arrivée (f) (Higher)	*arrival*
		le quai (Higher)	*platform*
		louer (Higher)	*to hire*

Grammar — 'monter', 'descendre'

Use 'monter dans' to say 'to get on'. Use 'descendre de' to say 'to get off'.

Je monte dans le train.
I get on the train.

Il descend du bus.
He gets off the bus.

Nous descendons à la prochaine gare. — *We're getting off at the next station.*

À quelle heure arrive le bus ? — *What time does the bus arrive?*

Nous ne pouvons pas retourner sur l'île parce que nous avons manqué le bateau. — *We can't go back to the island because we missed the boat.*

Son vol part à 18h00 et arrivera à 19h30 s'il n'est pas en retard. — *Her flight leaves at 18:00 and will arrive at 19:30 if it's not late.*

high-speed train — TGV (train à grande vitesse)

leave the island — quitter l'île

Practice Questions

Q1 *You are talking to your French friend about holiday accommodation. Respond to your friend's questions in French.* (SPEAKING)

Quelle sorte de logement préfères-tu ?
Décris ton endroit préféré pour passer les vacances.
Quel est ton moyen de transport préféré ?
Qu'est-ce que tu penses du camping ?
H *Décris un logement où tu as passé quelques jours.*

[10 marks]

Top Tips for Higher Students
✓ Use 'y' to talk about where you went.
✓ Use superlatives when giving opinions.

Higher

Q2 *Listen to Mark talking about a recent journey. What is mentioned? Put a cross in each one of the three correct boxes.* (LISTENING)

Listening Track 38

	A Mark flew from Marseille to Newcastle.
	B Mark's flight was late.
	C Mark will take the train back.
	D The plane ticket home was too expensive.
	E Mark prefers travelling by boat.
	F The boat is slower than the plane.

[3 marks]

Hope you've got all that vocab packed and ready for the exam...

French examiners are like travel websites — they want you to share your views on where you've stayed and how you got there. Keep them happy by including lots of opinions and extra details about your travels.

Quick Quiz

What to Do

Stuck for things to do while you're on holiday? Got a burning desire to describe your favourite tourist attraction in French? If so, you're in luck. These pages are full of things to do while you're away.

En vacances, j'ai visité... — On holiday, I visited...

Use 'nouvel' and 'bel' before masculine words that start with a vowel.

Vocabulary

la capitale	*capital city*	la piscine	*swimming pool*	historique	*historical*
la ville	*town, city*	la tour	*tower*	nouveau / nouvel / nouvelle	*new*
le centre	*centre*	la carte	*map, menu*	beau / bel / belle	*beautiful, nice*
le quartier	*neighbourhood*	le site	*site*	central(e)	*central*
le bâtiment	*building*	l'endroit (m)	*place*	ancien(ne)	*former, ancient, old*
le château	*castle*	l'entrée (f)	*entrance*	la visite	*visit, excursion*
le marché	*market*	entrer	*to enter, go in*	H la frontière	*border*
le magasin	*shop*	fermer	*to close, shut (down)*		
le musée	*museum*				

Que faire à... ? — What is there to do in...?

Quand je vais en vacances, j'aime visiter les sites historiques et les châteaux de la région.
When I go on holiday, I like to visit the region's historic sites and castles.

Roman ruins — ruines romaines
nature reserves — réserves naturelles

On peut acheter des croissants au marché.
You can buy croissants at the market.

Les enfants aiment tous la nouvelle piscine du centre-ville.
The children all like the new swimming pool in the town centre.

the new cafés — les nouveaux cafés

Le musée d'art se situe dans un bâtiment ancien plein de beaux tableaux.
The museum of art is located in an ancient building full of beautiful paintings.

Jean-Marie still wasn't sure what it was supposed to be.

Grammar — beau and nouveau

Some adjectives have irregular feminine and plural forms, e.g. beau and nouveau — see p.155 for more.

la belle tour	***the beautiful tower***
les beaux quartiers	***the beautiful neighbourhoods***
les belles îles	***the beautiful islands***
la nouvelle ville	***the new town***
les nouveaux musées	***the new museums***
les nouvelles piscines	***the new swimming pools***

Q&A Audio

Question

Qu'est-ce que tu as fait en vacances ?
What did you do on holiday?

Simple Answer

J'ai visité un château et je suis allé(e) à la plage.
I visited a castle and I went to the beach.

Extended Answer

J'ai décidé d'aller au musée pour découvrir l'histoire de la région. Ça m'a beaucoup intéressé(e). J'ai fait aussi une visite du centre-ville à pied.
I decided to go to the museum to discover the history of the region. It interested me a lot. I also went on a walking tour of the town centre.

Les activités (f) — Activities

Vocabulary

la cuisine	*cooking*	le souvenir	*souvenir, memory*	accueillir	*to welcome*
la glace	*ice cream*	prendre	*to take*	attirer	*to attract*
la culture	*culture*	la photo	*photo*	profiter de	*to take advantage, profit, make the most of*
la nature	*nature*	passer	*to spend (time)*		
le tourisme	*tourism*	se passer	*to happen, take place*		
le / la touriste	*tourist*	se trouver	*to be situated*	découvrir	*to discover*

(Higher: accueillir, attirer, profiter de, découvrir)

Axelle a pris de belles photos du lac — elle aime bien la nature. — *Axelle took some beautiful photos of the lake — she really likes nature.*

Traoré déteste nager dans la mer à cause des grandes vagues. — *Traoré hates swimming in the sea because of the big waves.* (*of the cold water* — de l'eau froide)

Cette ville est connue pour sa culture riche et sa cuisine unique. — *This town is known for its rich culture and unique cuisine.*

Normalement, je m'achète une glace quand je vais à la plage. — *Normally, I buy myself an ice cream when I go to the beach.* (*order* — commande)

Practice Questions

Q1 Read the following text about Lizzie's holiday plans, then answer the questions below in English.

READING

Cet été, je vais passer deux semaines à Cherbourg pour améliorer mon français. Je vais habiter chez une famille française. Leur appartement se trouve dans un bâtiment ancien. À Cherbourg, je vais visiter un musée intéressant avec d'autres touristes et aller au centre-ville. S'il fait beau, je vais probablement aller manger une glace dans un café. Le week-end, je veux passer du temps à la plage.

a) How long will Lizzie stay in Cherbourg? *[1 mark]*

b) Why will she go to Cherbourg? *[1 mark]*

c) Give two details about Lizzie's accommodation. *[2 marks]*

d) What will Lizzie do in Cherbourg? Give **two** details. *[2 marks]*

e) When will Lizzie go to the beach? *[1 mark]*

Q2 Write a blog post about a tourist attraction you visited recently. You should write about 80-90 words ***in French****. Describe:*

WRITING

- *where you went*
- *your opinion of the area with reasons*
- *what you did there*
- *where you will go next.* *[18 marks]*

Top Tip for Higher Students
✓ Use both the perfect and the imperfect tenses.

Have a go at writing about what there is to do in your local area...

Use the vocabulary on these pages to jot down a list of what there is to see and do in the area where you live, and then write a sentence in French about each place to let any tourists know what you think about it.

Speaking Questions

If at first you don't succeed, try and try again. You'll be working against the clock in the exam, so knowing what you're likely to come across is essential — the last thing you want to do is panic.

Candidate's Material

Scenario:

- You are at a tourist office in the south of France.
- Find a friend to play the part of the employee. They will speak first.
- Your friend will ask questions **in French** and you must answer **in French**.
- You are expected to say a few words or a short phrase / sentence in response to each prompt. One-word answers will not be sufficient to gain full marks.

Task:

1. Say what transport you need.
2. Ask for the price of a ticket.
3. Tell the employee about your holiday plans.
4. Say what accommodation you will be staying in during your trip.
5. Ask a question about transport options in the area.

Teacher's Material

- Begin the role play with the following introduction:
  'You are at a tourist office, and you are talking to a member of staff.
  I will play the part of the member of staff and speak first.'

1	*Bonjour. Je peux vous aider ?* Allow the candidate to tell you what transport they need.
2	*D'accord. Vous avez une question ?* Allow the candidate to ask about the price of a ticket. *Give an appropriate brief response.*
3	*Avez-vous organisé des activités pour vos vacances ?* Allow the candidate to tell you about their holiday plans.
4	*Très bien. Quel type de logement avez-vous réservé ?* Allow the candidate to tell you about their accommodation.
5	*Je comprends. Vous avez une autre question ?* Allow the candidate to ask a question about local transport options. *Give an appropriate brief response.*

Listening Questions

1 Yasmina, Mehdi and Chloé are talking about their holidays. Listen to the recording and complete the sentences by putting a cross in the correct box for each question.

Listening Track 39

1 a Yasmina and her friends take...

	A a map.
	B a tent.
	C suitcases.

[1 mark]

1 b Mehdi prefers...

	A a camping holiday.
	B a seaside holiday.
	C a mountain holiday.

[1 mark]

1 c Chloé's apartment...

	A was in a quiet neighbourhood.
	B was very clean.
	C didn't cost much.

[1 mark]

2 Listen to this information about a French tourist attraction. Then answer the questions in **English**.

Listening Track 40

2 a Name the tourist attraction that the caller talks about.

.... *[1 mark]*

2 b Name **one mode** of transport you can't use to get to the attraction.

.... *[1 mark]*

2 c Name **one thing** you can do when you visit the site.

.... *[1 mark]*

2 d What is prohibited at the attraction?

.... *[1 mark]*

Reading Questions

Foundation

1 Read these online reviews of a local museum.

> ***Léa****: Je ne recommande pas ce musée — il est assez cher et je l'ai trouvé ennuyeux.*
>
> ***Dorian****: Si vous êtes au centre-ville, vous devez visiter le musée. Il a beaucoup d'objets intéressants qui viennent du passé. C'est une visite vraiment agréable.*
>
> ***Fathia****: Le musée est une bonne idée s'il pleut, mais s'il fait beau, je préfère passer mon temps à la campagne.*

Who says what? Choose the correct answers.
Put a cross in the correct column for each question.

	Who ...	**Léa**	**Dorian**	**Fathia**	
a)	... thinks the museum is sometimes worth visiting?				*[1 mark]*
b)	... thinks the museum is definitely worth visiting?				*[1 mark]*
c)	... feels that the museum is not worth visiting?				*[1 mark]*

2 Read this online advert for holiday jobs. Answer the questions below in **English**.

> *Vous avez beaucoup de temps libre pendant les vacances d'été ?*
>
> *Les jeunes en France partent souvent en vacances avec leur famille parce qu'ils pensent que partir seul coûte cher.*
>
> *Alors, vous êtes un de ces jeunes qui n'ont pas beaucoup d'argent ? Pourquoi ne pas trouver un travail d'été ? Vous pouvez travailler dans un restaurant à l'étranger. Comme ça, vous pouvez apprendre une autre langue et gagner un peu d'argent en même temps.*

2 a Why do young French people often choose to go on holiday with their parents?

.... *[1 mark]*

2 b What job does the advert suggest that young people do?

.... *[1 mark]*

2 c What does the advert say are the **two** advantages of holiday jobs?

1. ....

2. .... *[2 marks]*

Writing Questions

Foundation

1 Describe the photo.

Write **four** short sentences **in French**.

1 a .... *[2 marks]*

1 b .... *[2 marks]*

1 c .... *[2 marks]*

1 d .... *[2 marks]*

2 Translate the following sentences **into French**.

2 a I'm going on holiday.

.... *[2 marks]*

2 b Normally, I prefer to travel by plane.

.... *[2 marks]*

2 c My hotel room has a beautiful view.

.... *[2 marks]*

2 d Yesterday, I bought a ticket at the station.

.... *[2 marks]*

2 e If I miss the train, I can take the bus.

.... *[2 marks]*

Higher

3 Write about tourist destinations for an online magazine.
You **must** include the following points:

- what makes an ideal tourist destination
- the pros and cons of travelling abroad
- a place you have visited and how you got there
- where you will visit next and what you will do there.

Write your answer **in French**. You should aim to write between 130 and 150 words. *[22 marks]*

Travel and Tourism — Vocabulary

Learning vocab isn't quite as fun as going on holiday, but you'll be glad you did it when it comes to the exam...

Where to Go

le pays	*country*
l'Angleterre (f)	*England*
l'Algérie (f)	*Algeria*
le Canada	*Canada*
la France	*France*
la France d'Outre-mer (f)	*overseas France*
le Madagascar	*Madagascar*
la Martinique	*Martinique*
le Royaume-Uni	*United Kingdom*
l'Afrique (f)	*Africa*
l'Amérique (f)	*America*
l'Asie (f)	*Asia*
l'Europe (f)	*Europe*
la région	*region*
la province	*province*
Paris	*Paris*
le monde	*world*
global(e)	*global*
national(e)	*national*
international(e)	*international*
francophone	*francophone*
la francophonie	*French-speaking world*

le temps	*time, weather climate*
le soleil	*sun*
chaud(e)	*hot*
froid(e)	*cold*
la saison	*season*
l'hiver (m)	*winter*
le printemps	*spring*
l'été (m)	*summer*
l'automne (m)	*autumn*
aller	*to go*
à l'étranger	*abroad*
les vacances (f)	*holiday(s)*
l'échange (m)	*exchange*
le projet	*plan, project*
rêver (à / de)	*to dream (about)*
pratiquer	*to practise*
la langue	*language*

Higher

mondial(e)	*global, world (adj.)*
climatique	*climate (adj.)*
humide	*wet, humid, moist*
étranger / étrangère	*foreign*
annuel(le)	*yearly*

To say 'in summer / autumn / winter', it's 'en été', 'en automne' and 'en hiver'. There's an exception to learn, though — 'in spring' is 'au printemps'.

Use 'rêver de' if you want to follow it with a verb. E.g. 'rêver de manger' (*to dream about eating*).

Accommodation

le logement	*accommodation*
l'hôtel (m)	*hotel*
l'appartement (m)	*apartment, flat*
la place	*room, space*
la chambre	*bedroom*
le sol	*floor, ground*
le camping	*camping, campsite*
la tente	*tent*
propre	*clean*
réserver	*to reserve, book*
chercher	*to look for, search*
organiser	*to organise*

rester	*to stay*
dormir	*to sleep*
coûter	*to cost*
le coût	*cost*
la monnaie	*change, currency*
l'euro (m)	*euro*
cher / chère	*expensive, dear*
complet / complète	*full, complete*
la vue	*view*
la mer	*sea*
le bord	*edge, side*
la côte	*coast*

la plage	*beach*
l'île (f)	*island*
la campagne	*countryside*
la forêt	*forest*
la montagne	*mountain*

Higher

la valise	*suitcase*
le chapeau	*hat*
l'étage (m)	*floor (of a building)*
le paysage	*landscape*
la piste	*track, trail*
la rivière	*river*
le sable	*sand*
se plaindre	*to complain*

Travel

le transport	(public) transport, transportation
l'avion (m)	plane
la voiture	car
le bateau	boat
le train	train
le bus	bus
le car	coach
le métro	underground, tube
le vélo	bike, bicycle, cycling
l'aéroport (m)	airport
la gare	station
la station	(bus) stop, (tube)station
le port	port, harbour
voyager	to travel
le voyage	journey, trip, travel
partir	to leave
retourner	to return, come back
revenir	to come back
arriver	to arrive
descendre (de)	to go down
traverser	to cross
manquer	to miss (public transport)
le billet	ticket, bank note
l'aller (m)	single ticket
l'aller-retour (m)	return ticket
le passeport	passport
le départ	departure
le retour	return
direct(e)	direct
la distance	distance
le retard	delay
suivant(e)	next, following
debout	standing
où	where
la direction	direction
rapide	fast, quick
vite	fast, quickly
lent(e)	slow
le sac	bag, sack

Higher

le vol	flight
voler	to fly
l'arrivée (f)	arrival
le quai	platform
louer	to hire
autour	around
communiquer	to communicate
complexe	complex, difficult

To say 'by bike', 'by car' etc., you use 'en', e.g. 'en vélo'. The exception is 'à pied' (on foot).

What to Do

la capitale	capital city
la ville	town, city
le centre	centre
le quartier	neighbourhood
la zone	zone
le bâtiment	building
le château	castle
le lac	lake
le marché	market
le magasin	shop
acheter	to buy
l'argent (m)	money
le musée	museum
la piscine	swimming pool
la tour	tower
la Tour Eiffel	The Eiffel Tower
la carte	map, menu
le restaurant	restaurant
le café	café
l'office (m)	office
le site	site
l'endroit (m)	place
entrer	to enter, go in
l'entrée (f)	entrance
fermer	to close, shut (down)
fermé(e)	closed
historique	historical
nouveau / nouvel / nouvelle	new
neuf / neuve	(brand) new
beau / bel / belle	beautiful, nice
central(e)	central
ancien(ne)	former, ancient, old
calme	quiet
visiter	to visit
la visite	visit, excursion
le tour	tour
la cuisine	cooking, cuisine
la glace	ice cream, ice
la culture	culture
la nature	nature
le tourisme	tourism
le / la touriste	tourist
le souvenir	souvenir, memory
prendre	to take
la photo	photo
apprendre	to learn
passer	to spend (time)
se passer	to happen, take place
se trouver	to be situated
commander	to order

Higher

la frontière	border
le lieu	place
se situer	to be situated, to be located
accueillir	to welcome
attirer	to attract
profiter de	to take advantage, profit, make the most of
découvrir	to discover
accompagner	to accompany, go with
apercevoir	to see, notice
la foule	crowd
goûter	to taste, try
l'addition (f)	bill

Revision Summary Test for Section Ten

Before you jet off to the next section, here are some questions to test your holiday knowledge.

- These questions are **really tricky**, but they'll help you see **how well you know your stuff**.
- Tackle the **revision summary test** below, or scan the QR code to do it **online**. You can **keep track of your progress** online and see **which areas need more work**.
- There are **sample answers** here: www.cgpbooks.co.uk/MerciExtras

Summary Test

Where to Go

1) Your best friend asks you: 'Quels sont tes projets pour les vacances ?' Translate the question, then answer it in French, giving as much detail as you can.
2) How many countries can you name in French? There are 6 you need to know.
3) Imagine two of your friends are going on holiday to two different places. Say where each of them will go and what they plan to do there.
4) Translate this sentence into English: 'Pendant les vacances d'été, Camille va faire un échange à l'étranger pour apprendre une nouvelle langue.'
5) Write down the French for these places:
a) overseas France b) America c) Africa d) Asia e) Europe
6) What are the names of the seasons in French? Explain in French which one is your favourite.

Accommodation and Travel

7) Write down the English for these verbs: a) voyager b) partir c) revenir d) chercher e) arriver
8) You're on the phone to your French friend who is planning on visiting you. Tell them that the fast train costs forty euros and that they can book a space when they're at the station.
9) Give the French for the verbs below:
a) to reserve b) to cross c) to organise d) to stay e) to sleep f) to cost g) to return
10) Imagine you are going to Paris. In French, ask what there is to do in Paris and say that you're looking for a flat with two bedrooms that isn't too expensive.
11) You're ringing a hotel. Say that you'd like to reserve a room and ask if there is:
a) a large swimming pool. b) a beautiful view. c) an island near the hotel.
12) Translate these words into French: a) return ticket b) bag c) journey d) sand e) track
13) Describe a type of accommodation that you have stayed in. Give as much detail as possible.
14) 'Quel moyen de transport utilises-tu normalement pour partir en vacances ?' Answer in French.

Higher

15) 'I dream of travelling to Martinique, a region of overseas France. However, you have to go there by plane so you can't take a lot of suitcases.' How would you say this in French?
16) Write these phrases in French: a) I would like to hire a bike. b) I can't find the platform.
17) Translate this announcement into English: 'Il y a un retard de trente minutes. Le vol durera deux heures et nous arriverons à onze heures du matin.'

What to Do

18) You're on holiday in Brittany. In French, ask a local where you can find:
a) the museum b) the shop c) the tower d) historical sites e) the market
19) Give the English for these French verbs: a) visiter b) se passer c) se trouver d) commander
20) Claire is telling you about her holiday: 'Nous sommes allés à la plage tous les jours, et le week-end nous avons marché dans la forêt. Mon père a organisé une visite du château — j'ai pensé que c'était un très bel endroit.' Translate her sentences into English.
21) 'Qu'est-ce que tu aimes faire en vacances ?' Answer in French.

H

22) 'We like to make the most of the restaurants beside the lake and buy ice creams at the café in the town centre.' How would you say this in French?

Nouns

Quick Quiz

Nouns are words for people and objects. In French, all nouns are divided up by gender.

Every noun in French is masculine or feminine

1) Whether a noun is masculine or feminine affects loads of things. The words for 'the' and 'a' are different and, if that wasn't enough, adjectives change to match the gender too.
2) 'Le' in front of a noun means it's masculine. 'La' in front means it's feminine.

le livre (m) bleu *the blue book*   la table (f) bleue *the blue table*

3) When you learn a noun, learn the article too — don't think 'chien = dog', think 'le chien = the dog'.
4) If you have to guess whether a noun is masculine or feminine, use these rules of thumb:

Masculine nouns often end in...
-age, -al, -er, -eau, -ing, -in, -ment, -ou, -ail, -ier, -et, -isme, -oir, -eil

Feminine nouns often end in...
-aine, -ée, -ense, -ie, -ise, -tion, -ance, -elle, -esse, -ière, -sion, -tude, -anse, -ence, -ette, -ine, -té, -ure

For more on how adjectives change to fit the gender, see p.155.

Some words have masculine and feminine versions

1) Words for people often have masculine and feminine versions to show whether the person is male or female. To form a feminine noun, add 'e' to the masculine noun and change the article. →

le président *the president (m)*
la présidente *the president (f)*

2) Some nouns follow a different pattern. Here are a few common examples:

Masc. ending	Change	Example
-e	article only	le touriste → la touriste *(tourist)*
-eur	'eur' → 'rice' or 'euse'	l'acteur → l'actrice *(actor)* le chanteur → la chanteuse *(singer)*
-en	add '-ne'	le Canadien → la Canadienne *(Canadian)*

Nouns can also be made plural

1) Nouns in French are usually made plural by adding an 's' — the same as in English.

le chien *the dog* → les chiens *the dogs*

2) Masculine nouns ending in '-(e)au' and '-eu' need an 'x' rather than an 's' in the plural form.

le jeu *the game* → les jeux *the games*

3) Nouns already ending in 's' or 'x' do not change in the plural.

le choix *the choice* → les choix *the choices*

When you make a noun plural, you need to use 'les' rather than 'le' or 'la'.

Grammar Questions

Add 'le' or 'la' to these words and then put the whole thing into its plural form.

1. cadeau (*present*) **3.** maison (*house*) **5.** voiture (*car*) **7.** langue (*language*)
2. piscine (*pool*) **4.** pays (*country*) **6.** prix (*price*) **8.** gâteau (*cake*)

These rules don't work every time — there are some exceptions...
No need to panic though — the gender of each noun is included in the vocab lists throughout the book.

Quick Quiz

Articles

'The' and 'a' are some of the most common words in a language, so you should revise them well...

'Un', 'une', 'le', 'la', 'l'', 'les' — 'A' and 'the'

'Le', 'la' and 'les' are definite articles.
'Un' and 'une' are indefinite articles.

1) The word for 'a' depends on the gender of the noun (see p.143).

'Un' is used with masculine words... un café (m) *a coffee* ...and 'une' is used with feminine ones. une boisson (f) *a drink*

2) The word for 'the' is different depending on the gender and number of the noun:

Masculine singular	Feminine singular	Before vowels / 'h' (sometimes)	Masc. or fem. plural
le	la	l'	les

3) For words starting with a vowel, 'le' or 'la' is shortened to 'l''. This makes them easier to say.

l'avion (m) *the plane* l'émission (f) *the programme*

4) Most words starting with 'h' also take 'l'' instead of 'le' or 'la'. Sadly, there's no rule for when this happens — you just have to learn it.

l'homme (m) *the man*

'À' and 'de' change before 'le' and 'les'

1) 'À' (*to / at*) and 'de' (*of / from*) are prepositions (see p.150).

2) Be careful when you use them before a definite article (le/la/l'/les). They combine with 'le' and 'les' to make new words.

	le	la	l'	les
à +	au	à la	à l'	aux
de +	du	de la	de l'	des

Je reste à + le collège. = Je reste au collège. *I'm staying at school.*
Je viens de + le Canada. = Je viens du Canada. *I come from Canada.*
Je parle à + les élèves. = Je parle aux élèves. *I'm talking to the students.*

'Du', 'de la', 'de l'' or 'des' — 'Some' or 'any'

1) If you want to say 'some' or 'any', use 'de' combined with the correct definite article. These are called partitive articles.

Je veux des livres. *I want some books.*

2) In negative sentences (see p.175), you only use 'de', regardless of the gender or whether it's singular or plural.

Je n'ai pas de pain. *I haven't got any bread.*

3) You just use 'de' after most quantities — such as 'beaucoup de' (*lots of*) or 'un peu de' (*a bit of*).

J'ai un peu de pain. *I have a little bread.*

H 4) In French, you have to include a partitive article before uncountable nouns.

Je bois de l'eau. *I drink water.*

Uncountable nouns are nouns that you can't count, e.g. 'water' or 'nature'.

Grammar Questions

Fill in the gaps with either 'de', 'du', 'de la' 'des', 'au' or 'à la'.

1. L'homme a un peu ...... pain.
2. L'étudiant vient ...... Canada.
3. Je vais ...... piscine.
4. Il va ...... marché.
5. Elle mange ...... viande.
6. On a ...... légumes.

Using a definite article before certain adjectives can form a noun...

For example, if you add 'le' to the adjective 'seul' (*alone*), you get the noun 'le seul' (*the only one*).

Quick Quiz

Subject and Emphatic Pronouns

There are lots of pronouns to learn, but they're useful and they'll make your French less repetitive.

Subject pronouns replace the subject of the sentence

1) Subject pronouns are words like 'I' and 'you':

I	je
You (informal, singular)	tu
He / she / it / one / we	il / elle / on
We	nous
You (formal, plural)	vous
They	ils / elles

'Il' means 'he', or 'it' for a masculine noun. 'Elle' means 'she', or 'it' for a feminine noun.

'On' is a bit like 'one' in English. It often means 'we', e.g. 'on doit recycler' (*we must recycle*).

Use 'vous' in formal situations, e.g. when talking to your teacher, or when you're talking to more than one person. Use 'tu' when talking to one person in an informal situation.

'Ils' is for a group of masculine nouns, or a mixture of masculine and feminine. 'Elles' is for a group of feminine nouns.

2) Subject pronouns can replace the subject (the person or thing doing the action in a sentence). Using them means you don't have to keep saying the same noun over and over again.

Mon frère est médecin. Il travaille à l'hôpital. *My brother is a doctor. He works at the hospital.*

'My brother' can be replaced with 'he' to sound less repetitive.

Emphatic pronouns emphasise who you are talking about

1) Emphatic pronouns make it really clear who you're talking about.
2) They can be used in lots of different ways:

Me	moi
You (informal singular)	toi
Him / her / it	lui / elle
Us	nous
You (formal, plural)	vous
Them (m / f)	eux / elles

Higher

C'est qui ? Moi ! C'est moi !
Who is it? Me! It's me!

Use them if the word is on its own or comes after 'c'est'.

Écoutez-moi ! *Listen to me!*

Use them for giving orders (see p.176 for more on how to do this).

Il est plus petit que toi. *He's smaller than you.*

They're used for comparing people or things — the emphatic pronoun goes after 'que' (*than*).

Ce sac est pour moi. *This bag is for me.*

They can come after prepositions such as 'for' or 'with'.

Higher

3) You can add '-même(s)' on the end of an emphatic pronoun to say '-self' or '-selves'.

Je le fais moi-même. *I do it myself.*

Elles l'ont écrit elles-mêmes. *They wrote it themselves.*

Grammar Questions

Unscramble the words in these sentences and then translate them into **English**.

1. un achète il billet
2. pour cadeau est le toi
3. moi plus que est elle contente
4. avez joué moi vous avec
H **5.** elle eux mange avec
H **6.** la lui-même il envoyé lettre a

Subject pronouns will stop you repeating yourself again and again...

You'll soon get to know subject pronouns as they're frequently used in spoken and written French. If you're struggling to find the subject in a sentence, it'll be the person or thing performing the action of the verb.

Quick Quiz

Object Pronouns

Now that you've mastered subject and emphatic pronouns, object pronouns are up next. They're a bit different from subject pronouns — they replace the person or thing affected by an action.

There are different pronouns for the direct object...

The direct object is the person or thing that the action is being done to — direct object pronouns replace the noun used as the direct object:

Me	You (inf. sing.)	Him / her / it	You (formal, sing.)
me	te	le / la	vous

H

Us	You (formal, pl.)	Them
nous	vous	les

Remember, if me, te, le or la are followed by a word beginning with a vowel they become m', t', or l'.

Il voit son amie. *He sees his friend.* → Il la voit. *He sees her.*

...and for the indirect object

Indirect objects are things that are affected by the action being done, but not directly. They often have 'to' or 'for' before them in English:

Me	You (inf. sing.)	Him / her / it	You (formal, sing.)
me	te	lui	vous

H

Us	You (formal, pl.)	Them
nous	vous	leur

Il donne le cadeau à son amie.
He gives the present to his friend.
→
Il lui donne le cadeau.
He gives the present to her.

Object pronouns usually go before the verb

1) In French, you put the object pronoun before the verb.

Je la mange. *I eat it.*

2) The perfect tense is a compound tense — a tense which uses 'avoir' or 'être' before the main verb. With compound tenses, the pronouns go before both verbs.

Elle l'a acheté. *She bought it.*

3) Certain verbs (e.g. 'vouloir', 'pouvoir', 'devoir') are often used with the infinitive of another verb. The object pronouns go between them.

Je peux le faire. *I can do it.*

4) In negative sentences, 'ne' goes before the object pronoun and 'pas' goes after the verb. See p.175 for more about negatives.

Il ne l'aime pas. *He doesn't like him.*

Grammar Questions

Rewrite each sentence below, replacing the word or phrase in **bold** with the correct pronoun.

E.g. Lola donne le livre **à son frère**. → *Lola lui donne le livre.*

1. Maria aime **le chien.**
2. J'ai lu **le livre**.
3. Je ne vois pas **toi et ton ami**.
4. Elle a envoyé l'e-mail **à son père**.
H **5.** Ils parlent **à moi et Pierre**.
H **6.** Il ne visite pas **les musées**.

Pronouns are tricky, so make sure you learn this page...

Keep an eye out for the difference between direct object pronouns and indirect object pronouns in the third person singular form. Use 'le' / 'la' for direct object pronouns and 'lui' for indirect object pronouns.

Relative and Interrogative Pronouns

Quick Quiz

These pronouns help link bits of a sentence together so you're not stuck with lots of short phrases.

Relative pronouns add detail

1) Relative pronouns introduce extra information about something you've mentioned in your sentence.
2) 'Qui' is used if you're referring to the subject of a clause — the person or thing doing the action.

la femme qui a acheté le livre *the woman who bought the book*

A clause is a group of words that has a subject and a verb. For more on verbs, see p.165.

Higher

3) 'Que' is used to refer to the object of the clause — the person or thing that something's being done to.

le livre que la femme a acheté *the book that the woman bought*

4) You can also use 'où' as a relative pronoun to mean both 'where' and 'when'.

La ville où il habite est jolie.
The town where he lives is pretty.

le jour où je suis parti(e)
the day when I left

5) 'Dont' means 'of which' or 'whose' — it's often left out in English, but you need it in French.

le chat dont j'ai parlé *the cat of which I spoke*

You can use 'qui' and 'que' to ask questions

1) In questions, 'qui' and 'que' are interrogative pronouns. 'Qui' means 'who', and 'que' means 'what'.

Qui parle ? *Who is speaking?*

Que savez-vous ? *What do you know?*

See p.8-9 for more on questions.

2) After prepositions (words such as 'with' or 'for' — see p.150), 'qui' stays the same but 'que' changes to 'quoi'.

Tu parles avec qui ? *Who are you talking to?*

De quoi parles-tu ? *What are you talking about?*

There are a few ways to say 'this', 'that' and 'it'

1) 'Ce' can be used with 'est' or 'sont' to mean 'it is' or 'they are'.

C'est génial. *It's great.*

Ce sont bons. *They are good.*

2) 'Ça' can be used in a sentence to mean 'this' or 'that'.

Je n'aime pas faire ça. *I don't like doing that.*

3) 'Cela' means 'that' or 'it'. It doesn't have to agree with the noun it replaces. It usually refers to non-specific things.

Cela n'est pas vrai ! *That isn't true!*

Grammar Questions

Translate these sentences and phrases into **French**, making sure you're using the correct pronouns.

1. It is a big house.
2. I really love that.
3. Who do you run with?
4. What do you want to do?
H **5.** the hotel where I slept
H **6.** the food that I like to eat

Make sure you learn the difference between 'qui' and 'que'...

It's handy to remember that 'qui' is often followed by a verb, whilst 'que' is followed by a noun or pronoun.

Quick Quiz

Indefinite and Adverbial Pronouns

There are even more pronouns for unspecified things — read on for more...

Use indefinite pronouns for unspecified things

Indefinite pronouns refer to general, unspecific things, such as 'everyone' and 'something'.

quelqu'un	*someone*	plusieurs	*several*
tout le monde	*everyone*	tout	*all, everything*
quelque chose	*something*		

Tout le monde aime le chocolat.
Everyone likes chocolate.

Y — There, it, them

'Y' and 'en' are adverbial pronouns.

Higher

1) 'Y' can mean 'there'. It replaces the noun for a location which has already been mentioned.

Elle va à la banque. *She's going to the bank.* → Elle y va. *She's going there.*

2) It can also mean 'it' or 'them' when it replaces 'à' + a noun after a verb.

Je pense à cette idée. *I'm thinking about this idea.* → J'y pense. *I'm thinking about it.*

En — Of it, of them, some, any

1) 'En' has a few meanings — depending on the context, it can mean 'of it', 'of them', 'some' or 'any'.

As-tu peur des lapins ? Oui, j'en ai peur. *Are you scared of rabbits? Yes, I'm scared of them.*

As-tu des légumes ? Non, je n'en ai pas. *Have you got any vegetables? No, I don't have any.*

Higher

2) It means 'it' or 'them' when it replaces 'de' + a noun after a verb.

Tu as besoin d'aide. *You need help.* → Tu en as besoin. *You need it.*

3) 'En' can be used alongside 'y' in the phrase 'il y a' to say 'there are some'.

Il y a... *There is / There are...* → Est-qu'il y a des fleurs ? Oui, il y en a.
Are there any flowers? Yes, there are some.

Grammar Questions

Translate these sentences into **French**, making sure you're using the correct pronouns.

1. Several finished their homework.
2. Everyone knows that it is true.
3. Someone bought the book.

Higher

4. I'm reflecting on it.
5. Do you know the castle? I've been there.
6. There are lots of them.

Watch out for singular and plural indefinite pronouns...

Remember that some indefinite pronouns, such as 'tout le monde' (*everyone*), are singular, even though they refer to multiple people or things. You'll need to conjugate the verb that follows with this in mind.

Conjunctions

Quick Quiz

Conjunctions link words together. They help make your French sound more natural and more sophisticated too — because nothing says sophistication like accurate French conjunctions...

Use conjunctions to make longer sentences

1) Here are some common conjunctions:

mais	*but*	ou	*or*	ensuite	*then*	ne...ni...ni (H)	*neither...nor*
et	*and*	donc	*therefore, so*	alors	*so, then, well*	puis (H)	*then, next*

2) Some conjunctions link two clauses or sentences together. They make the sentences sound more natural.

J'aime protéger la planète. — donc — Je recycle le papier. → J'aime protéger la planète, donc je recycle le papier.

I like to protect the planet. — *so* — *I recycle paper.* → *I like to protect the planet, so I recycle paper.*

3) 'Ou' (*or*) is used to give more than one option.

Houéfa veut être médecin. — ou — Houéfa veut être policière. → Houéfa veut être médecin ou policière.

Houéfa wants to be a doctor. — *or* — *Houéfa wants to be a police officer.* → *Houéfa wants to be a doctor or a police officer.*

Make sure you don't mix up 'ou' (*or*) and 'où' (*where*).

Some conjunctions add extra information to a sentence

1) Some conjunctions can also add extra detail to a sentence.
2) Often these conjunctions introduce a reason for something happening, a contradiction or a condition.

parce que	*because*	par contre	*however*	puisque (Higher)	*because, since*
car	*because*	comme	*like, as, in terms of*	cependant (Higher)	*however*
si	*if*	même si	*even if*	par exemple (Higher)	*for example*

Je déteste la drogue parce que c'est mauvais pour la santé.
I hate drugs because they're bad for your health.

Some conjunctions can go at the beginning of sentences too.

Même si l'exercice est difficile, il faut le faire. *Even if exercise is difficult, you must do it.*

Grammar Questions

Fill in the gaps with either 'comme', 'si', 'et' or 'mais'. You can only use each conjunction once.

1. Je voudrais un thé ...... une glace.
2. ...... tu prends mon pain, je vais être triste.
3. Je veux sortir, ... je dois finir mes devoirs.
4. ...... il est tard, je vais me reposer.

Using conjunctions will make your sentences sound more natural...

You probably already know lots of the conjunctions on this page — it's good practice to add them into your work as much as you can. Keep doing that, and you'll be sounding fluent in no time. Got it? Great.

Quick Quiz

Prepositions

Prepositions may not be much to look at, but size is no guarantee of power. These fellas are some of the most useful words in French — and, luckily, they're also some of the easiest to pronounce.

À — 'to', 'in' or 'at'

1) Prepositions are short words like 'to' and 'from'. They let you add extra information to sentences.
2) 'À' can mean 'to', 'in' or 'at'. It changes to 'au' and 'aux' when it's followed by 'le' and 'les' (see p.144).

Je suis à la maison.
I'm at home.

Il va aux toilettes.
He's going to the toilet.

J'habite au Canada.
I live in Canada.

You can't use 'à' for feminine countries, or singular countries beginning with a vowel. Look at the section on 'en' below to find out more.

3) Some verbs are followed by 'à' when they go before a noun or another verb. Here are some examples:

répondre (à)	*to answer, reply (to)*	réussir à	*to succeed in*
jouer à	*to play (a game)*	penser à	*to think about*

En — 'in' or 'to'

1) 'En' is used instead of 'à' for feminine countries and singular countries starting with a vowel.

Hugo habite en Angleterre.
Hugo lives in England.

Je vais en France en mai.
I'm going to France in May.

2) You should use 'en' to say how long an action takes:

Elle a lu la page en cinq minutes. *She read the page in five minutes.*

Higher

3) You don't need 'le', 'la' or 'les' after 'en'.

Il partira en hiver. *He will leave in the winter.*

4) 'En' is also used before present participles to mean 'while' or 'by' (see p.177 for more).

Elle est tombée en courant. *She fell while running.*

Tom regretted not checking the weather forecast before he jetted off on holiday.

De — 'of' or 'from'

French doesn't use apostrophes to show belonging — it uses 'de' instead.

1) 'De' often means 'of'.

un groupe d'étudiants *a group of students*

les vêtements de ma sœur *my sister's clothes*

2) 'De' can also mean 'from'. It changes to 'du', 'de la' or 'des' when used with a definite article (see p.144).

Chérif revient de la plage. *Chérif is coming back from the beach.*

3) Some verbs are followed by 'de' when they go before a noun. Learn these important examples:

changer de	*to change*	partir de	*to leave*
jouer de	*to play (an instrument)*	H avoir besoin de	*to need*

Chez Natalie — At Natalie's

These prepositions are really important for your exams — try to learn them all.

avec	*with*	à cause de	*because of*	H malgré	*despite*	H parmi	*amongst*
sans	*without*	chez	*at / to (the house of)*	H par	*by, for*	H vers	*towards*

Lots of prepositions relate to time

1) Prepositions of time tell you when something happened in relation to something else.

pour	*for*	avant	*before*	H jusque	*until*
pendant	*during*	après	*after*	H depuis	*for, since*

'Jusque' is normally followed by 'à' or 'en', e.g. 'jusqu'à la fin' (*until the end*).

2) Use 'pendant' for actions that have already happened, or will happen in the future, but aren't happening now.

J'ai travaillé dans un hôtel pendant deux ans. *I worked in a hotel for two years.*

3) 'Pour' (*for*) is used very similarly to in English, but with time, it's only used in the future tense.

Myriam va aller en Algérie pour une semaine. *Myriam is going to go to Algeria for a week.*

Higher

4) Use 'depuis' for actions that began in the past, but are still continuing today (see p.167).

J'habite à la campagne depuis trois mois. *I've lived in the countryside for three months.*

5) You can use 'avant de' with an infinitive to say 'before doing something'.

Avant de partir, j'ai mangé avec ma famille. *Before leaving, I ate with my family.*

To say 'after doing something' see p.177.

Use prepositions to describe position

1) Some prepositions describe the location of something or someone.

sur	*on*	à côté de	*next to*	dans	*in*
sous	*under*	derrière	*behind*	devant	*in front of*

'Dans' is also used to say how much time will pass before an event. E.g. 'dans cinq minutes' (*in five minutes*).

'En' also means 'in', but it can't mean 'inside' — see p.150.

2) 'Dans' (*in*) is normally used to describe when something is actually inside something else.

Mon livre est dans mon sac. *My book is in my bag.*

Grammar Questions

Choose the correct preposition to complete each sentence below.

1. Je suis (à / chez) Nadia avec Tom.
2. La route passe (sous / dans) le pont.
3. Je joue (au / du) football.
4. Il était en vacances (pendant / pour) deux semaines.
5. Il y a un train (à / dans) deux minutes.
H **6.** Je travaille à la boulangerie (depuis / par) six mois. H

Now that you've got these prepositions under your belt...
Make sure you learn them all — they'll help you to express time, location or direction in your answers.

Nouns, Articles & Linking Words — Grammar List

All the essential info from this grammar section is listed on these pages — they're handy to turn to for a quick recap.

Determiners

A determiner is a word that comes before a noun in a sentence. They provide extra information about the quantity of the noun, and what it is referring to.

le	*the (m)*
la	*the (f)*
les	*the (pl.)*
un	*a, an (m)*
une	*a, an (f)*
du	*some (m)*
de la	*some (f)*
des	*some (pl.)*
ce / cet	*this, that (m)*
cette	*this, that (f)*
ces	*these, those*

Nouns

In French, all nouns are either masculine or feminine. Common endings for masculine nouns are:
-age, -al, -er, -eau, -ing, -in, -ment,
-ou, -ail, -ier, -et, -isme, -oir, -eil

Common endings for feminine nouns are:
-aine, -ée, -ense, -ie, -ise, -tion, -ance, -elle, -esse,
-ière, -sion, -tude, -anse, -ence, -ette, -ine, -té, -ure

Most masculine nouns describing people can be made feminine:

le président → la présiden**te**	*president*
le touriste → la touriste	*tourist*
le chant**eur** → la chant**euse**	*singer*
l'act**eur** → l'act**rice**	*actor*
l'Européen → l'Européen**ne**	*European*

There are also different ways of making singular nouns plural:

le chien → les chien**s**	*dog(s)*
le château → les château**x**	*castle(s)*
le concours → les concours	*competition(s)*

You can add definite articles (le/la/les) before some adjectives to form nouns. E.g. 'français' (*French*) becomes 'les Français' (*French people*).

Subject Pronouns

Subject pronouns replace the person or thing doing the action.

je	*I*
tu	*you (sing. informal)*
il	*he, it (m)*
elle	*she, it (f)*
on	*everyone, you, one, we (informal)*
nous	*we*
vous	*you (formal, pl.)*
ils	*they (m)*
elles	*they (f)*

'À' and 'de'

Some articles change when combined with 'à' or 'de':

à + le → au
à + les → aux
de + le → du
de + les → des

Negative Subject Pronouns

H

personne ne + verb	*nobody + verb*
rien ne + verb	*nothing + verb*

See p.157 for more on possessive adjectives.

Possessives

Possessive adjectives show that something belongs to someone.

mon	*my (m)*	notre	*our (m/f)*
ma	*my (f)*	nos	*our (pl.)*
mes	*my (pl.)*	votre	*your (m/f)*
ton	*your (m)*	vos	*your (pl.)*
ta	*your (f)*	leur	*their (m/f)*
tes	*your (pl.)*	leurs	*their (pl.)*
son	*his / her / its (m)*		
sa	*his / her / its (f)*		
ses	*his / her / its (pl.)*		

Higher

Possessive pronouns also show belonging.

le/la mien(ne)	*mine (m/f)*
les miens/miennes	*mine (pl.)*
le/la tien(ne)	*yours (m/f)*
les tiens/tiennes	*yours (pl.)*
le/la sien(ne)	*his / hers (m/f)*
les siens/siennes	*his / hers (pl.)*

Direct Object Pronouns

Direct object pronouns replace the person or thing the action is being done to.

me	*me*	nous (H)	*us*
te	*you (sing. informal)*	vous (H)	*you (pl.)*
vous	*you (sing. formal)*	les (H)	*them*
le	*him, it (m)*		
la	*her, it (f)*		

Indirect Object Pronouns

Indirect object pronouns replace the person or thing that is being affected by the action, but not directly.

me	*me*	nous (H)	*us*
te	*you (sing. informal)*	vous (H)	*you (pl.)*
vous	*you (sing. formal)*	leur (H)	*them*
lui	*him, her, it*		

Emphatic Pronouns

Emphatic pronouns emphasise who you are talking about.

moi	*me*	nous	*us*
toi	*you (sing. inf.)*	vous	*you (formal, pl.)*
lui	*him, it (m)*	eux	*them (m)*
elle	*her, it (f)*	elles	*them (f)*

(Higher: lui, elle, nous, vous, eux, elles)

H: You can add '-même(s)' to an emphatic pronoun to mean '-self' or '-selves', e.g. 'moi-même' or 'eux-mêmes'.

Reflexive Pronouns

See p.174 for more on forming reflexives.

Reflexive pronouns refer back to a person or thing and mean 'self'.

me	*myself*
te	*yourself (sing. informal)*
se	*himself / herself* *itself / oneself*
nous	*ourselves, each other*
vous	*yourselves, each other*
se	*themselves, each other*

(H: nous, vous, se)

Indefinite Pronouns

Indefinite pronouns refer to nouns that are general and unspecific.

quelqu'un	*somebody, someone*
tout le monde	*everybody, everyone*
quelque chose	*something*
plusieurs	*several, many*
tout	*all, everything*

Adverbial Pronouns

(Higher)

'Y' and 'en' replace nouns and adverbs. 'Y' replaces the noun for a location that has already been mentioned. 'Y' is also used with verbs followed by 'à'.

E.g. Il est allé à Nice. → Il y est allé.
He went to Nice. → *He went there.*

'En' replaces the noun after expressions of quantity.

E.g. Nous avons trois chats. → Nous en avons trois.
We have three cats. → *We have three of them.*

'En' is also used with verbs followed by 'de'.

Relative Pronouns

Relative pronouns introduce extra information about something already mentioned in the sentence.

'Qui' refers to the subject of a clause — the person or thing doing the action.

E.g. J'ai un frère qui est médecin.
I have a brother who is a doctor.

(Higher)

'Que' refers to the object of the clause — the person or thing that something's being done to.

E.g. L'ordinateur que j'utilise est cassé.
The computer that I use is broken.

'Où' can mean 'where' or 'when'.

E.g. Le collège où j'ai étudié a fermé.
The school where I studied has closed.

'Dont' can mean 'of which' or 'whose'.

E.g. l'homme dont le nez est grand
the man whose nose is big

'Qui' and 'que' can also be used as interrogative pronouns — see p.147.

Demonstrative Pronouns

Demonstrative pronouns replace things in a sentence that are unspecific. They don't have to agree in gender or number.

ça	*that, it*	→ J'aime ça.
ce	*it*	→ C'est bon.
cela	*that, it*	→ J'adore cela.

Prepositions

à	*at, to, in, on*	derrière	*behind, at the back*
en	*in, by, to*	devant	*in front of*
de / d'	*of, from*	dans	*in, inside*
avec	*with*	entre	*between*
sans	*without*	voilà	*there, there you are*
à cause de	*because of*	depuis (Higher)	*since, for*
chez	*at (the house of)*	vers (Higher)	*towards*
avant	*before*	dès (Higher)	*as soon as*
après	*after, afterwards*	parmi (Higher)	*amongst*
pour	*for, in order to*	sauf (Higher)	*except*
contre	*against*	par (Higher)	*by, for*
pendant	*during*	malgré (Higher)	*despite*
sur	*on, upon*	jusque (Higher)	*until*
sous	*under*		
à côté de	*next to*		

Conjunctions

mais	*but*
et	*and*
ou	*or*
donc	*so, therefore*
ensuite	*then*
parce que	*because*
car	*because*
par contre	*however*
comme	*like, as, in terms of*
si	*if*
même si	*even if*
ne...ni...ni (Higher)	*neither...nor*
puisque (Higher)	*because, since*
puis (Higher)	*then, next*
cependant (Higher)	*however*
toutefois (Higher)	*yet*
par exemple (Higher)	*for example*
afin de (Higher)	*in order to*
soit (Higher)	*either*
lorsque (Higher)	*while, when*
sinon (Higher)	*otherwise*
quoique (Higher)	*although*

Revision Summary Test for Section Eleven

You've powered through this grammar section. Before a well-earned rest, try these questions.

- These questions are **hard**, but they'll really help you see **how well you know your stuff**.
- Tackle the **revision summary test** below, or scan the QR code to do it **online**. You can **track your progress** online and see **which areas need more work**.
- There are **sample answers** for the test here: www.cgpbooks.co.uk/MerciExtras

Summary Test

Nouns and Articles

1) For each of these words, swap the indefinite article ('un' or 'une') for the definite article ('le', 'la', or 'l''): a) une maison b) un thé c) un hôpital d) une heure
2) Make these nouns feminine: a) le chef b) l'étudiant c) l'acteur d) le canadien
3) Make these nouns plural: a) la rue b) le pays c) le chien d) le jeu e) le niveau
4) Fill in the blanks with 'à' combined with the correct definite article ('le', 'la', 'l'', 'les'), then translate each sentence into English. a) Je vais ...... campagne. b) Elle habite ...... Canada. c) Tu as demandé ...... profs ? d) Je participe ...... activités.
5) Fill in the blanks with the correct article ('de', 'du', 'de la' or 'des'). a) Je viens ...... parc. b) Je mange beaucoup ...... fromage. c) Il n'a pas ...... chevaux. d) J'ai acheté ...... viande.
6) (H) Translate these phrases into French: a) I want some bread and water. b) I won some money.

Pronouns

7) In French, list all the subject pronouns and emphatic pronouns you need to know for your tier.
8) Rewrite the sentences below, replacing each phrase in bold with the correct object pronoun. a) Je regarde **la série**. b) Tom lit **le journal**. c) Tu envoies la lettre **à ton oncle**.
9) Translate these indefinite pronouns into French: a) everyone b) something c) several
10) Translate this sentence into French: 'I watched that yesterday — it's funny.'
11) Fill in the gaps in these sentences with 'quoi', 'qui' or 'que': a) ...... aime le théâtre ? b) ...... font-ils ? c) On a besoin de ...... pour la recette ?

Higher

12) Find the relative pronoun in each phrase and then translate the phrase into English. a) le pays où j'ai passé mes vacances b) le site que j'ai lu hier soir c) le sang dont il a besoin
13) How do you say this in French: 'Me? I prefer to do it myself.'
14) Rewrite the sentences below, replacing each phrase in bold with the correct object pronoun. a) Elle déteste **les chiens**. b) Je vais parler **à mes amis** demain.
15) Use 'y' or 'en' to fill in the gaps in these sentences. Then translate them into English.
    a) Tu ...... es déjà allée ?
    b) J'ai oublié les gâteaux. Est-ce que tu peux m'...... acheter ?
    c) On va ...... aller demain.

Conjunctions and Prepositions

16) Translate these conjunctions into English: a) ensuite b) par contre c) donc d) comme
17) Fill in the gaps using an appropriate conjunction, then translate each sentence into English.
    a) Je vais rester à la maison ...... j'ai mal à la tête.
    b) J'ai oublié mon sac ...... je dois retourner au collège.
18) Fill in each gap with 'à' or 'de': a) aider ...... b) avoir besoin ...... c) réussir ......
19) Translate these sentences into French:
    a) The dog is under the table.
    b) There's a café next to the park.
    c) It's my brother's bag.
    d) I think about you.
    e) The party is at Camille's.
    f) She's going to France for two days.
20) (H) Translate the following sentences into French:
    a) Before dancing, I would like to run. b) She's been waiting for you since 09:30.

Quick Quiz

Adjective Agreement

Adjectives are useful for adding detail to your sentences, which will help you get the higher marks.

French adjectives agree with the thing they're describing

1) Adjectives are words used to describe things, for example 'beautiful', 'sad', 'funny' and 'difficult'.
2) In French, most adjectives change to match the gender and number of the noun they're describing.
3) You often add '-e' to the adjective if the noun being described is feminine (see p.143).

le livre vert *the green book* — la table verte *the green table*

You don't need to add an 'e' if the adjective already ends in 'e', or an 's' if the adjective already ends in 's' or 'x'.

4) Add '-s' to the adjective if the noun being described is plural (see p.143). This means that with feminine plurals, you're adding '-es'.

des films intéressants *interesting films* — des idées intéressantes *interesting ideas*

Some adjectives have their own rules

Adjectives with certain endings follow different rules:

Ending	Examples	Masculine singular	Feminine singular	Masculine plural	Feminine plural
-al	génial (*brilliant*), normal (*normal*)	génial	géniale	géniaux	géniales
-x	heureux (*happy*), sérieux (*serious*)	heureux	heureuse	heureux	heureuses
-en	ancien (*former*), végétarien (*vegetarian*)	ancien	ancienne	anciens	anciennes
-er	dernier (*last*), cher (*expensive*)	dernier	dernière	derniers	dernières
-el	réel (*real*), essentiel (*essential*)	réel	réelle	réels	réelles
-f	sportif (*sporty*), positif (*positive*)	sportif	sportive	sportifs	sportives

Some adjectives are irregular

1) These adjectives are irregular.
2) Some change before masculine singular nouns starting with a vowel or a mute 'h' because it's easier to say.
3) Some adjectives never change, e.g. 'sympa' (*nice*).

Masc. sing.	Before a masc. sing. noun starting with a vowel	Fem. sing.	Masc. plural	Fem. plural
vieux (*old*)	vieil	vieille	vieux	vieilles
beau (*beautiful*)	bel	belle	beaux	belles
nouveau (*new*)	nouvel	nouvelle	nouveaux	nouvelles
long (*long*)	long	longue	longs	longues

Grammar Questions

Translate these phrases into **French**, making sure the adjectives agree.

1. a regular week
2. a traditional meal
3. a sad girl
4. a blue door
5. the dangerous dogs
6. the new neighbours
7. the first day
8. an international star

Adjectives and their nouns — always in agreement...

The ending of your adjective depends on the gender and number of the noun you're describing — the adjective almost always needs to agree. Don't forget that this applies to those tricky irregular adjectives too.

Quick Quiz

More Adjectives

Adjectives have various functions — they can be indefinite, possessive or demonstrative. Or they can just be descriptive. It's also important you know whether to put them before or after the noun.

Most adjectives go after the word they're describing...

1) In French, most adjectives follow the noun (the word they're describing).

J'ai une voiture rapide. *I have a fast car.*

Adjectives are always masculine singular after 'c'est', e.g. 'c'est nouveau' (*it's new*).

2) You can also use adjectives in sentences with verbs such as 'être' (*to be*) and 'devenir' (*to become*). The adjective still needs to agree with the noun though.

Ils sont célèbres maintenant.
They are famous now.

Elle devient grande.
She is becoming tall.

...but there are some odd ones which go before

1) These adjectives almost always go before the noun:

bon(ne)	*good*	vieux / vieil / vieille	*old*	petit(e)	*small, short*
mauvais(e)	*bad*	nouveau / nouvel / nouvelle	*new*	grand(e)	*big, tall*
jeune	*young*	beau / bel / belle	*beautiful*	gros(se)	*big, large*
haut(e)	*high*	premier / première	*first*	faux / fausse	*false*
cher / chère	*dear*	dernier / dernière	*last*	seul(e)	*only*

Adjectives have to agree, regardless of whether they come before or after the noun.

J'ai une petite maison avec un gros jardin et une belle vue.
I have a small house with a big garden and a beautiful view.

2) Some adjectives change meaning depending on whether they go before or after a word. For example, 'ancien(ne)' means 'former' before a noun, but 'ancient' after it. 'Propre' is another example:

ma propre maison *my own house*

ma maison propre *my clean house*

Indefinite adjectives describe words in a more general way

1) 'Quelque' (*some*), 'chaque' (*each, every*), 'plusieurs' (*several, many*), 'même' (*same*), 'autre' (*other*) and 'tout' (*all*) are all examples of indefinite adjectives.

2) 'Chaque' and 'plusieurs' are invariable — they never change form to agree with the gender or quantity of the word they're describing.

3) 'Quelque', 'même' and 'autre' don't have a set of different forms for masculine or feminine, but they do add an '-s' when they change from singular to plural.

J'ai acheté quelques bonbons au magasin. *I bought some sweets at the shop.*

4) 'Tout' has different forms for masculine, feminine and plural.

Masc. sing.	Fem. sing.	Masc. pl.	Fem. pl.
tout	toute	tous	toutes

Words like 'my' and 'your' show who an object belongs to

1) Possessive adjectives show that something belongs to someone. They go before the noun.

notre tante *our aunt*

2) They match the thing being described — NOT the person it belongs to. The different forms are in the table on the right.

3) So, for example, it's always 'mon père' (*my father*) even if a girl is talking.

Voici mon père et ma mère.
Here are my dad and my mum.

	My	Your (inf. sing.)	His / her / its	Our	Your (formal, pl.)	Their
Masculine singular	mon	ton	son	notre	votre	leur
Feminine singular	ma	ta	sa	notre	votre	leur
Plural	mes	tes	ses	nos	vos	leurs

This means that 'son', 'sa' or 'ses' could all mean either 'his', 'her' or 'its'. You can usually tell which one it's meant to be by using the context.

For possessive pronouns like 'mine', 'yours', 'his' and 'hers', see p.152.

4) Before vowels, or words starting with 'h' that take 'l'', you use the masculine possessive adjective — even if the noun is feminine. It's easier to say.

Mon amie s'appelle Akiko.
My friend's called Akiko.

Ce, cet, cette, ces — This, these

1) To say 'this' or 'these', you need the right form of 'ce':

Masculine singular	Masc. words that take 'l''	Feminine singular	Masculine or feminine plural
ce	cet	cette	ces

Choose the one that matches the noun you're describing.

2) These are demonstrative adjectives — they're used when you use 'this' as a describing word.

Ce film est excellent. *This film is excellent.*

Cet homme est grand. *This man is tall.*

Aucun(e) — no, none (of them)

Higher

1) Aucun(e) can refer to both objects and people. Like most adjectives, it agrees with the gender of the noun it's describing.

2) However, it is only used in the singular form, even when it's describing plural nouns.

3) When you use 'aucun(e)', you have to put 'ne' before the verb.

Je n'ai aucune idée. *I have no idea.*

Aucun de mes amis ne veut partir. *None of my friends want to leave.*

You use 'veut' here because the verb needs to agree with 'aucun', not 'amis'.

Grammar Questions

Complete these sentences using the correct translations of the words in brackets.

1. ...... père n'aime pas ...... nouvelle voiture. (my, his)

2. ...... tes amis habitent dans ...... quartier. (all, our)

3. ...... hôtel est grand. (this)

4. ...... policière a ...... chats. (this, their)

You need to know how and where to use adjectives correctly...

You should be using adjectives all the time, so it's vital you can use them correctly and earn those marks in the exams. Remember, proper placement is key — otherwise you may change the meaning entirely...

Quick Quiz

Comparative and Superlative Adjectives

Adjectives have other functions too — they're useful for comparing things or making strong statements. For example, you might want to say this book is the best you've ever read...

Plus...que, moins...que, aussi...que — More than, less than, as...as

1) '<u>Plus</u>', '<u>moins</u>' and '<u>aussi</u>' can be used with adjectives to <u>compare things</u>. Add '<u>que</u>' after the adjective to say '<u>than</u>'.

These are called comparative adjectives.

Je suis plus rapide que toi.
I am faster than you.

Layla est moins forte que moi.
Layla is weaker than me.

When using comparatives, the adjectives still need to agree with the noun they're describing.

2) If you want to say something is the <u>same</u>, use '<u>aussi</u>...<u>que</u>' (*as...as*).

Ce film est aussi passionnant que le premier. *This film is as exciting as the first one.*

There are some exceptions

1) There are some <u>odd ones out</u> when it comes to making <u>comparisons</u> — just like in English.
2) With these adjectives, you <u>don't</u> use '<u>plus</u>' or '<u>moins</u>':

bon(ne)	*good*	→	meilleur(e)	*better*
mauvais(e)	*bad*	→	pire	*worse*

Les légumes sont meilleurs qu'hier. *The vegetables are better than yesterday.*

Adding 'le', 'la' or 'les' makes it 'the most' or 'the least'

Higher

1) '<u>Le plus</u>' and '<u>le moins</u>' form <u>superlative adjectives</u> — they're used to say something is '<u>the most</u>' or '<u>the least</u>', rather than directly <u>comparing</u> it to something else.
2) If you're using a <u>superlative adjective</u>, you have to make the <u>article</u> (*the*) <u>agree</u> as well.

Cette fleur est la plus belle. *This flower is the most beautiful.*

Mokhtar et Françoise sont les plus jeunes. *Mokhtar and Françoise are the youngest.*

3) You can also add an <u>article</u> to the adjectives '<u>meilleur</u>' and '<u>pire</u>' to make them <u>superlatives</u>. In this case, they mean '<u>the best</u>' and '<u>the worst</u>'.

Ses nouvelles chansons sont les meilleures. *Her new songs are the best.*

Grammar Questions

Translate these phrases into **French**. Remember those pesky adjective agreements...

1. Théo is smaller than Pauline.
2. I am younger than you.
3. Julie is as rich as Léa.
4. Spring is better than winter.
H **5.** His ideas are the worst.
H **6.** Poole is the biggest town.

Make sure you can use comparatives (and superlatives) accurately...

Hopefully it's *plus* clear *que* before when it comes to using comparative adjectives. Remember — 'plus', 'moins' or 'aussi' + adjective + 'que' is the way to go. Unless something is 'meilleur' or 'pire', of course...

Adverbs

Quick Quiz

Words that describe actions are called adverbs. Like adjectives, they're useful for adding more detail to your French and gaining you marks. Nifty. Just keep an eye out for those bothersome exceptions.

Adverbs describe how something's being done

Gérard had finally found the perfect dance partner.

1) In English, you don't say 'I dance perfect' — you add '-ly' on the end to say 'I dance perfectly'. 'Perfectly' is an adverb.
2) In French, you add '-ment' on the end of an adjective to make an adverb. But first you have to make sure it's in the feminine form (see p.155).

parfait (*perfect*) ⟶ parfaite (feminine form) + -ment ⟶ parfaitement (*perfectly*)

3) Unlike adjectives, adverbs don't have to agree — they're describing an action, not the person doing it.

Il danse parfaitement.
He dances perfectly.

Elle danse parfaitement.
She dances perfectly.

Elles dansent parfaitement.
They dance perfectly.

There are a few exceptions

1) Some adverbs don't follow the rules above.
2) If an adjective ends in '-ant' or '-ent', the 'ant' or 'ent' is replaced with '-amment' or '-emment'.

récent (*recent*) ⟶ réc- + -emment ⟶ récemment (*recently*)
patient (*patient*) ⟶ pati- + -emment ⟶ patiemment (*patiently*)
indépendant (*independent*) ⟶ indépend- + -amment ⟶ indépendamment (*independently*)

Some adverbs don't use '-ment'

Some adverbs are quite different from their adjectives.

bon(ne)	*good*	⟶	bien	*well*
mauvais(e)	*bad*	⟶	mal	*badly*
rapide	*fast, quick*	⟶	vite	*fast, quickly*

Je joue bien. *I play well.*
Il écrit mal. *He writes badly.*

Grammar Questions

Turn these adjectives into adverbs, then translate the **adverb** into **English**.

1. triste
2. négatif
3. sérieux
4. général
5. exact
6. essentiel
7. ordinaire
8. certain
9. heureux

[Higher]
10. actuel
11. évident
12. rare

Remember, adverbs don't have to agree...

It can get confusing remembering which rules apply to adjectives and adverbs. The important thing to remember is that adverbs describe the action of the subject — so they don't need a feminine or plural form.

Quick Quiz

More Adverbs

As well as describing how something's done, adverbs can also specify when and where it's done.

Adverbs can describe when something's being done

1) Adverbs can also describe when or how frequently something happens. They are usually placed at the beginning or end of the sentence, or after the verb they are describing.

souvent	*often*	déjà	*already*	maintenant	*now*
jamais	*never*	tard	*late*	bientôt	*soon*
avant	*before*	tôt	*early*	H parfois	*sometimes*

2) You can also form phrases to describe the day, month, season or year something happens using the adjectives 'dernier' (*last*) and 'prochain' (*next*). They can go at the start or end of a sentence.

L'année dernière, je suis allé(e) à Paris. — *Last year, I went to Paris.*

See p.172 for more on the future tense and p.168-171 for more on the past tenses.

3) Words to describe different days can be used as adverbs.

hier	*yesterday*	aujourd'hui	*today*	demain	*tomorrow*

Some adverbs describe location

Adverbs of place usually come after the verb in a phrase or sentence.

ici	*here*
là	*there*
là-bas	*over there*
loin	*far*
près	*nearby*
H partout	*everywhere*

Sa voiture est là-bas. — *His car is over there.*

Je fais mes devoirs ici. — *I do my homework here.*

If there's a direct object, e.g. 'mes devoirs', the adverb of place normally goes after it.

Phrases can be used as adverbs

Adverbial phrases are often really handy when you're giving your opinion on something.

You can often use adverbial phrases in the same way as adverbs. Longer adverbial phrases usually come at the beginning of a sentence.

en général	*in general*
tous les jours	*every day*
H par exemple	*for example*

En général, j'aime les chiens. — *In general, I like dogs.*

Grammar Questions

Translate these sentences into **French**. Make sure you use the right adverbs.

1. I play football over there.
2. You ('tu') work every day.
3. I often go to town by bus.
4. There are animals everywhere.
5. I leave tomorrow.
6. Last year, I went to France.

Adverbs — learn them <u>well</u>, revise them <u>often</u> and you'll go <u>far</u>...

It's useful to remember that adverbs don't always end in '-ment', so the best way to figure out if a word is an adverb is to look at the type of word it's modifying. From there, you'll be able know where it should go.

Comparative and Superlative Adverbs

Quick Quiz

Adverbs can be used to compare how you do things, or to say you're the best or worst at something.

Comparative adverbs compare actions

1) 'Plus' is used to say someone is doing something 'more...' than someone else. Use 'que' to say 'than'.

'Que' becomes 'qu'' before a vowel.

Fatima lit plus vite qu'Axel. *Fatima reads more quickly than Axel.*

2) You can use 'moins' to say 'less...' — use it in the same way as 'plus'.

Axel lit moins souvent que Diane. *Axel reads less often than Diane.*

3) When something is done equally, use 'aussi...que' to say 'as...as'.

Diane lit aussi lentement que Jules. *Diane reads as slowly as Jules.*

Emmanuel and Agathe were starting a new chapter together...

4) You can also use 'plus' or 'moins' without an adverb.

Jules lit plus que Marie. *Jules reads more than Marie.*

5) 'Bien' (*well*) doesn't follow the rules. You just need to learn its comparative form.

bien *well* → mieux *better*

The most, the best, the worst...

Higher

1) 'Le plus...' and 'le moins...' are superlatives — you use them to say someone does something 'the most...'or 'the least...'.

C'est Lola qui court le plus regulièrement. *Lola is the one who runs the most regularly.*

2) You always use 'le' because adverbs don't have to agree with the person doing the action — they're describing the action itself. This is different from adjectives.

3) 'Bien' and 'mal' also have irregular superlative forms:

mieux *better* → le mieux *the best*

pire *worse* → le pire *the worst*

Grammar Questions

Fill in the gaps in these sentences by translating the words in brackets into **French**.

1. Je travaille .... toi. (as quickly as)

2. Lucie court .... Dorian. (more often than)

3. Elle mange .... vous. (less than)

Higher

4. Morgane chante .... (the best)

5. Je nage .... régulièrement. (the least)

6. Qui marche .... rapidement ? (the most)

Use comparatives to make sure you write as well as possible...

...and in the reading exam keep your eyes peeled for them — they can change the meaning of a sentence.

Quick Quiz

Quantifiers and Intensifiers

Using intensifiers and quantifiers with adjectives and adverbs can make descriptions more precise.

Intensifiers strengthen what you're saying

1) Adverbs such as '<u>trop</u>' (*too*) and '<u>assez</u>' (*quite*) can add <u>detail</u> to your sentences. They're called <u>intensifiers</u>.

trop	*too (much, many)*	Higher	particulièrement	*particularly*
très	*very*		entièrement	*entirely, completely*
assez	*quite*		plutôt	*rather*
vraiment	*really*		tellement	*so much*
extrêmement	*extremely*			

2) <u>Intensifiers</u> can be used with <u>adjectives</u> — they always go <u>before</u> them. You can use them to <u>emphasise</u> the <u>adjective</u>, or to say <u>what</u> something's like.

Camille est trop sérieuse.
Camille is too serious.

La géographie est assez intéressante.
Geography is quite interesting.

3) The <u>adjectives</u> still have to <u>agree</u> but the <u>intensifiers don't</u>.

Cette montagne est très petite. *The mountain is very small.*

4) You can also use intensifiers with other <u>adverbs</u>. They go <u>before</u> the adverb they modify.

Il mange vraiment lentement. *He eats really slowly.*

J'écris assez vite. *I write quite quickly.*

Quantifiers help you say how many or how much

1) <u>Quantifiers</u> let you say roughly how much of something you have, without being specific, e.g. '<u>lots</u>' or '<u>not many</u>'.

2) Many are formed using <u>adverbs</u>, followed by '<u>de</u>'.

J'ai beaucoup de lapins. *I have lots of rabbits.*

trop de	*too much*
beaucoup de	*a lot of*
un peu de	*a few, a little*
plusieurs	*several, many*

3) With <u>quantifiers</u>, '<u>de</u>' doesn't change to agree with the noun, but it changes to '<u>d'</u>' before a <u>vowel</u>.

Nous avons un peu d'argent. *We have a bit of money.*

Il a trop de temps. *He has too much time.*

Grammar Questions

Translate these sentences into French.

1. She is very beautiful.
2. They have lots of friends.
3. He has a bit of water.
4. The teacher is really old.
5. The man eats too much cheese.
6. His house is quite large.

Intensifiers will make your French incredibly good...

It's worth remembering to scatter some of these quantifiers and intensifiers throughout your written and spoken French when you can — it'll show the examiner you're a real grammar pro. Full marks all round.

Adjectives and Adverbs — Grammar List

Here's a roundup of the words you need to describe people, things, actions... and just about anything else.

Regular Adjectives

In French, adjectives usually change to match the gender and number of the word they're describing. To make an adjective feminine, you normally add '-e' to the end.

général(e)	*general*
normal(e)	*normal, usual*
original(e)	*original*
vrai(e)	*true, correct*
lourd(e)	*heavy*
léger / légère	*light*
exact(e)	*exact*
haut(e)	*high, tall*
Higher	
suffisant(e)	*sufficient, enough*
évident(e)	*obvious*
plein(e)	*full*
étroit(e)	*narrow*

Other adjectives follow different rules — see p.155.

essentiel(le)	*essential*
possible	*possible*
impossible	*impossible*
faux / fausse	*false*
nécessaire	*necessary, essential*
régulier / régulière	*regular*
ordinaire	*ordinary*
positif / positive	*positive*
négatif / négative	*negative*
Higher	
entier / entière	*whole, full, entire*
indispensable	*essential*
rare	*rare*
pareil(le)	*same*

Make most adjectives plural by adding '-s'. E.g. grande → grande<u>s</u>
However, there are some exceptions. E.g. normal → norm<u>aux</u>

See p.155 for more on how to form plural adjectives.

Irregular Adjectives

Some adjectives follow irregular patterns in French.

vieux / vieil / vieille / vieux / vieilles *old*
beau / bel / belle / beaux / belles *beautiful*

Adverbs

Adverbs are usually formed by taking the feminine version of an adjective and adding '-ment', although some are irregular.

rapidement	*quickly, fast*
facilement	*easily*
seulement	*only*
simplement	*simply*
exactement	*exactly*
absolument	*absolutely*
complètement	*completely*
certainement	*certainly, surely*
parfaitement	*perfectly*
totalement	*totally*
réellement	*really*
clairement	*clearly*
bien	*well, a lot*
mal	*badly*
vite	*fast, quickly*
même	*even*
aussi	*also, as well*
encore	*again, yet, still*
déjà	*already*
alors	*so, well, then*
ensuite	*then*
souvent	*often*
Higher	
actuellement	*currently, at the moment*
autrement	*otherwise, differently in a different way*
différemment	*differently*
évidemment	*obviously*
apparemment	*apparently*
uniquement	*only*
ailleurs	*somewhere else, besides, by the way*
pourtant	*yet, nonetheless*
également	*also, too, as well, equally*
puis	*then, next*
surtout	*especially*
d'abord	*firstly*
ainsi	*so, thus*

Indefinite Adjectives

quelque	*some*
même	*same*
autre	*other*
chaque	*each, every*
certain(e)	*certain*
tout(e)	*all*
H	
nombreux / nombreuses	*many, numerous*

Quantifiers & Intensifiers

trop (de)	*too (much, many)*
très	*very*
assez	*quite, enough*
beaucoup de	*a lot of, many*
un peu de	*a few, a little*
peu (de)	*few, little*
plusieurs	*several, many*
vraiment	*really*
extrêmement	*extremely*
Higher	
plutôt	*rather*
particulièrement	*particularly*
entièrement	*entirely, completely*
presque	*nearly*
tant	*so much, so many*
tellement	*so much*

Comparative & Superlative Adjectives and Adverbs

plus de	*more*
moins de	*less*
plus...que	*more...than*
moins...que	*less...than*
aussi...que	*as...as*
meilleur(e)	*better (adj.)*
mieux	*better (adv.)*
pire (adj.)	*worse, worst*
Higher	
le / la / les plus	*the most*
le / la / les moins	*the least*
le / la / les meilleur(e)(s)	*the best (adj.)*
le mieux	*the best (adv.)*
le / la / les pire(s)	*the worst (adj.)*

Revision Summary Test for Section Twelve

You've hopefully got to grips with another big chunk of grammar. Have a go at some questions.

- Yep, these questions are **hard** — they'll really help you see **how well you know your stuff**.
- Tackle the **revision summary test** below, or scan the QR code to do it **online**. Use the CGP RevisionHub to **track your progress** and see **which areas need more work**.
- You can find **sample answers** here: www.cgpbooks.co.uk/MerciExtras

Summary Test

Adjectives

1) Choose the correct adjective in brackets, then translate each sentence into English.
   a) Axel a les yeux (bleu / bleus).
   b) La (premier / première) question est difficile.
   c) J'aime les maisons (moderne / modernes).
   d) Mes frères sont assez (sportifs / sportives).
2) Fill in each gap by translating the adjective in brackets into French.
   a) Ces rues sont très .... (long)
   b) Je dors .... la journée. (all)
   c) Hugo a une .... partenaire. (new)
   d) Elle adore les .... forêts. (beautiful)
3) What's the French for... a) my small dog? b) your grey car? c) their room? d) our meal?
4) [H] Translate these phrases into French using 'aucun' or 'aucune':
   a) None of my friends are here.
   b) We have no cars.

Adverbs

5) Find the adverbs in these sentences, then translate each sentence into English.
   a) Aujourd'hui, je vais manger au café.
   b) Tu parles calmement.
   c) Il se lève souvent à six heures.
   d) Je dois aller à l'hôpital bientôt.
6) Translate these sentences into French, using the adverb form of the adjective in the brackets:
   a) He plays well. (bon) b) She sings badly. (mauvais) c) You run quickly. (rapide)
7) Turn these adjectives into adverbs: a) facile b) normal c) récent d) vrai
8) Translate into French:
   a) The airport is quite far from the town.
   b) Yesterday, I ran in the park.
   c) I saw the castle over there.
   d) I returned late last night.
9) [H] Turn each of these adjectives into adverbs:
   a) actif b) entier c) aigre d) plein e) rare f) évident

Comparatives and Superlatives

10) Translate these sentences into French:
    a) I'm taller than you.
    b) Eva writes as well as Toni.
    c) The films are worse than the books.
    d) They go out less often than us.
11) Choose the correct option to complete each sentence.
    a) Elle est aussi sympa **que / qui** son ami.
    b) Cette maison est plus **petit / petite** que l'autre.
    c) Cette idée est **meilleur / meilleure** .
    d) Tu joues **mieux / meilleur** que lui.

Higher

12) Translate these sentences into French:
    a) His new songs are the best.
    b) These clothes are the least expensive.
    c) She is the youngest but I am the smallest.
    d) This region is the most beautiful.
13) What do these sentences mean in English?
    a) Hier, le cours de maths était le pire.
    b) Nous sommes les plus forts.
14) Translate this sentence into French:
    'Katie studies more regularly than Léo, but Léo studies the most seriously.'

Quantifiers and Intensifiers

15) Use quantifiers or intensifiers to fill in the gaps, using the clues in brackets to help you.
    a) Elle a .... argent. (more than she needs)
    b) L'acteur a eu .... succès. (a small amount)
    c) Mon ami a .... livres. (a large amount)
    d) J'ai acheté .... cafés. (quite a few)

Verbs in the Present Tense

Quick Quiz

You need to know the present tense inside out and back to front — it crops up all over the place.

Verbs are action words

1) A verb is an action word. 'Eat', 'sing' and 'jump' are all examples of English verbs.
2) Actions can take place in different times — or tenses — the past, present or future.
3) To put a verb in a tense, you need to know its infinitive, e.g. 'être' (*to be*). They're in this form in the dictionary.

The present describes something happening now

1) Use the present tense to describe something that's occurring now.

Je mange du pain. *I am eating bread. / I eat bread.*

You can use the French present tense to say that something 'is happening' or that something 'happens'.

2) You should also use the present tense to describe something that happens regularly.

Le lundi, je joue au football. *I play football on Mondays.*

3) Verbs in the present tense have different endings, but you always start by finding the verb's stem.

regarder *to look* — Begin by putting the verb in the infinitive. − -er — Remove the last two letters of the infinitive. = regard- *the stem* — You're left with the stem.

Infinitive	Stem
parler	parl-
choisir	chois-
entendre	entend-

4) Then you add the correct endings to the stem.
5) In French, there are three groups of verbs — verbs ending in '-er', '-ir' and '-re':

The 'il'/'elle'/'on' form of the present tense for '-re' verbs doesn't have an ending.

'-er' endings

I	je	-e
you (inf. sing.)	tu	-es
he/she/it/one	il/elle/on	-e
we	nous	-ons
you (formal, pl.)	vous	-ez
they (m/f)	ils/elles	-ent

E.g. 'regarder' (*to watch*)
'regard-' (the stem)
+ '-ons' ('nous' ending)
nous regardons (*we watch*)

'-ir' endings

I	je	-is
you (inf. sing.)	tu	-is
he/she/it/one	il/elle/on	-it
we	nous	-issons
you (formal, pl.)	vous	-issez
they (m/f)	ils/elles	-issent

E.g. 'choisir' (*to choose*)
'chois-' (the stem)
+ '-issent' ('elles' ending)
elles choisissent (*they choose*)

'-re' endings

I	je	-s
you (inf. sing.)	tu	-s
he/she/it/one	il/elle/on	—
we	nous	-ons
you (formal, pl.)	vous	-ez
they (m/f)	ils/elles	-ent

E.g. 'entendre' (*to hear*)
'entend-' (the stem)
+ nothing ('elle' ending)
elle entend (*she hears*)

Some '-ir' and '-re' verbs follow different patterns — see p.180-182.

Grammar Questions

Put the verbs below into the present tense. The subject is given in brackets.

1. parler (je)
2. trouver (tu)
3. vendre (vous)
4. répondre (je)
5. finir (elles)
6. commencer (vous)
7. perdre (on)
8. remplir (nous) H

You can't avoid the present tense, so make sure you learn it...

Regular verbs are absolutely everywhere. Do yourself a favour and learn these conjugations off by heart.

Quick Quiz

Irregular Verbs in the Present Tense

Irregular verbs don't follow a set pattern. This means that there aren't any concrete rules you can apply to them. The only way to revise them properly is to learn them off by heart. Off you go...

Some of the most useful verbs are irregular

Lots of important verbs are irregular — this means that they don't follow the usual rules. Here are some of the most common ones that you need to know for your exams:

avoir (to have)

I have	j'ai
you (inf. sing.) have	tu as
he/she/it/one has	il/elle/on a
we have	nous avons
you (formal, pl.) have	vous avez
they have	ils/elles ont

You sometimes use 'avoir' in French when you would use 'to be' in English. E.g. 'j'ai peur' (*I'm scared*), 'il a froid' (*he's cold*).

être (to be)

I am	je suis
you (inf. sing.) are	tu es
he/she/it/one is	il/elle/on est
we are	nous sommes
you (formal, pl.) are	vous êtes
they are	ils/elles sont

faire (to make / do)

I make	je fais
you (inf. sing.) make	tu fais
he/she/it/one makes	il/elle/on fait
we make	nous faisons
you (formal, pl.) make	vous faites
they make	ils/elles font

Remember, you don't usually pronounce the last letter of a word in French if it's a consonant. This means that some endings (e.g. 'fais' and 'fait') are spelt differently but sound exactly the same.

aller (to go)

I go	je vais
you (inf. sing.) go	tu vas
he/she/it/one goes	il/elle/on va
we go	nous allons
you (formal, pl.) go	vous allez
they go	ils/elles vont

devoir (must / to have to)

I must	je dois
you (inf. sing.) must	tu dois
he/she/it/one must	il/elle/on doit
we must	nous devons
you (formal, pl.) must	vous devez
they must	ils/elles doivent

'Devoir' is a verb, but 'les devoirs' is a noun meaning 'homework'.

vouloir (to want)

I want	je veux
you (inf. sing.) want	tu veux
he/she/it/one wants	il/elle/on veut
we want	nous voulons
you (formal, pl.) want	vous voulez
they want	ils/elles veulent

pouvoir (to be able to / can)

I can	je peux
you (inf. sing.) can	tu peux
he/she/it/one can	il/elle/on peut
we can	nous pouvons
you (formal, pl.) can	vous pouvez
they can	ils/elles peuvent

Don't mix up 'savoir' and 'connaître' — 'savoir' means to know something. To say that you know somebody, use 'connaître'.

savoir (to know / can)

I know	je sais
you (inf. sing.) know	tu sais
he/she/it/one knows	il/elle/on sait
we know	nous savons
you (formal, pl.) know	vous savez
they know	ils/elles savent

Grammar Questions

Each verb below is spelt incorrectly. Using the verb tables above, rewrite each of the phrases correctly.

1. nous doivons
2. je veut
3. vous êtez
4. tu doix
5. elle vat
6. ils faient
7. elles pouvent
8. on saix
9. ils avont
10. nous faions

These verbs crop up everywhere, so you need to learn them...

It's pretty hard to speak or write French without these verbs — read this page through again, then close the book and try to write down as many of them as you can without looking. Repeat until you've got them all.

More about the Present Tense

Quick Quiz

There's still more to learn about the present tense — round off your knowledge with these points.

Verbs sometimes stay in their infinitive

1) When one verb follows another in a sentence or phrase, the first verb needs to be in the right form, but the second verb is always in the infinitive.

> Je veux aider les autres. *I want to help other people.*
>
> 'Veux' is the first verb in the sentence — it's in the first person singular form of the present tense. Because 'aider' comes directly after 'veux', it's in the infinitive form.

2) Some verbs can be followed directly by an infinitive, but a few verbs need a preposition in between.

				Higher	
commencer à	*to begin*	essayer de	*to try*	éviter de	*to avoid*
réussir à	*to succeed*	décider de	*to decide*	encourager à	*to encourage*
apprendre à	*to learn*	arrêter de	*to stop*	tenter de	*to try, attempt*

> J'apprends à conduire la voiture de mon père. *I'm learning to drive my dad's car.*

3) You can also use the infinitive as a noun where you'd use an '-ing' word in English.

> Faire du sport, c'est amusant. *Doing sport is fun.*

'Depuis' can be used with the present tense

Higher

1) 'Depuis' means 'since' or 'for' (see p.151).
2) If the action you're talking about is still going on today, use the present tense.

> Il habite à Belfast depuis 1997. *He's lived in Belfast since 1997.*

Even though the action began in the past, the person is still living in Belfast — so you need the present tense.

Verb phrases can tell you when something happened

Higher

1) Use 'être en train de' to say that you're in the middle of doing something.

> Je suis en train de manger. *I am in the middle of eating.*

2) 'Venir de' followed by an infinitive means 'to have just done something'.

> Je viens de quitter l'école. *I've just left school.*

Marguerite could usually be found in the middle of eating.

Grammar Questions

Translate these sentences into **French**.

1. I like eating.
2. Studying is boring.
3. They ('elles') try to sing.
4. He continues to speak.
H **5.** He has just left.
H **6.** You've ('vous') been here since yesterday.

Remember — infinitives always end in '-er', '-ir' or '-re'...

There's no hard and fast way of knowing which preposition goes with which verb. They're often different to what you'd use in English, so it's best just to learn any prepositions whenever you come across a new verb.

Quick Quiz

The Perfect Tense

Now you've got the hang of the present, it's time to look at the past — that's if you can remember what life was like before revision, of course. The perfect tense can be tricky, so read carefully.

Use the perfect tense for completed actions

1) Use the perfect tense to describe an action that started and finished in the past.
2) In French, it has three parts — a subject, the present tense of 'avoir' or 'être' and a past participle.

il (*he*)		a (*has*)		regardé (*watched*)		il a regardé (*he has watched / he watched*)
This is the subject. The subject could also be a noun, e.g. someone's name.	+	This is the present tense of 'avoir'. Its form depends on the subject.	+	This is the past participle. There's more about this below.	=	

3) You don't always need the 'have' part in English, but you must have it in French. For example, 'il a regardé' can be translated as 'he has watched' or 'he watched'.

Most verbs use 'avoir' in the perfect tense

1) Use the present tense of 'avoir' to make the 'have' part of the perfect tense:

avoir (to have)

I have	j'ai
you (inf. sing.) have	tu as
he/she/it/one has	il/elle/on a
we have	nous avons
you (formal, pl.) have	vous avez
they have	ils/elles ont

Remember that the present tense of 'avoir' is irregular. See p.166 for other irregular verbs.

Elle a mangé. *She has eaten. / She ate.*

Nous avons parlé. *We've spoken. / We spoke.*

2) Get the past participle of a verb by finding the verb's stem (see p.165) and adding on the correct ending.
3) Verbs ending in '-er', '-ir' and '-re' each have a different ending:

Past participles

'-er' verbs	stem	+	é	e.g. regarder:	regard + é = regardé
'-ir' verbs	stem	+	i	e.g. choisir:	chois + i = choisi
'-re' verbs	stem	+	u	e.g. entendre:	entend + u = entendu

j'ai cherché *I have searched / I searched*

vous avez dormi *you have slept / you slept*

ils ont perdu *they have lost / they lost*

4) Many '-ir' and '-re' verbs have irregular past participles — see the next page.

Irregular past participles look a bit different

1) Some verbs have irregular past participles — they don't use the same endings as regular verbs.
2) These are the most important ones:

avoir *(to have)*	→ eu	lire *(to read)*	→ lu
boire *(to drink)*	→ bu	mettre *(to put)*	→ mis
dire *(to say / tell)*	→ dit	prendre *(to take)*	→ pris
être *(to be)*	→ été	venir *(to come)*	→ venu
faire *(to do / make)*	→ fait	traduire (to translate)	→ traduit

H

devoir *(to have to / must)*	→ dû	savoir *(to know)*	→ su
pouvoir *(to be able to / can)*	→ pu	vouloir *(to want)*	→ voulu

Look out for the past participle of 'être' — it's spelt exactly the same way as the noun 'été' *(summer)*.

Some verbs take 'être' instead of 'avoir'

To see how the present tense of 'être' is formed, see p.166.

1) A few verbs use 'être' instead of 'avoir' to form the perfect tense.

aller	*to go*	partir	*to leave*	monter	*to go up*	entrer	*to go in*
venir	*to come*	sortir	*to go out*	devenir	*to become*	rentrer	*to go back*
revenir	*to come back*	descendre	*to go down*	rester	*to stay*	naître	*to be born*
arriver	*to arrive*	retourner	*to return*	tomber	*to fall*		

2) Just like with 'avoir' verbs, the correct present tense form of 'être' is needed.

Tao est allé à l'école. *Tao went to school.*

Il s'est levé. *He got up.*

All reflexive verbs (see p.174) take 'être' in the perfect tense.

Verbs that take 'être' have to agree

1) All verbs that take 'être' in the perfect tense have to agree with their subject.
2) The past participle gains an 's' if the subject is plural, an 'e' if it's feminine and 'es' if it's feminine and plural.

Les filles sont parties. *The girls have left.*

When a reflexive verb is in the perfect tense, the present tense of 'être' always goes between the reflexive pronoun and the past participle.

Elle s'est reposée près de la rivière. *She rested near the river.*

Grammar Questions

Translate these phrases into **French**, using the **perfect tense**.
Remember to check if each verb takes 'avoir' or 'être'.

1. they ('elles') put
2. I went
3. you ('tu') said
4. we've ('nous') recycled
5. she arrived
6. he took
7. they ('ils') came back
H **8.** I injured myself H

It's vital you know which verbs take 'être' and which take 'avoir'...

Grab some paper, cover up the list of 'être' verbs above and write down as many as you can. Repeat until you can get them all without looking. For an extra challenge, write down the past participle for each one.

Quick Quiz

The Imperfect Tense

Like English, French has more than one past tense — time is complicated, after all. The imperfect tense is really useful, and dead easy to form. Once you've got the hang of it, you won't look back.

Get the stem from the present tense 'nous' form

1) To form the imperfect tense, you have to find the stem of the verb you want and add on the correct ending.

The only verb that's irregular in the imperfect tense is 'être' (see below).

2) To get the stem, find the present tense 'nous' form of the verb and take off the '-ons'.

regardons *we look / we are looking* Begin by putting the verb in the 'nous' form of the present tense.	–	-ons Remove the '-ons' from the end.	=	regard- *the stem* You're left with the stem.

See p.165 for how to find the 'nous' form of the present tense.

3) When you've got the stem, add on the ending you need. The endings are the same for all verbs:

Imperfect tense endings

I	je	-ais
you (inf. sing.)	tu	-ais
he/she/it/one	il/elle/on	-ait
we	nous	-ions
you (formal, pl.)	vous	-iez
they (m/f)	ils/elles	-aient

Higher

Tu m'attendais. *You were waiting for me.*

Il venait le mardi. *He used to come on Tuesdays.*

Higher

Nous faisions beaucoup de bruit.
We were making a lot of noise.

'Être', 'avoir' and 'faire' crop up a lot

1) Some verbs crop up more than others, so it's a good idea to become really familiar with them.

2) 'Être' is irregular in the imperfect tense — its stem is 'ét-'. It uses the regular endings, though:

être (to be)

I	j'	étais
you (inf. sing.)	tu	étais
he/she/it/one	il/elle/on	était
we	nous	étions
you (formal, pl.)	vous	étiez
they (m/f)	ils/elles	étaient

Higher

C'était génial. *It was great.*

'C'était' (*it was*) is the past tense of 'c'est' (*it is*). 'C'était' + an adjective is useful for descriptions.

La salle était propre. *The room was clean.*

H

Nous étions travailleurs. *We were hard-working.*

3) All the other verbs are regular — they form the imperfect tense following the normal rules.

4) Make sure you learn 'avoir' and 'faire' inside out. They're used in lots of handy phrases.

Il y avait... *There was... / There were...*

Il faisait froid. *It was cold.*

Use the imperfect for descriptions in the past

Imperfect	Perfect
I was going	I went
she was running	she ran
we were waiting	we waited

1) Use the imperfect tense to describe something or someone in the past.

C'était rouge. *It was red.*

Il faisait chaud. *It was hot.*

Yann était heureux de la voir. *Yann was happy to see her.*

2) The imperfect tense can also describe an action that 'was happening' in the past. It's different to the perfect tense (see p.168) because the action isn't complete.

J'attendais le train. *I was waiting for the train.*

Il parlait au président. *He was talking to the president.*

The person hadn't finished waiting for the train, so the action is incomplete.

Higher

3) When one action interrupts another action in a past tense sentence, the first action is left unfinished. This means that it needs to be in the imperfect tense.

The second action is in the perfect tense.

Je lisais quand elle est arrivée. *I was reading when she arrived.*

Il dormait quand il a plu. *He was sleeping when it rained.*

Use the imperfect for what used to happen

You also use the imperfect tense to talk about what you used to do.

You can use the imperfect for something you used to do regularly, or something you used to do in general.

J'allais au cinéma tous les jeudis. *I used to go to the cinema every Thursday.*

Nous habitions dans la capitale de l'Algérie. *We used to live in the capital of Algeria.*

Quand j'avais dix ans, je jouais de la guitare. *When I was ten, I used to play the guitar.*

Grammar Questions

Decide whether the verbs below should be in the perfect or the imperfect tense, then translate each sentence.

1. I ran.
2. It was fun.
3. We ('on') were dreaming.
4. He was boring.
5. They ('ils') have eaten.
6. She has studied.
7. I used to play football.
8. I was buying bread.

Learn the difference between the perfect and imperfect tenses...

It's important you know which tense to use in different situations — generally, you use the perfect tense for completed actions and the imperfect tense for actions that took place over a longer time period. Simple.

Quick Quiz

Talking about the Future

You need to be able to talk about things that'll happen in the future, too. Don't worry — there are no crystal balls, just some good old verb conjugations. Everything you need to know is on this page.

Use 'I'm going' + infinitive

The immediate future is the easiest future tense — it uses the present tense form of 'aller' and an infinitive.

je vais (*I am going*) This is the present tense of 'aller' (see p.166).	+	danser (*to dance*) The next verb goes in the infinitive (see p.167).	=	Je vais danser. (*I am going to dance.*) A sentence about the future.

Il va couper le pain. *He's going to cut the bread.*

Ces étudiants vont voyager cet été. *These students are going to travel this summer.*

'I will' — the proper future tense

Higher

1) Using the proper future tense in French is the same as saying 'will' in English, e.g. 'I will bake'.
2) To form the future tense of regular '-er' verbs, you need to find the verb's infinitive (see p.167) and add on the correct endings. The endings are the same for all verbs:

The endings might look familiar because they're similar to the present tense of 'avoir'.

Future tense endings

I	je	-ai	we	nous	-ons
you (inf. sing.)	tu	-as	you (formal, pl.)	vous	-ez
he/she/it/one	il/elle/on	-a	they (m/f)	ils/elles	-ont

je regarderai *I will look*

il signera *he will sign*

Ils mangeront des fruits. *They will eat fruit.*

Lucie made it very clear that she definitely wouldn't eat the fruit.

3) Some important verbs are irregular in the future tense — their stems aren't in the infinitive form:

avoir (to have)	
j'	aurai
tu	auras
il/elle/on	aura

être (to be)	
je	serai
tu	seras
il/elle/on	sera

aller (to go)	
j'	irai
tu	iras
il/elle/on	ira

faire (to do)	
je	ferai
tu	feras
il/elle/on	fera

The stems are the only irregular part of these verbs — they all use the normal endings listed above.

Grammar Questions

Put these phrases into the immediate future tense. If you're taking the Higher-tier exams, put the ones marked 'H' into the proper future too.

1. tu choisis **2.** ils sont **3.** nous finissons **4.** tu regardes (H) **5.** elles disent **6.** vous faites **7.** il va (H) **8.** elle vient **9.** j'ai (H) **10.** on vend

Sometimes you use the present tense to describe a future event...

Just like in English, French speakers often use the present tense to talk about something that'll happen in the near future, e.g. 'je sors ce soir' (*I'm going out this evening*) or 'ça commence demain' (*it starts tomorrow*).

The Conditional

The conditional is a bit of a mishmash of different tenses. Fortunately, you already know half of it...

'Je voudrais' — I would like

1) The French conditional is used when you say 'would' in English.
2) 'Vouloir' is really useful in the conditional — you can use it lots in your speaking assessment:

vouloir (to want)	
I would like	je voudrais
you (inf. sing.) would like	tu voudrais
he/she/it/one would like	il/elle/on voudrait

'Vouloir' is often followed by an infinitive. Look at p.167 for more on infinitives.

Je voudrais partir. *I'd like to leave.*

Elle voudrait du lait. *She would like some milk.*

The conditional for '-er' verbs = infinitive + imperfect endings

Higher

1) Forming the conditional is pretty straightforward for '-er' verbs — you take the verb's infinitive and add on the endings you learnt for the imperfect tense.

regarder (to look) This is an infinitive ending in '-er'. + *ais* This is the ending for the first person singular imperfect tense (see p.170). = *je regarderais* (I would look) This is the first person singular conditional of 'regarder'.

2) Here's a reminder of the endings:

Conditional endings		
I	je	-ais
you (inf. sing.)	tu	-ais
he/she/it/one	il/elle/on	-ait
we	nous	-ions
you (formal, pl.)	vous	-iez
they (m/f)	ils/elles	-aient

Some important verbs have irregular stems

Higher

Some important verbs are irregular in the conditional tense — their stems aren't in the infinitive form:

avoir (to have)	
j'	aurais
tu	aurais
il/elle/on	aurait

être (to be)	
je	serais
tu	serais
il/elle/on	serait

aller (to go)	
j'	irais
tu	irais
il/elle/on	irait

faire (to do)	
je	ferais
tu	ferais
il/elle/on	ferait

The stems are the only irregular part of these verbs — they all use the normal endings listed above.

Grammar Questions

Put these verbs into the conditional. The subject has been given to you in brackets.

H
1. améliorer (vous)
2. goûter (il)
3. manger (il)
4. organiser (je)
5. aller (elle)
6. annoncer (tu)
7. être (on)
8. décider (elle)
9. s'identifier (ils)
10. chercher (nous)
H

The examiner would like to see that you can use the conditional...

If you're taking the Foundation paper, you need to know 'je voudrais', 'tu voudrais' and 'il/elle/on voudrait'. If you're taking the Higher one, you also need to know regular '-er' verbs and the irregulars above.

Quick Quiz

Reflexive Verbs and Pronouns

Don't be put off by reflexives — they're actually pretty simple. You just need a few basic rules...

Reflexive verbs have an extra part

Reflexive pronouns	
myself	me
yourself (inf. sing.)	te
himself/herself/itself/oneself	se
ourselves (Higher)	nous
yourselves (formal, pl.) (Higher)	vous
themselves (m/f) (Higher)	se

You can tell which verbs are reflexive by checking in the dictionary. If you look up 'to get up', it'll say 'se lever'.

1) Reflexive verbs describe actions that you do to yourself, like washing yourself or getting yourself up.
2) These verbs look different because they've got an extra part — a pronoun that means 'self', e.g. 'se demander' (*to ask oneself*). The pronoun changes form depending on who's doing the action.
3) [H] Reflexive pronouns can also mean 'each other', e.g. 'ils se regardent' (*they look at each other*).
4) Reflexive verbs can end in '-er', '-ir' or '-re'. They form tenses in exactly the same way as other verbs:

se demander (to ask oneself)

I ask myself	je me demande	one asks oneself	on se demande
you (inf. sing.) ask yourself	tu te demandes	[H] we ask ourselves	nous nous demandons
he asks himself	il se demande	[H] you (formal, pl.) ask yourselves	vous vous demandez
she asks herself	elle se demande	[H] they ask themselves (m/f)	ils/elles se demandent

Reflexives keep their pronouns in all tenses

1) All reflexive verbs take 'être' in the perfect tense — this means they agree with their subject (see p.169).
2) The reflexive pronoun (me, te, se, etc.) always goes between the subject and the present tense of 'être'.

Je me suis levé(e) à sept heures ce matin.
I got up at seven o'clock this morning.

Elle s'est reposée.
She rested.

'Reposée' has an 'e' on the end here because its subject ('elle') is feminine.

3) In the immediate future tense (see p.172), the reflexive infinitive needs the pronoun that matches its subject.

Je vais m'amuser. *I'm going to enjoy myself.*

Il va s'habiller. *He's going to get dressed.*

'Se' becomes 's'' before a word starting with a vowel.

Grammar Questions

Translate these phrases into **French**. Make sure you put the reflexive pronouns in the right places.

1. he's interested in
2. she got married
3. you ('tu') get on with
4. I'm going to get dressed
[H] **5.** they ('elles') get up
[H] **6.** we ('nous') will escape

Learn to express yourself with reflexive verbs...

Learn this page, and before you know it, sticking a pronoun before the verb will be, erm, a reflex...

Negative Forms

Quick Quiz

You've reached the page where you can grumble and moan. Take your stress out on two of the most important French words — 'ne' and 'pas'. (Don't worry — they're only little but they can take it.)

'ne...pas' — not

Clémentine was not 'd'accord'.

1) In English, you change a sentence to mean the opposite by adding 'not'. In French, you add two words — 'ne' and 'pas'. They go either side of the verb.

je suis d'accord → je ne suis pas d'accord
I agree → *I do not agree*

'Suis' is the verb. The 'ne' goes before it, and the 'pas' goes after it.

2) For verbs in the perfect tense (see p.168-169), put the 'ne' and 'pas' around the bit of 'avoir' or 'être'.

Je n'ai pas aimé l'école. *I did not like school.*

3) To make an infinitive negative, put the 'ne' and the 'pas' in front of it.

Elle préfère ne pas parler de son travail. *She prefers not to talk about her work.*

'ne...jamais' — never

There are other negatives that work in the same way as 'ne...pas'. Here are some of the most common ones:

ne...jamais	*never, not ever*	ne...plus (H)	*not any more, no longer*	ne...ni...ni (H)	*neither...nor*
ne...rien	*nothing, not anything*	ne...pas encore (H)	*not yet*	ne...que (H)	*only, nothing but*
ne...personne	*no-one, not anyone*				

Je ne vais jamais à York.
I never go to York.

Il n'y a rien ici.
There's nothing here.

Elle ne voit personne.
She doesn't see anyone.

Higher

Je ne vais plus au collège.
I don't go to school any more.

Nous n'allons ni à York ni à Leeds.
We're neither going to York nor Leeds.

Tu n'as que deux heures.
You only have two hours.

Articles change to 'de' after a negative

After a negative, indefinite articles ('un / une') and partitives ('du', 'de la', 'des' — see p.144) become 'de'.

Elle n'a pas de pain. *She doesn't have any bread.*

'Ne...que' doesn't follow this rule — it keeps its articles. E.g. 'Je n'ai que du café.' (*I only have coffee.*)

Grammar Questions

Translate these sentences into **French**, using the negative phrases you've learnt on this page.

1. I never eat meat.
2. He doesn't like anyone.
3. I don't listen any more. (H)
4. They ('ils') only drink tea. (H)
5. She has neither a dog nor a cat. (H)
6. He has not yet gone. (H)

This page should help you feel more positive about being negative...

Don't forget that you need two words to make French verbs negative — 'ne' before the verb, and then one of the words from above after the verb. The end result? A tasty verb sandwich. Right, time for lunch...

Quick Quiz

Giving Orders

Learning to order other people about is an important life skill, whatever language you're speaking. Putting verbs in the imperative lets you do just that — it's really useful and very easy to form.

Imperatives use the present tense

1) Imperatives are words that give an order. They often tell someone to do something (e.g. 'sit down').

For when to choose 'tu' or 'vous', see p.145.

2) In French, imperatives are formed using the present tense of the 'tu' and 'vous' forms of a verb. Be careful — the 'tu' form of '-er' verbs loses its final '-s' in the imperative.

regarder (to watch)	
regarde !	*watch! (inf. sing.)*
regardez !	*watch! (formal, pl.)*

choisir (to choose)	
choisis !	*choose! (inf. sing.)*
choisissez !	*choose! (formal, pl.)*

attendre (to wait)	
attends !	*wait! (inf. sing.)*
attendez !	*wait! (formal, pl.)*

Regardez ça !
Watch this!

Choisis la rouge !
Choose the red one!

Attends le bus !
Wait for the bus!

3) The imperative forms of 'aller' and of 'être' are a bit different:

aller (to go)	
va !	*go! (inf. sing.)*
allez !	*go! (formal, pl.)*

Va dans le jardin ! *Go to the garden!*

Higher

être (to be)	
sois !	*be! (inf. sing.)*
soyez !	*be! (formal, pl.)*

Sois sympa ! *Be nice!*

Negative imperatives use 'ne...pas' normally

To make an imperative verb negative, put 'ne' before the verb and 'pas' or another negative after it (see p.175).

Ne volez pas mon tableau ! *Don't steal my painting!*

Ne sers personne ! *Don't serve anyone!*

To say 'let's', use the 'nous' form of the imperative

Higher

If you want to suggest doing something together, you use the 'nous' form of the imperative, which is the same as the present.

Travaillons ensemble !
Let's work together!

Faisons du gâteau !
Let's make cake!

Construisons un château !
Let's build a castle!

Grammar Questions

Translate these phrases into **French**.

1. Finish your homework! (pl.)
2. Don't organise a party! (pl.)
3. Listen! (sing.)
4. Don't drink! (pl.)
5. Don't go! (sing.)
6. Leave! (sing.)
H **7.** Let's dance!
H **8.** Let's eat!

It's imperative that you learn this page...

Imperatives are really useful things. Next time you hear one used in English, have a think about what the French version might be — keep doing that, and you'll be an imperative expert in no time at all.

Quick Quiz

'-ing' Verbs

'But what if I'm doing two things at the same time and want to talk about them both?' I hear you cry. Well, dry your eyes and read on — present participles are the solution to your problem...

'Doing', 'saying' and 'thinking' are present participles

Higher

1) To form the present participle, get the imperfect stem of the verb (see p.170) and add '-ant':

Verb	Imperfect stem	Present participle
regarder	*regard-*	regardant (*watching*)
choisir	*choisiss-*	choisissant (*choosing*)
partir	*part-*	partant (*leaving*)
venir	*ven-*	venant (*coming*)
ouvrir	*ouvr-*	ouvrant (*opening*)
entendre	*entend-*	entendant (*hearing*)
prendre	*pren-*	prenant (*taking*)
traduire	*traduis-*	traduisant (*translating*)
connaître	*connaiss-*	connaissant (*knowing*)
écrire	*écriv-*	écrivant (*writing*)

Careful — to say you're 'doing something', e.g. 'I am dreaming', you should use the present tense (see p.165-167). If you use two verbs together, e.g. 'I like writing', you use the present tense with an infinitive (see p.167).

2) 'En' + the present participle usually means 'while doing something' or 'by doing something'.

Il lit le journal en écoutant la musique. *He reads the paper while listening to music.*

3) Some verbs have irregular stems in the present participle.

Verb	Irregular stem
avoir (*to have*)	*ay-*
être (*to be*)	*ét-*
faire (*to do / make*)	*fais-*

Elle est devenue riche en faisant des vidéos.
She became rich by making videos.

Après avoir mangé — After having eaten

Higher

'Avoir' + past participle means 'having done something'.

Il regrette d'avoir envoyé le message.
He regrets having sent the message.

Après avoir payé, elles ont quitté le restaurant.
After having paid, they left the restaurant.

Grammar Questions

Translate the following phrases into **French**.

H **1.** while helping
H **2.** by discovering
3. after having eaten
4. by staying
5. by constructing
6. after having seen
7. after having chosen H
8. while training H

After having learnt the page, the student attempted the questions...

Present participles aren't used anywhere near as much in French as they are in English — most of the time, you'll just need the present tense. You still need to learn them though — they pop up every now and then.

Quick Quiz

Impersonal Verbs and the Passive

Passive sentences in French are structured just like passive sentences in English, so they're dead easy to recognise. But before we get there, there's some impersonal verbs to get your teeth into...

Impersonal verbs only work with 'il'

1) Impersonal verbs always have 'il' as their subject. Here are some common examples:

il y a	*there is / are*	Higher	il est (adjective) de	*it's (adjective) to*
il faut	*you must / it is necessary to*	Higher	il manque	*...is missing*
il fait (beau)	*it is (nice)*	Higher	il vaut mieux	*it's better*
		Higher	il vaut la peine de	*it's worth (doing something)*

Use 'il fait' to talk about the weather. For more about the weather, see p.75.

Il y a des cravates noires. *There are some black ties.*

Il y aura des gâteaux. *There will be cakes.*

Make sure you know how to use 'il y a' in the future ('il y aura') and the imperfect ('il y avait') too.

Il vaut la peine de trouver un emploi. *It's worth finding a job.*

2) 'Il faut' and impersonal verb phrases ending in 'de' are always followed by an infinitive:

Il faut aller au lycée tous les jours.
You must go to school every day.

Il est important de recycler tes déchets.
It's important to recycle your rubbish.

See p.167 to learn more about infinitives.

Le film est regardé par... — The film is watched by...

Higher

1) In most sentences, there's a person or thing doing the verb, e.g. 'The fly bites the man'. These are active sentences. In a passive sentence, the person or thing has something done to it, e.g. 'The man is bitten by the fly'.
2) The present passive is formed of a person or thing followed by the present tense of 'être' + a past participle.

Il est aidé par ses parents. *He is helped by his parents.*

See p.168-169 for more on past participles.

3) The past participle has to agree with the person or thing that is having the action done to it.

La série est regardée par beaucoup de gens.
The series is watched by lots of people.

This is passive — 'the series' is having something done to it. 'Regardée' has an 'e' at the end as it agrees with 'la série'.

4) The passive isn't used as often in French. French speakers often use 'on' (*one*) with an active sentence instead.

'One didn't see' sounds quite formal in English, so you'd normally use the passive voice instead.

On n'a pas vu l'homme. *One didn't see the man. / The man wasn't seen.*

Grammar Questions

Rewrite these sentences in French so they use the passive.

H: **1.** The students love the dog.
H: **2.** The influencer makes a video.
3. The family hires the bikes.
4. The teacher adores the pupils.
H: **5.** The boy eats cheese.
H: **6.** Anna is buying trousers.

The past participle needs to agree when you use the passive...

Remember to add '-e' if it's feminine, '-s' if it's masculine and plural and '-es' if it's feminine and plural.

Verbs and Tenses — Grammar List

Regular Verbs

Regular verbs that end in 'er', 'ir' or 're' follow the patterns of 'parler', 'choisir' and 'entendre'.

parler (to speak)

Present
je parle
tu parles
il/elle/on parle
nous parlons
vous parlez
ils/elles parlent

Imperative
parle !
H parlons !
parlez !

Participles
(avoir) parlé
H (en) parlant

Imperfect
je parlais
tu parlais
il/elle/on parlait
H nous parlions
H vous parliez
H ils/elles parlaient

Future (Higher)
je parlerai
tu parleras
il/elle/on parlera
nous parlerons
vous parlerez
ils/elles parleront

Conditional (Higher)
je parlerais
tu parlerais
il/elle/on parlerait
nous parlerions
vous parleriez
ils/elles parleraient

choisir (to choose)

Present
je choisis
tu choisis
il/elle/on choisit
nous choisissons
vous choisissez
ils/elles choisissent

Imperative
choisis !
H choisissons !
choisissez !

Participles
(avoir) choisi
H (en) choisissant

Imperfect
je choisissais
tu choisissais
il/elle/on choisissait
H nous choisissions
H vous choisissiez
H ils/elles choisissaient

entendre (to hear)

Present
j'entends
tu entends
il/elle/on entend
nous entendons
vous entendez
ils/elles entendent

Imperative
entends !
H entendons !
entendez !

Participles
(avoir) entendu
H (en) entendant

Imperfect
j'entendais
tu entendais
il/elle/on entendait
H nous entendions
H vous entendiez
H ils/elles entendaient

Modal Verbs

Modal verbs crop up all over the place and are used to show possibility or necessity. They're often followed by an infinitive verb.

devoir (to have to / must)

Present
je dois
tu dois
il/elle/on doit
nous devons
vous devez
ils/elles doivent

H **Past Participle**
H (avoir) dû

pouvoir (to be able to / can)

Present
je peux
tu peux
il/elle/on peut
nous pouvons
vous pouvez
ils/elles peuvent

H **Past Participle**
H (avoir) pu

vouloir (to want to)

Present
je veux
tu veux
il/elle/on veut
nous voulons
vous voulez
ils/elles veulent

Conditional
je voudrais
tu voudrais
il/elle/on voudrait

H **Past Participle**
H (avoir) voulu

savoir (to know / can)

Present
je sais
tu sais
il/elle/on sait
nous savons
vous savez
ils/elles savent

H **Past Participle**
H (avoir) su

Verbs and Tenses — Grammar List

Important Irregular Verbs

There are lots of verbs that don't behave themselves. Some of them, like 'être', 'faire', 'avoir' and 'aller', are pretty key.

être (to be)

Present
je suis
tu es
il/elle/on est
nous sommes
vous êtes
ils/elles sont

Imperfect
j'étais
tu étais
il/elle/on était
nous étions
H vous étiez
ils/elles étaient

Imperative
H sois !
soyez !

Participles
(avoir) été
H (en) étant

Higher

Future
je serai
tu seras
il/elle/on sera

Conditional
je serais
tu serais
il/elle/on serait

avoir (to have)

Present
j'ai
tu as
il/elle/on a
nous avons
vous avez
ils/elles ont

Imperfect
j'avais
tu avais
il/elle/on avait
nous avions
H vous aviez
ils/elles avaient

Participles
(avoir) eu
H (en) ayant

Higher

Future
j'aurai
tu auras
il/elle/on aura

Conditional
j'aurais
tu aurais
il/elle/on aurait

If only Zoe had learnt all the conjugations on the grammar list...

aller (to go)

Present
je vais
tu vas
il/elle/on va
nous allons
vous allez
ils/elles vont

Imperfect
j'allais
tu allais
il/elle/on allait
nous allions
H vous alliez
ils/elles allaient

Imperative
va !
H allons !
allez !

Participles
(être) allé
H (en) allant

Higher

Future
j'irai
tu iras
il/elle/on ira

Conditional
j'irais
tu irais
il/elle/on irait

faire (to do / make)

Present
je fais
tu fais
il/elle/on fait
nous faisons
vous faites
ils/elles font

Imperfect
je faisais
tu faisais
il/elle/on faisait
nous faisions
H vous faisiez
ils/elles faisaient

Imperative
fais !
H faisons !
faites !

Participles
(avoir) fait
H (en) faisant

Higher

Future
je ferai
tu feras
il/elle/on fera

Conditional
je ferais
tu ferais
il/elle/on ferait

'Être', 'avoir', 'faire' and 'aller' all have irregular stems in the future and conditional.

Anchor Verbs

Anchor verbs give you the pattern you need to be able to conjugate verbs with similar endings.

ouvrir (to open)

Verbs ending in 'vrir' normally conjugate like 'ouvrir'.

Present
j'ouvre
tu ouvres
il/elle/on ouvre
nous ouvrons
vous ouvrez
ils/elles ouvrent

Imperative
ouvre !
H ouvrons !
ouvrez !

Participles
(avoir) ouvert
H (en) ouvrant

Imperfect
j'ouvrais
tu ouvrais
il/elle/on ouvrait
H nous ouvrions
H vous ouvriez
H ils/elles ouvraient

partir (to leave)

Verbs ending in 'tir' normally conjugate like 'partir'.

Present
je pars
tu pars
il/elle/on part
nous partons
vous partez
ils/elles partent

Imperative
pars !
H partons !
partez !

Participles
(être) parti
H (en) partant

Imperfect
je partais
tu partais
il/elle/on partait
H nous partions
H vous partiez
H ils/elles partaient

prendre (to take)

Verbs ending in 'dre' sometimes conjugate like 'prendre'.

Present
je prends
tu prends
il/elle/on prend
nous prenons
vous prenez
ils/elles prennent

Imperative
prends !
H prenons !
prenez !

Participles
(avoir) pris
H (en) prenant

Imperfect
je prenais
tu prenais
il/elle/on prenait
H nous prenions
H vous preniez
H ils/elles prenaient

connaître (to know)

H Verbs ending in 'aître' conjugate like 'connaître'.

Present
je connais
tu connais
il/elle/on connaît
H nous connaissons
H vous connaissez
H ils/elles connaissent

Imperative
H connais !
H connaissons !
H connaissez !

Participles
H (avoir) connu
H (en) connaissant

Imperfect (Higher)
je connaissais
tu connaissais
il/elle/on connaissait
nous connaissions
vous connaissiez
ils/elles connaissaient

traduire (to translate)

Verbs ending in 'ire' often conjugate like 'traduire'.

Present
je traduis
tu traduis
il/elle/on traduit
nous traduisons
vous traduisez
ils/elles traduisent

Imperative
traduis !
H traduisons !
traduisez !

Participles
(avoir) traduit
H (en) traduisant

Imperfect
je traduisais
tu traduisais
il/elle/on traduisait
H nous traduisions
H vous traduisiez
H ils/elles traduisaient

venir (to come)

Verbs ending in 'nir' normally conjugate like 'venir'.

Present
je viens
tu viens
il/elle/on vient
nous venons
vous venez
ils/elles viennent

Imperative
viens !
H venons !
venez !

Participles
(être) venu
H (en) venant

Imperfect
je venais
tu venais
il/elle/on venait
H nous venions
H vous veniez
H ils/elles venaient

écrire (to write)

H Verbs ending in 'crire' conjugate like 'écrire'.

Present
j'écris
tu écris
il/elle/on écrit
H nous écrivons
H vous écrivez
H ils/elles écrivent

Imperative
H écris !
H écrivons !
H écrivez !

Participles
H (avoir) écrit
H (en) écrivant

Imperfect (Higher)
j'écrivais
tu écrivais
il/elle/on écrivait
nous écrivions
vous écriviez
ils/elles écrivaient

Verbs and Tenses — Grammar List

Other Irregular Verbs

The verb forms on this page are high frequency irregular verbs, so it's important you know them well.

dire (to say)

Present
je dis
tu dis
il/elle/on dit

Imperative
dis !
H disons !

Past Participle
(avoir) dit

boire (to drink)

Present
je bois
tu bois
il/elle/on boit

Imperative
bois !

Past Participle
(avoir) bu

rire (to laugh)

Present
je ris
tu ris
il/elle/on rit

Imperative
ris !

Past Participle
(avoir) ri

croire (to believe)

Present
je crois
tu crois
il/elle/on croit

Imperative
crois !

Past Participle
(avoir) cru

suivre (to follow)

Present
je suis
tu suis
il/elle/on suit

Imperative
suis !

Past Participle
(avoir) suivi

courir (to run)

Present
je cours
tu cours
il/elle/on court

Imperative
cours !

Past Participle
(avoir) couru

recevoir (to receive)

Present
je reçois
tu reçois
il/elle/on reçoit

Imperative
reçois !

Past Participle
(avoir) reçu

voir (to see)

Present
je vois
tu vois
il/elle/on voit

Imperative
vois !

Past Participle
(avoir) vu

mettre (to put)

Present
je mets
tu mets
il/elle/on met

Past Participle
(avoir) mis

Other Irregular Past Participles

Higher:
- se plaindre (*to complain*) ⟶ plaint
- découvrir (*to discover*) ⟶ découvert
- convaincre (*to convince*) ⟶ convaincu
- se taire (*to be quiet, keep quiet*) ⟶ tu
- pleuvoir (*to rain*) ⟶ plu

Jérôme might have been irregular, but he was still a hoot.

Revision Summary Test for Section Thirteen

This is it. The last revision summary. It's been an honour and a privilege... *Cries in French*

- These questions are **really tricky**, but they'll help you see **how well you know your stuff**.
- Tackle the **revision summary test** below, or scan the QR code to do it **online**. You can **keep track of your progress** online and see **which areas need more work**.
- There are **sample answers** here: www.cgpbooks.co.uk/MerciExtras

Summary Test

The Present Tense

1) Give all the present tense conjugations of these French verbs: a) jouer b) réussir c) attendre
2) Translate these verb phrases into French:
   a) I go b) we ('nous') are c) she wants d) they ('elles') know e) you ('vous') have
3) Correct these phrases: a) J'ai décidé partir. b) Elle veut à sortir. c) Nous apprenons de chanter.
4) [H] Translate this sentence into French: 'I have just finished my history homework.'

The Perfect and Imperfect Tenses

5) Translate these sentences into French:
   a) She used to dance. b) They ('elles') danced all night. c) I was dancing.
6) Write down the past participles of these verbs: a) parler b) comprendre c) partir
   d) attendre e) dire f) avoir g) mettre h) prendre i) voir j) connaître
7) Excluding reflexive verbs, how many verbs can you think of that take 'être' in the perfect tense? There are at least 15 you need to know.
8) Translate these verb phrases into French: a) you ('tu') ate b) I was sleeping c) I used to write
   d) they ('ils') walked e) you ('vous') drank f) I have seen g) he was doing

The Future and the Conditional

9) Translate these sentences into French: a) He is going to leave. b) They ('ils') are going to eat.

Higher

10) Write down all the proper future tense conjugations of the verb 'rêver'.
11) How do you say the following phrases in French? Use the proper future tense or the conditional.
    a) he will be b) you ('tu') will go c) one would look d) she would ask e) I will have

Reflexives and Negation

12) Give the French translations for these sentences:
    a) She rested. b) I am called Axel. c) It is going to happen. d) You ('tu') got changed.
13) Translate this passage into English: 'Il n'y avait personne sur la côte — je n'ai jamais vu la plage comme ça en été. C'est parce qu'il n'y a rien à faire là-bas. J'ai décidé de ne pas acheter une glace car je n'avais pas d'argent.'
14) [H] Write a sentence that includes the phrase: a) ne...plus. b) ne...ni...ni. c) ne...que.

Imperatives, Present Participles and the Passive

15) Write down the 'tu' and 'vous' imperative forms of these verbs (plus the 'let's' form for Higher tier):
    a) apprendre b) étudier c) venir d) aller e) prendre
16) Translate this sentence into English: 'Il faut vite rentrer chez toi parce qu'il fait mauvais.'

Higher

17) Write down the present participles of these verbs:
    a) conduire b) découvrir c) être d) se taire e) nettoyer f) remplir
18) Rewrite these sentences using the passive voice:
    a) Joël mange un poisson. b) Sophie achète une voiture. c) La pollution menace les animaux.
19) Translate this sentence into French: 'It's worth going to the restaurant because after having eaten well, you always feel better.'

Spelling and Pronunciation

French pronunciation isn't easy, so use this page to help if you're unsure how to pronounce a word. You can scan the QR code to hear the sounds and words in the tables spoken aloud.

Listening Track 41

French words aren't always pronounced as they're written

The table below shows some of the main ways of spelling common sounds in French.

Listen to the audio and practise pronouncing each sound out loud as you hear it.

Spelling	Example 1	Example 2
silent final consonant	temps	froid
a	avril	avenir
i/y	ici	lycée
eu	heure	bleu
e	me	se
au/eau/closed o/ô	bureau	côte
ou	court	trouver
u	futur	nul
silent final e	belle	publique
é/-er/-ez	passé	écouter
en/an/em/am	seulement	emporter
on/om	pont	nom
ain/in/aim/im	terrain	simple
è/ê/ai	problème	faible
oi/oy	coin	moyen
ch	proche	rechercher
ç/soft 'c'	garçon	lycée
qu	manquer	pratiquer
j	juste	juin
-tion	tradition	addition
-ien	bien	chien
h	hiver	hôtel
un	lundi	emprunter
-gn-	en ligne	gagner
r	revenir	apprendre
open eu/œu	couleur	sœur
open o	tort	d'accord
-s-	chemise	surprise
th	thé	théâtre
-ill-/-ille	billet	fille
-aill-/-ail	taille	travail

If you add an 'e' to a word ending in a silent consonant, the consonant will no longer be silent. E.g. you don't pronounce the 'd' in 'froid', but you do pronounce it in 'froide'.

In French, you don't pronounce the 'h' at the beginning of some words.

Sam decided now was the perfect time to read the French dictionary from start to finish.

You often pronounce the final letter of a word if the word after it begins with a vowel. This is called 'liaison'.

s-liaison	des espaces	vos amis
t-liaison	tout en	cent euros
n-liaison	ton oncle	son avenir
x-liaison	aux animaux	deux équipes

For example, in the phrase 'vos amis', you pronounce the 's' at the end of 'vos'.

The Speaking Exam

'But what will my exams actually be like?' I hear you cry. Well, the next four pages are just what you need...

There are four exams for GCSE French

1) Your Edexcel French GCSE is assessed by four separate exams — Speaking, Listening, Reading and Writing.
2) Each exam is worth 25% of your final mark. You'll get a grade between 1 and 9 (with 9 being the highest).
3) You'll probably have your speaking exam a couple of weeks before the rest of your exams.

The speaking exam has three parts

During your preparation time, you can make notes to use at any point during the exam.

1) Your speaking exam will be conducted and recorded by your teacher.
2) The exam is in three parts. Before you start, you'll get 15 minutes of preparation time.
The time allowed for the exam is 10-12 minutes at Higher tier and 7-9 minutes at Foundation tier.

① Read aloud

You'll get a card with several sentences on it, in French. You'll read the sentences out loud, then your teacher will ask you two questions in French related to the topic of the sentences. See p.190 for an example.

② Role play

You'll get a card with a scenario on it. At Higher tier, there are three questions for you to answer and two to ask (see p.191). At Foundation tier, you'll have four questions to answer and one to ask.

③ Picture task

Before the exam, you'll get a card with two photos on it (see p.192). You'll describe one photo and answer questions on it, and then you'll have a discussion on the same theme.

Try to be imaginative with your answers

You need to find ways to show off the full extent of your French knowledge. You should try to:

1) Use a range of tenses — e.g. for a question on daily routine, think of when something different happens.

   Mais demain je vais jouer au foot. *But tomorrow I am going to play football.*

2) Talk about other people, as well as yourself — it's fine to make people up if that helps.

   J'aime le sport, mais ma mère le déteste. *I like sport, but my mum hates it.*

3) Give loads of opinions and reasons for your opinions.

   À mon avis, il faut faire plus de recyclage. *In my opinion, we must do more recycling.*

You can use non-binary or gender-neutral pronouns in the exam — just make sure you use them consistently and that your adjectives agree.

If you're really struggling, ask for help in French

1) If you get really stuck trying to think of a word or phrase, you can ask for help — as long as it's in French.
2) For example, if you can't remember how to say 'homework' in French, ask your teacher.
You won't get any marks for vocabulary your teacher's given you though.

   Comment dit-on 'homework' en français ? *How do you say 'homework' in French?*

3) If you don't hear something clearly, just ask:

   Est-ce que tu peux répéter, s'il te plaît ? *Could you repeat that, please?*

You could also ask this if you're desperately in need of time to think of an answer.

Making mistakes isn't the end of the world...

You won't lose marks for correcting yourself, so show the examiner that you know where you went wrong.

The Listening Exam

This page is crammed full of advice to help you tackle your listening exam head on — so listen up.

The listening exam has two sections

1) For the listening paper, you'll listen to various recordings of people speaking in French.
2) The paper is 60 minutes long for Higher-tier students and 45 minutes long for Foundation-tier students. It's split into Section A and Section B:

Section A is the longer section — it's worth 40 marks. It contains comprehension questions in English, and you'll write your answers in English.

Section B is a shorter dictation section — it's worth 10 marks. You'll hear some short sentences and write them down in French.

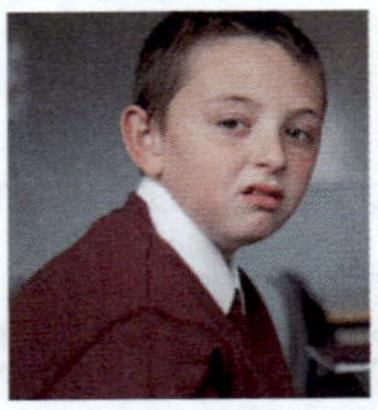

James realised a little too late that he was sitting the Spanish paper rather than the French one.

Read through the paper carefully at the start of the test

1) Before the recording begins, you'll be given five minutes to read through the paper.
2) In particular, look at the questions in Section A. Use this time to read each question carefully. Some are multiple choice, and others require you to write some short answers — make sure you know what each one is asking you to do.
3) Reading the question titles, and the questions themselves, will give you a good idea of the topics you'll be asked about. This should help you predict what to listen out for.
4) You can write on the exam paper, so scribble down anything that might be useful.
5) You'll be given 2 minutes at the end of Section B to check your work.

Make notes while listening to the recordings

1) For Section A you'll hear each audio track three times, and then there'll be a pause for you to write down your answer.

- While you're listening, it's a good idea to jot down a few details — e.g. dates, times, names or key words. But make sure you keep listening while you're writing down any notes.
- Listen right to the end, even if you think you've got the answer — sometimes the person will change their mind or add an important detail at the end.
- Don't worry if you can't understand every word that's being said — just listen carefully each time and try to pick out the vocabulary you need to answer the question.

2) For Section B you will hear each sentence three times.

- For the first group of sentences, you have to fill in the missing words. For the second group, you need to write down the whole sentence.
- Keep in mind that you'll be marked for accurate spelling.

Don't worry if you didn't quite catch the answer...

If you're still not sure of the answer after you've heard the track three times, scribble one down anyway — it's worth a shot and you might pick up some extra marks, especially if it's a multiple-choice question. Neat.

The Reading Exam

The reading exam is split into two parts, so make sure you know what to do for each section.

In Section A, you'll answer questions about texts

1) The Higher-tier reading paper is 1 hour long, and the Foundation-tier paper is 45 minutes. Both are worth 50 marks and have two sections.
2) In Section A, you'll be given a variety of French texts and then asked questions about them. The texts could include things like blog posts, emails, newspaper reports and adverts. The questions and answers will be in English.
3) Scan through each text first to get an idea of what it's about. Then read the questions that go with it carefully, making sure you understand what information you should be looking out for.
4) Next, go back through the text. You're not expected to understand every word, so don't get distracted by trying to work out what everything means — focus on finding the information you need. If you're having trouble with a particular question, you might want to move on and come back to it later.

Don't give up if you don't understand something

1) Use the context of the text to help you understand what it might be saying. You might be able to find some clues in the title of the text or the type of text.
2) Knowing how to spot different word types (e.g. nouns, verbs) can help you work out what's happening in a sentence. See the grammar sections (p.143-182) for more.
3) Make sure you put an answer down for every question — some of the questions are multiple choice, so even if you can't work out the answer, it's always worth putting down one of the options.
4) You can guess some French words that look or sound the same as English words, e.g. le problème (*problem*), la musique (*music*), dangereux (*dangerous*).
5) Be careful though — you might come across some 'false friends'. These are French words that look like an English word, but have a completely different meaning:

le coin	*corner*	le genre	*type / kind*	le / la médecin	*doctor*	les affaires (f)	*business*
grand(e)	*big*	demander	*to ask*	attendre	*to wait*	la journée	*day*

In Section B, you'll translate from French to English

1) Section B asks you to translate short French sentences (Foundation tier) or a short paragraph (Higher tier) into English. The sentences will be on topics you've studied, so the vocabulary should be familiar.
2) Here are some top tips for doing your translations:

- Translate a whole sentence at a time, rather than word by word — this will avoid any of the French word order being carried into the English.
- Keep an eye out for different tenses — there will be a variety throughout the sentences.
- Read through your translations to make sure they sound natural. Some words and phrases don't translate literally, so you'll need to make sure that your sentences sound like normal English.

Familiarise yourself with the structure of the exam...

It's good to be prepared and know what you'll be facing in the exam, so remember that Section A is reading French texts and Section B is translating sentences. Have a look at the Practice Papers for an example.

The Writing Exam

The writing exam is a great way of showing off what you can do — try to use varied vocabulary, include a range of tenses, and pack in any clever expressions that you've learnt over the years. You've got this.

There are various types of questions in the writing exam

1) The Higher-tier writing paper is 1 hour and 20 minutes long and the Foundation-tier paper is 1 hour and 15 minutes long. Some tasks are only for one tier, but others appear in both — these are explained below.
2) Each task is worth a different number of marks, so you should spend more time on the higher-mark tasks.

F

Photo Response Task (8 marks)

You'll be asked to write four short sentences in French to describe a photo.

Foundation

40 to 50-word Writing Task (14 marks)

You'll produce a short piece of writing in response to three bullet points. You'll need to choose between two questions and write about 40-50 words. Remember to write about each bullet point.

Both tiers

80 to 90-word Writing Task (18 marks)

You'll write about 80-90 words in response to four bullet points. You'll have a choice between two questions. It's really important that you write about each bullet point.

Higher

130 to 150-word Writing Task (22 marks)

You'll need to write about 130-150 words in French, based on four bullet points. There will be two questions to choose from. This task is more creative, so don't forget to include some opinions with reasons.

Both tiers

Translation Task (10 marks)

You'll translate five sentences (Foundation) or a short passage (Higher) into French. It could be on any topic you've studied. See p.187 for some top tips for translation tasks.

Plan out your answers and carefully check them

1) In the writing paper, you'll have to translate English sentences into French. Read each sentence fully before you start. Don't worry — the translation will only include the vocab and grammar you've learnt.
2) For the longer writing tasks, spend a few minutes for each question planning out your answer. Decide how you're going to cover every bullet point and in what order you're going to write things.
3) Write the best answers you can, using the French that you know — it doesn't matter if it's not true. It's your chance to show off your French knowledge.
4) Once you've got something that you're happy with, go back through and check your answer. Here's a checklist of useful things to look out for:

Remember — you can use non-binary or gender-neutral pronouns in the exam (see p.185).

- Are all the verbs in the right tense and do they have the correct endings?
- Do your adjectives agree with their nouns and are they in the right place?
- Is your word order correct, including any negative structures?
- Have you spelt everything correctly, including using the right accents?

Make sure you cover every aspect of the tasks...

When you're nervous and stressed, it's easy to miss out something the question has asked you to do. For questions with bullet points, try to write about each point in order — tick them off as you go along.

Practice Exams

Once you've been through all the questions in this book, you should be starting to feel prepared for the Edexcel exams. As a final piece of preparation, here are some practice exams for you to have a go at. There's a full set of Higher-tier papers in this book, or you can scan the QR code on the right to access them online. You'll find Foundation-tier practice papers online too — just scan the same QR code. Good luck!

Practice Papers

GCSE French Higher Tier

CGP Practice Exam Paper GCSE French

Speaking Paper

Time Allowed: 25-27 minutes, which includes 15 minutes preparation time

Instructions to candidates

- Find a friend or parent to read the teacher's part for you.
- The examination is made up of three tasks: one read aloud task, one role play, and one picture task.
- You have 15 minutes in total to prepare for the three tasks.
- You may ask for questions to be repeated.
- You must not use a dictionary or any other resources at any time.
- You may make notes on one sheet of A4 paper. For the read aloud task you may also make notes on the stimulus card.

Instructions to teachers

- The examination is made up of three tasks.
- The tasks must be conducted in the following order: read aloud, role play, picture task.
- The total examination will last between 10 and 12 minutes.
- Timings:
    - Read aloud and follow-up questions — between two and two-and-a-half minutes.
    - Role play — between one and one-and-a-half minutes.
    - Picture task — between two and two-and-a-half minutes for the picture description, and between five and five-and-a-half minutes for the conversation.

READ ALOUD
CANDIDATE'S CARD

Instructions to candidates

Katie has contributed to a blog about the environment.

Read out the text below.

Je m'inquiète pour l'environnement et pour l'avenir de notre planète.

Plusieurs espèces d'animaux sont en train de disparaître, donc les gouvernements du monde doivent travailler ensemble pour trouver une solution.

Il faut absolument réduire la quantité de ressources naturelles qu'on utilise.

Moi, j'essaie de protéger les animaux en faisant des dons à une association.

- Once you have read the text, you will then be asked two questions related to what you have read.
- You are expected to say a few words or a short phrase/sentence in response to each question. One-word answers will not be sufficient to gain full marks.

ROLE PLAY
CANDIDATE'S ROLE

Instructions to candidates

- You are in a clothes shop in France, and you are talking to a shop assistant.
- Your teacher will play the part of the shop assistant and will speak first.
- Your teacher will ask questions **in French** and you must answer **in French**.
- You are expected to say a few words or a short phrase/sentence in response to each prompt. One-word answers will not be sufficient to gain full marks.

1. Say what item of clothing you want to buy.

2. Ask if you can try the item on.

3. Say whether you like shopping.

4. Say which shops you will go to later.

5. Ask how much the item of clothing costs.

PICTURE TASK
CANDIDATE'S MATERIAL

Instructions to candidates

- Describe **ONE** of these pictures. You will tell your teacher which one you have chosen to describe.
- Your description must cover:
  - people
  - location
  - activity.
- When you have finished your description, your teacher will ask you two questions relating to your chosen picture. You are expected to say a few words or a short phrase/sentence in response to each question. One-word answers will not be sufficient to gain full marks.
- You will then move on to a conversation on the broader thematic context of **Studying and My Future**.
- During the conversation, your teacher will ask you questions in the present, past and future tenses. Your responses should be as full and detailed as possible.

Picture 1

Picture 2

READ ALOUD
TEACHER'S ROLE

- The candidate should be offered up to 1 minute additional preparation time in order to practise the read aloud task out loud.
- Teachers should not offer any guidance or correction to candidates during this time.
- When the candidate is ready to begin the test, you should state:
'The test will now begin. Please read the text.'
- The candidate should read aloud the following text.

Je m'inquiète pour l'environnement et pour l'avenir de notre planète. Plusieurs espèces d'animaux sont en train de disparaître, donc les gouvernements du monde doivent travailler ensemble pour trouver une solution. Il faut absolument réduire la quantité de ressources naturelles qu'on utilise. Moi, j'essaie de protéger les animaux en faisant des dons à une association.

Follow-on questions

Once the candidate has read the text aloud, you should ask the following questions.

- Est-ce que tu aimes passer du temps dans la nature ?
- Quel est ton avis sur les transports publics ?

ROLE PLAY
TEACHER'S ROLE

Setting: Clothes Shop

- The target language phrases below must be read out verbatim. There must be no supplementary questions and no re-phrasing, but teacher prompts may be repeated.
- Begin the role play with the following introduction:
  You are in a clothes shop in France, and you are talking to a shop assistant. I will play the part of the shop assistant and will speak first.

1	*Bonjour. Je peux vous aider ?* Allow the candidate to say what item of clothing they want to buy.
2	*D'accord. Vous avez une question ?* Allow the candidate to ask about trying the item of clothing on. *Give an appropriate brief response.*
3	*Vous aimez faire les magasins ?* Allow the candidate to say whether they like shopping.
4	*Quels autres magasins allez-vous visiter aujourd'hui ?* Allow the candidate to say what other shops they will go to later.
5	*Vous avez une autre question ?* Allow the candidate to ask how much the item costs. *Give an appropriate brief response.*

PICTURE TASK
TEACHER'S NOTES

Theme: Studying and My Future

- Start by asking the candidate which picture they have chosen to describe. Once their response is clear, continue with the instruction 'Describe the picture'.
- To encourage the candidate to address all the prompts and to develop their description, teachers may prompt by asking the following questions:
  - (Et) les personnes ?
  - (Et) c'est où ?
  - (Et) que font-ils ?
  - Autre chose ?
- These prompts must not be rephrased. Each prompt can be used a maximum of three times.

Compulsory questions related to pictures

- When the candidate has finished their description, ask the **two** questions below that relate to the candidate's chosen picture.
  - **Questions for Picture 1**
    (a) Où veux-tu travailler à l'avenir ?
    (b) Qu'est-ce que tu as fait récemment comme travail pour gagner de l'argent ?
  - **Questions for Picture 2**
    (a) Où est-ce que tu étudies normalement ?
    (b) Quelles matières as-tu choisi pour tes examens ?
- The questions must not be rephrased. If the candidate does not respond, the question may be repeated twice. Where a candidate answers incorrectly, do not repeat the question.

Follow-on conversation on the broader thematic context

- You must begin the follow-on conversation by asking the candidate to talk about **SCHOOL**, for example '*Parle-moi de ton école.*'
- Use the candidate's responses to continue the conversation about this subject as well as other areas of the thematic context, and the interests and experiences of the candidate.
- Give the candidate the opportunity to respond in the present, past and future tenses and to develop full and detailed responses.

The questions below are examples of questions in the past, present and future tenses that you may also wish to ask during the conversation. They are not compulsory and do not have to be asked consecutively or in the order given.

- *À ton avis, quel est le plus grand problème à ton école ?*
- *Quelle est ta matière préférée ?*
- *Pourquoi as-tu décidé d'étudier le français ?*
- *Qu'est-ce que tu vas faire l'année prochaine ?*
- *Parle-moi de ton emploi idéal.*
- *Quel était ton métier de rêve quand tu étais petit(e) ?*
- *Selon toi, est-il important de mettre de la distance entre sa vie privée et sa vie professionnelle ?*

End of test

GCSE French
Higher Tier

Listening Paper

CGP Practice Exam Paper GCSE French

Centre name						
Centre number						
Candidate number						

Surname	
Other names	
Candidate signature	

Instructions

- Use **black** ink or ball-point pen.
- **Fill in the boxes** at the top of this page with your name, centre number and candidate number.
- Answer **all** questions in Sections A and B.
- All questions in Section A (Listening comprehension) are set in English and must be answered in English.
- The task in Section B (Dictation) is set in French.
- Answer the questions in the spaces provided — there may be more space than you need.
- You must **not** use a dictionary.

Information

- The total mark for this paper is 50.
- You have 5 minutes to read through the paper before the first extract starts.
- You may make notes during these 5 minutes.
- The marks for each question are shown in brackets — use this as a guide as to how much time to spend on each question.

Higher Listening

Section A: Listening comprehension

- You will hear each extract three times. Each extract will end with one, two or three beeps. There will be a pause between each question.
- You may write at any time during the test.

Section B: Dictation

- You will write in French what you hear in the spaces provided.
- The number of each sentence will be announced.
- You will hear each sentence three times. You may write at any time during the test. There will be a pause between each question.
- You will have 2 minutes to check your answers at the end of this section.

Advice

- Read each question carefully before you start to answer it.
- Try to answer every question.
- Use the third play of the recording and/or the additional time given at the end of each extract to check your answer.

Section A

Listening comprehension

School subjects

1 Léa is talking about school subjects.

What does she say?

Listen to the recording and complete the sentences by putting a cross in the correct box for each question.

a) Léa says that English is...

	A the most boring subject.
	B the easiest subject.
	C the most problematic subject.

[1 mark]

b) According to Léa, physics is...

	A very difficult.
	B as enjoyable as music.
	C interesting.

[1 mark]

c) According to Léa, music...

	A was not a very useful subject.
	B is beneficial for the future.
	C was not offered at her school.

[1 mark]

Restaurants

2 Théo is talking about restaurants.

What does he say?

Complete the gap in each sentence using a word or phrase from the box below. There are more words/phrases than gaps.

town centre	village	shopping centre	farm
fruit	meat	fish	bread
welcomes you in	makes you hungry	brings back memories	

a) Théo's favourite restaurant is located in the .... *[1 mark]*

b) The restaurant's fresh produce comes from a nearby .... *[1 mark]*

c) At the restaurant, he normally orders .... *[1 mark]*

d) All meals are served with .... *[1 mark]*

e) When you enter the restaurant, the smell .... *[1 mark]*

Sports centre

3 Listen to this advert promoting a local sports centre.

What is mentioned?

Listen to the recording and put a cross in each one of the **three** correct boxes.

	A swimming
	B cycling
	C opening hours
	D outdoor sports pitches
	E group classes

[3 marks]

The local area

4 Sofiane, Inès and Rachid are talking about their town.

What do they say?

Listen to the recording and complete the sentences by putting a cross in the correct box for each question.

a) According to Sofiane, the town has...

	A two supermarkets.
	B everything necessary.
	C a lack of services.

[1 mark]

b) Sofiane also says the town has...

	A a stadium.
	B rail links.
	C a university.

[1 mark]

c) According to Inès, the town...

	A draws lots of visitors.
	B has a long history.
	C is not very attractive.

[1 mark]

d) Rachid says a new hospital will...

	A enhance healthcare.
	B have little impact.
	C improve the town centre.

[1 mark]

Holidays

5 Louis, Jade and Zoé are talking about tourism.

What do they say?

Listen to the recording and complete the following table **in English**.

You do not need to write in full sentences.

a)

	Why he goes abroad
Louis	....

[1 mark]

b)

	Her view on winter sports
Jade	....

[1 mark]

c)

	Her plans for the summer
Zoé	....

[1 mark]

Social media

6 Mehdi is talking about social media.

What does he say?

Complete the gaps in each sentence using a word or phrase from the box below.

There are more words/phrases than gaps.

photos	articles	videos	music
relatives overseas	friends abroad	former colleagues	

a) Mehdi's friends post .... on social media and

use it to share ....*[2 marks]*

b) Mehdi's mum uses social media to stay in touch with ....*[1 mark]*

Exercise

7 Nadia, Yanis and Sarah are talking about the advantages and disadvantages of exercise.

What do they say?

Listen to the podcast and complete the following tables **in English**.

You do not need to write in full sentences.

a) Nadia

Advantage	....
Disadvantage	....

[2 marks]

b) Yanis

Advantage	....
Disadvantage	....

[2 marks]

c) Sarah

Advantage	....
Disadvantage	....

[2 marks]

School life

8 Lucie and Tom are talking about their views on school.

What do they say?

Listen to the recordings and complete the sentences by putting a cross in the correct box for each question.

a) Lucie

i) Lucie's school...

	A offers a range of classes.
	B employs uninteresting staff.
	C recently got a new headteacher.

[1 mark]

ii) The school's extra-curricular activities include...

	A sports clubs.
	B a drama group.
	C reading groups.

[1 mark]

iii) Lucie intends to...

	A start a band.
	B play music.
	C act in a play.

[1 mark]

b) Tom

i) The biggest problem at Tom's school is...

	A a lack of resources.
	B student conduct.
	C poor teaching.

[1 mark]

ii) The school has also struggled with...

	A drugs.
	B fighting.
	C racism.

[1 mark]

iii) The headteacher...

	A is less strict than previously.
	B has made a big difference.
	C has recently taken up the position.

[1 mark]

Future careers

9 **a)** Yasmina is talking about her future.

What does she say?

Listen to the podcast and put a cross in each one of the **three** correct boxes.

	A Artists make a lot of money.
	B Her parents weren't in favour of her choice of career.
	C She wants to work with animals.
	D She would like a more active job.
	E She wants to make a difference in the world.
	F Working for the police is straightforward.

[3 marks]

b) You also hear this report on post-16 options.

Listen to the recording and answer the following questions **in English**.

You do not need to write in full sentences.

i) According to the recording, what did people normally do in the past?

.... *[1 mark]*

ii) According to the recording, what does university allow you to do?

.... *[1 mark]*

iii) According to the recording, why might you choose to do on-the-job training?

.... *[1 mark]*

iv) Give **one** benefit of spending time abroad.

.... *[1 mark]*

Section B

Dictation

10 You are going to hear someone talking about family and home life.

Sentences 1 and 2: Write down the missing words in the gaps provided.
In each gap, you will write one word **in French**.

Example: Ma <u>mère</u> <u>travaille</u> dans un <u>bureau</u>.

1. Ma .... a de ....

2. Mon .... et mon .... sont ....

Sentences 3, 4, 5 and 6: Write down the full sentences that you hear in the spaces provided, **in French**.

Example: <u>Mon père est professeur.</u>

3. ....

....

4. ....

....

5. ....

....

6. ....

....

[10 marks]

GCSE French
Higher Tier

Reading Paper

CGP Practice Exam Paper GCSE French

Centre name					
Centre number					
Candidate number					

Surname	
Other names	
Candidate signature	

Time allowed: 60 minutes

Instructions
- Use **black** ink or ball-point pen.
- **Fill in the boxes** at the top of this page with your name, centre number and candidate number.
- Answer **all** questions in Sections A and B.
- All questions in Section A (Reading comprehension) are set in English and must be answered in English.
- The question in Section B is a translation task set in French and must be answered in English.
- Answer the questions in the spaces provided — *there may be more space than you need.*
- You must **not** use a dictionary.

Information
- The total mark for this paper is 50.
- The marks for **each** question are shown in brackets
  - *use this as a guide as to how much time to spend on each question*
  - *you should spend approximately 10 minutes on the translation question.*

Advice
- Read each question carefully before you start to answer it.
- Try to answer every question.
- Check your answers if you have time at the end.

Section A

Reading comprehension

Holidays

1 Read the email that Enzo wrote to his French friend.

> Bonjour,
>
> Je viens de revenir de mon voyage en Angleterre où je suis allé avec mes frères. Le pays était plein d'histoire, mais l'hôtel était nul. Il n'y avait pas d'eau chaude ! Si j'y retourne un jour, je trouverai un autre logement.
>
> Quand j'avais douze ans, j'ai passé des vacances chez ma tante. Elle habite dans la campagne française, mais malheureusement c'est assez loin de la mer. Pendant notre visite, on a visité un musée de verre.
>
> Enzo

Complete the gap in each sentence using a word from the box below.

There are more words/phrases than gaps.

unsatisfactory	full of history	modern	hot
by the sea	in the country	in town	in England

a) According to Enzo, England is .... *[1 mark]*

b) Enzo thought his accommodation was .... *[1 mark]*

c) Enzo's aunt lives .... *[1 mark]*

Online Shopping

2 Read Gabrielle's blog about online shopping.

Dans le passé j'allais dans les magasins pour faire des achats, mais maintenant j'achète la plupart de mes vêtements en ligne. C'est pratique parce qu'on peut le faire sans quitter la maison. En plus, on peut comparer les différents sites pour trouver le meilleur prix.

Cependant, certains de mes amis préfèrent aller au centre-ville. Selon eux, c'est un bon moyen de soutenir des entreprises indépendantes et de sauver la rue principale. On peut essayer les ***habits*** avant d'en acheter. Malheureusement pour moi, tous les magasins sont fermés dans ma ville.

a) Complete the sentences below.

Put a cross in the correct box for each question.

i) Gabrielle no longer...

	A buys online.
	B shops in person.
	C spends money on clothes.

[1 mark]

ii) Online she can find...

	A lower prices.
	B more choice.
	C customer reviews.

[1 mark]

iii) Her friends shop locally in order to...

	A discover new styles.
	B purchase designer clothes.
	C boost the local economy.

[1 mark]

iv) All the shops in Gabrielle's town are...

	A old.
	B shut.
	C expensive.

[1 mark]

b) Which of these is the best translation for the word ***habits***?
Put a cross in the correct box.

	A clothes
	B money
	C sales

[1 mark]

Relationships

3 Charlie writes a letter to a problem page in a French magazine.

> Ma partenaire et moi sommes ensemble depuis l'école. Nous nous sommes rencontrés à la fête d'un de mes amis. J'essaie de la soutenir et nous avons une relation forte. Pourtant récemment, elle semble m'ignorer et je ne comprends pas pourquoi.

a) Complete the gap in each sentence using a word from the box below.
There are more words than gaps.

a music festival	a party	school	
support	relate to	understand	avoid

i) Charlie met his partner at .... *[1 mark]*

ii) He tries to .... her. *[1 mark]*

iii) He thinks she is starting to .... him. *[1 mark]*

The letter continues.

Normalement, nous passons du temps ensemble tous les deux jours, et les jours où nous ne nous voyons pas, nous parlons en ligne. Récemment, chaque fois que j'ai proposé une activité, elle a dit qu'elle avait trop à faire. Vous pensez qu'elle ne veut plus être avec moi ?

b) Complete the sentences below. Put a cross in the correct box for each question.

i) They usually exchange messages...

	A when they don't see each other.
	B if they have free time.
	C to organise dates.

[1 mark]

ii) Charlie is worried that his girlfriend...

	A has a new partner.
	B wants to end their relationship.
	C will stop speaking to him entirely.

[1 mark]

c) Answer the following question **in English**. You do not need to write in full sentences.

Give **one** reason why Charlie's girlfriend says she can't see him.

.... *[1 mark]*

Directions

4 Read Manon's email to her friend Camille.

> Salut Camille,
>
> Ma maison est au centre-ville. Va à l'école, et puis prends la rue à droite. Après, pars à gauche et traverse le pont. Passe devant la boulangerie et tourne à gauche.
>
> Ma maison se situe à côté de la poste sur la Rue du Lac. Le bâtiment est grand et bleu. Il y a une ***clôture*** blanche autour de mon jardin — j'ai deux chiens donc je les garde là-bas.
>
> À bientôt !
> Manon

a) Answer the following questions **in English**.
You do not need to write in full sentences.

i) After reaching the school, what should Camille do next?

.... *[1 mark]*

ii) What **two** things should Camille do after she crosses the bridge?

1. ....

2. .... *[2 marks]*

iii) Where exactly is Manon's house on the Rue du Lac?

.... *[1 mark]*

b) Which of these is the best translation of the word ***clôture*** ?
Put a cross in the correct box.

	A fence
	B door
	C garage

[1 mark]

Future Study and Work

5 Alessandro has sent you an email about his plans for after his exams.

> Salut !
>
> Je n'ai que deux semaines avant le début de mes examens. J'ai étudié très dur donc j'espère obtenir de bonnes notes. Cependant, je me sens très stressé — les épreuves sont fatigantes. Après les examens, j'irai en vacances pour me reposer. Pourtant, je ne sais pas quoi faire après les vacances.

a) What does Alessandro mention in his email?

Put a cross next to each one of the **three** correct statements.

	A His exams started two weeks ago.
	B He thinks he could have worked harder.
	C He is hopeful he will do well.
	D He doesn't feel too worried about his exams.
	E He is going on holiday to rest after his exams.
	F He is unsure about his long-term plans.

[3 marks]

Alessandro's email continues.

> Je peux aller à l'université, mais je dois choisir une matière intéressante et je n'arrive pas à décider. Mon père pense qu'une formation pratique serait mieux, mais pour ça j'aurais besoin d'avoir une idée du travail que je veux faire. Je crois que je vais travailler pour une association comme **bénévole*** pendant quelques mois et puis je vais prendre une décision plus tard.
>
> **un bénévole* = a volunteer

b) What does Alessandro say about his future plans?

Complete the tables **in English**. You do not need to write in full sentences.

i)

The issue with going to university
....

[1 mark]

ii)

A reason for doing an apprenticeship
....

[1 mark]

iii)

What he plans to do next
....

[1 mark]

Bastille Day

6 Maxime is talking about Bastille Day.

Aujourd'hui, c'est le 14 juillet, un jour où les Français fêtent leur pays. Le 14 juillet 1789 a été un moment historique de la Révolution française, quand les citoyens ont lutté pour obtenir plus de liberté.

Actuellement, mon frère, qui travaille pour le président, est en train de participer à un grand événement au centre-ville — ma mère et moi sommes là pour le soutenir, et le président est présent aussi. Il y a des **drapeaux*** partout — ils sont bleus, blancs et rouges.

**des drapeaux* = flags

a) What does Maxime say?

Put a cross next to each one of the two correct statements.

	A 14th July is next week.
	B French people celebrate their fight for freedom.
	C Maxime's brother is supporting him.
	D The family are going to the presidential event.

[2 marks]

Maxime continues.

> Ce soir ma famille et moi allons ensemble au concert dans notre quartier — beaucoup de chanteurs locaux vont être là et j'ai envie de les voir. Je préférerais y aller en bus, mais les rues sont fermées. Ma mère pense que le métro reste ouvert, mais elle a tort. C'est pourquoi nous devons y aller à pied.
>
> L'année dernière, les foules au concert étaient simplement énormes. J'ai détesté ça car je n'ai pas pu bouger. Peut-être la même chose arrivera cette année — je suis inquiet.

b) What else does Maxime mention?

Complete the tables in English. You do not need to write in full sentences.

i)

How he will spend his evening
....

[1 mark]

ii)

How he will get there
....

[1 mark]

iii)

How he feels about crowds
....

[1 mark]

Climate Change

7 Read this speech about the environment.

Hier, le gouvernement français a partagé un article sur les niveaux de pollution mondiale. L'article explique que les véhicules et l'industrie créent beaucoup de pollution. À cause de cela, la terre devient plus chaude, et, en conséquence, le niveau des mers monte. L'article a montré que **le réchauffement de la planète*** aura des résultats négatifs pour les citoyens du pays. En réponse à l'article, les organisations de protection de l'environnement ont partagé des informations en ligne pour encourager les gens à réduire la quantité d'énergie qu'ils utilisent, en faisant des petits changements dans la vie quotidienne. Elles nous conseillent de recycler nos déchets, d'adopter un régime végétarien et d'aller au travail en transports publics.

**le réchauffement de la planète* = global warming*

a) Complete the sentences below. Put a cross in the correct box for each question.

i) The article...

	A was shared yesterday.
	B will be shared today.
	C will be shared tomorrow.

[1 mark]

ii) The article mentioned...

	A the amount of rubbish in the sea.
	B changes to the climate.
	C the negative impact on wildlife.

[1 mark]

iii) According to the article, global warming will affect...

	A the lives of French people.
	B how many people visit France.
	C the amount of energy available.

[1 mark]

b) Answer the following questions **in English**.
You do not need to write in full sentences.

i) What did environmental groups do in response to the article?

.... *[1 mark]*

ii) Apart from lowering their energy usage, give **one** way people can reduce their environmental impact that is mentioned in the text.

.... *[1 mark]*

Unhealthy Living

8 A French newspaper has published an article about parents' concerns surrounding young people and their lifestyle choices.

Read what Sabrina and Richard say.

> Aujourd'hui, les jeunes reçoivent beaucoup de critiques sur leur choix de vie. La semaine dernière, notre journal a mené un entretien avec deux parents qui s'inquiètent pour leurs enfants.
>
> Sabrina nous a dit que de nombreux enfants mangent trop de nourriture malsaine. Ses enfants préfèrent le fastfood puisque c'est plus savoureux que les légumes. Souvent, elle trouve que ses efforts pour aider ses enfants n'ont pas réussi à cause de l'influence des autres jeunes.
>
> Richard s'inquiète car il est certain qu'un grand nombre de jeunes prend de la drogue. Il prévient que 37% des adolescents en prennent, même si Sabrina pense que ce nombre n'est pas exact. Les deux ont noté que c'est difficile pour les adolescents d'obtenir des conseils médicaux.
>
> Après l'entretien, Richard a invité Sabrina à devenir membre d'une organisation **caritative***. L'organisation commencera bientôt à visiter les collèges pour conseiller aux jeunes de s'occuper de leur santé.
>
> **caritative* = charitable

Answer the following questions **in English**.
You do not need to write in full sentences.

a) Name **one thing** Sabrina says about fast food.

.... *[1 mark]*

b) Why does Sabrina struggle to help her children?

.... *[1 mark]*

c) What concerns Richard?

.... *[1 mark]*

d) What do both parents agree on?

.... *[1 mark]*

e) How does the charity help children?

.... *[1 mark]*

Section B

Translation into English

9 Translate the following paragraph into English.

Chaque année, je vais en France pendant les vacances d'été. Cet été, je voudrais découvrir un autre pays francophone. Mes amis et moi profiterons d'un mois à Madagascar. Pour y arriver, il faut aller en métro jusqu'à l'aéroport, puis prendre l'avion. Le voyage dure plusieurs heures. Je viens de réserver un appartement dans la capitale.

....

....

....

....

....

....

....

....

....

....

[10 marks]

GCSE French Higher Tier

Writing Paper

CGP Practice Exam Paper GCSE French

Centre name					
Centre number					
Candidate number					

Surname
Other names
Candidate signature

Time Allowed: 1 hour 20 minutes

Instructions

- Use **black** ink or ball-point pen.
- **Fill in the boxes** at the top of this page with your name, centre number and candidate number.
- Answer Questions 1, 2 and 3.
- In Questions 1 and 2, answer **either** option (a) **or** option (b).
- Write your answers in full sentences.
- You must **not** use a dictionary.

Information

- The total mark for this paper is 50.
- The marks for each question are shown in brackets
  - *use this as a guide as to how much time to spend on each question*
  - *you should spend approximately 10 minutes on the translation question.*

Advice

- Read each question carefully before you start to answer it.
- Check your answers if you have time at the end.

Choose either Question 1(a) or Question 1(b).

1 (a) Write to your friend about travelling.

You **must** include the following points:

- things to see and do in your town
- your opinion of the countryside with reasons
- a place that you've visited in the past
- where you will go in the future.

Write your answer **in French**. You should aim to write between 80 and 90 words. *[18 marks]*

1 (b) Write to your friend about food.

You **must** include the following points:

- your favourite things to eat or drink
- your opinion of fast food with reasons
- a restaurant you went to recently
- a meal you will try in the future.

Write your answer **in French**. You should aim to write between 80 and 90 words. *[18 marks]*

Choose either Question 2(a) or Question 2(b).

2 (a) Write about sustainability for an online blog.

You **must** include the following points:

- the negative aspects of environmental change
- the pros and cons of walking instead of driving
- what your school has done recently to help protect the planet
- what measures you will take to preserve nature in your area.

Write your answer **in French**. You should aim to write between 130 and 150 words. *[22 marks]*

2 (b) Write about the internet for an online blog.

You **must** include the following points:

- what you use the internet for
- the pros and cons of streaming
- your social media use over the last week
- how technology will change in the future.

Write your answer **in French**. You should aim to write between 130 and 150 words. *[22 marks]*

3 Translate the paragraph into **French**. *[10 marks]*

My favourite sport is basketball because it is exciting. I recently started to play for my school's team, but we often lose. Last week, I went to watch a match at the stadium — the crowd was enormous! My sister accompanied me since she didn't have any plans. Unfortunately, a player injured himself.

....

....

....

....

....

....

....

....

....

....

....

....

....

....

....

Answers

The answers to the translation questions are sample answers only, just to give you an idea of one way to translate them. There may be different ways to translate these sentences that are also correct.

For dictation and translation questions, this symbol (|) shows where to divide the marks. There is 1 mark awarded for the first part of the text, and 1 mark awarded for the second.

Section One — General Stuff

Page 5: Numbers and Times

1) a) 16:50 b) film class c) music d) theatre / drama
2) a) Mon frère a | dix-sept ans.
   b) C'est ma sixième | visite au musée.
   c) Elle est née en | deux mille onze.
   d) Il est quatre heures | et demie.

Page 7: Days and Dates

2) a) 23rd March
   b) July
   c) Tuesdays and Thursdays
   d) 1995

Page 9: Questions

1) E.g. Le restaurant ferme à quelle heure ?
   E.g. Est-ce que tu veux des frites ?
   E.g. Combien coûte une glace ?
   E.g. Où sont les toilettes ?
2) Here are some questions you could have asked:
   Depuis combien de temps êtes-vous professeur ?
   Où travaillez-vous ?
   Quelle matière enseignez-vous ?
   Pourquoi aimez-vous être professeur ?
   Quelle est votre moment préféré de la journée scolaire ?

Page 11: Being Polite

1) a) (her husband's) birthday
   b) a cake
   c) in the garden
   d) a dance

Page 13: Opinions

1) a) i) true ii) false
   b) i) false ii) false
   c) i) true ii) false

Page 15: Listening Questions

1) a) 3 b) 8 c) €156 d) 16 e) around ten
2) a) B
   b) C
   c) A
   d) C

Page 16: Reading Questions

1) a) Toni b) Luis c) Eva d) Luis e) Eva
2) a) B b) C c) C

Page 17: Writing Questions

1) a) J'organise | une fête dimanche.
   b) Quelle heure | est-il ?
   c) La fête commence à | dix-neuf heures le douze juin.
   d) Mes amis sont en retard | — où sont-ils ?
   e) Combien coûte | un gâteau ?
3) Est-ce que je peux | te/vous présenter ma voisine ? | Elle a quatre-vingt-dix-neuf ans. | Auparavant, elle ne me parlait pas souvent. | Mais récemment, elle a commencé | à venir me voir chaque matin, | et elle m'a invité à une soirée. | Elle me raconte souvent des histoires de sa vie, | et je veux savoir plus | sur sa famille et ses amis.

Section Two — Identity and Relationships

Page 25: My Family and Friends

2) a) her mother and her father
   b) a rabbit
   c) She went to the cinema.
   d) They have a tradition of watching a film together every month.

Page 27: Describing People

1) a) A and D b) A and C c) B and D

Page 29: Relationships and Partnerships

2) a) Couples who get married seem happier.
   b) Weddings are too expensive.
   c) The number of same-sex marriages has increased.

Page 30: Role Models

1) a) A and B b) B and C

Page 31: Celebrations

1) a) C b) B c) C

Page 33: Listening Questions

1) a) Mon <u>frère</u> | est <u>petit</u>.
   b) Elle a | les cheveux noirs.
   c) J'habite avec mon frère <u>jumeau</u>, | ma <u>tante</u> et mon <u>cousin</u>.
   d) Je ressemble beaucoup | à ma grand-mère.
2) a) She wants to be independent.
   b) His girlfriend isn't ready to get married.

Page 34: Reading Questions

1) a) My brother is called Tom | and he is fifteen (years old).
   b) My step-father | is really nice.
   c) Charlie talks | more loudly than Lola.
2) I'm organising a party | for my best friend this weekend. | I would like to surprise her | for her birthday. | I've already invited | all of her family and friends. | Tomorrow I have to buy | a cake and flowers. | I think that it will be a nice opportunity | to show her that I love her.
3) a) hard-working
   b) She couldn't count on her last partner.
   c) He would love his job / He would be active.

Page 35: Writing Questions

1) Here are some examples of sentences you could have written:
   Il y a une femme célèbre.
   Elle a une voiture blanche.
   Les gens prennent des photos.
   Elle porte une robe rouge.
3) a) J'ai les cheveux marron | et les yeux bleus.
   b) J'ai trois frères | et une sœur.
   c) Quand j'étais jeune, | j'étais très indépendant(e).
4) Je passais beaucoup de temps | avec mon grand-père. | Il a un handicap et | il utilise un fauteuil roulant. | Il est né en France, | mais maintenant il habite en Angleterre. | Il est le membre de notre famille | le plus âgé et je suis le plus jeune. | Nous adorons la musique | et nous chantons souvent ensemble.

Section Three — Healthy Living and Lifestyle

Page 41: Physical and Mental Wellbeing

2) a) A new sports centre
   b) Swimming
   c) It makes the writer forget about their worries.
   d) It's a good way to enjoy oneself. / It's a good way to stay in shape.

Page 43: Illnesses and Treatments

1) A and C

Page 45: Food

1) a) B   b) C   c) A   d) A

Page 47: Listening Questions

1) A, C and F
2) a) It causes health problems.
   b) medical help
   c) It's difficult to keep a job.

Page 48: Reading Questions

1) a) Manon   b) Rachid   c) Ana   d) Rachid   e) Manon
   f) Manon
2) a) B   b) A   c) B

Page 49: Writing Questions

1) a) J'aime | le sport.
   b) Je suis membre | d'une équipe de basket.
   c) Hier, je suis allé(e) à | un rendez-vous médical.
   d) Le / La médecin travaille | à l'hôpital local.
   e) Je dois me reposer maintenant | mais je vais commencer à faire de l'exercice la semaine prochaine.

Section Four — Free-time Activities

Page 53: Music

1) a) listens to music on the internet
   b) i) quite difficult
      ii) She can see her progress. OR She wants to continue with lessons.
   c) i) ten years
      ii) writing lyrics for his group's songs

Page 55: Sport

1) a) À mon avis, l'exercice | est essentiel pour la santé.
   b) Je suis actif / active | et j'essaie de faire du sport tous les jours.
   c) Hier, ma sœur a dansé | avec ses amis.
   d) Cet été, je vais jouer | au tennis avec mon père.
2) a) running
   b) sports centre, athletics track and park
   c) She's improving her skills.
      She no longer gets injured.

Page 57: Cinema, Theatre and TV

1) A and D

Page 59: Hobbies and Going Out

2) a) She loves video games.
   b) She reads novels.
   c) He prefers staying at home and ordering a takeaway to going to a restaurant.
   d) He gets bored after an hour.
      There is never enough food.

Page 61: Listening Questions

1) a) Le <u>nouveau</u> cinéma | est <u>génial</u>.
   b) Je vais acheter | deux billets.
   c) Je préfère voir des <u>pièces</u> de théâtre — | c'est plus <u>intéressant</u>.
   d) À l'avenir | je voudrais être acteur.
2) a) He had to wait for a long time to get a table.
   b) The food was cold.

Page 62: Reading Questions

1) a) football   b) the news   c) follows
2) a) to learn to play a musical instrument
   b) transport / accommodation
   c) Any one from:
      - spend time with Camille
      - watch a football match at Wembley stadium
      - eat at a famous chef's restaurant

Page 63: Writing Questions

1) a) Je joue | au basket.
   b) Je pratique souvent | sur le terrain.
   c) Le sport | est bon pour la santé.
   d) Je participais à | des matchs de tennis.
   e) J'aime regarder | le tour de France avec ma mère.
3) Mon loisir préféré est la lecture. | J'aime particulièrement les histoires d'amour | ou les romans historiques. | Chaque soir j'essaie de lire | pendant une demi-heure. | Le week-end dernier, je suis allé(e) | à la bibliothèque et j'ai trouvé | une nouvelle série que je veux lire. | Cet été, je vais à | un festival du livre en France.

Section Five — Places in Town

Page 67: Where You Live

1) a) on the north-west coast
   b) It is beautiful.
      There are lots of large beaches.
   c) There is not much to do there in winter.
   d) It is hotter there.
      She loves the region's cuisine.

Page 69: The Home

1) a) J'habite dans | un immeuble moderne.
   b) C'est toujours très agréable | chez moi.
   c) Je veux acheter une maison | avec un jardin.
   d) J'avais | une chambre énorme.
   e) Je ne voudrais pas | construire ma propre maison.
   f) Mon appartement se situe | au quatrième étage.
2) a) B   b) C   c) C   d) A

Page 73: Shopping

1) a) B   b) B   c) C   d) A
2) a) J'aime porter | des vêtements confortables.
   b) Ce week-end, je vais aller | au centre commercial.
   c) Au travail, j'ai vendu | plusieurs robes.
   d) J'ai dépensé beaucoup d'argent | et fait beaucoup d'achats la semaine dernière.

Page 75: Directions and Weather

1) a) almost a million
   b) It is very mountainous.
   c) It is hot.
      It rains a lot.
   d) It is generally nice.
      It is colder.
2) a) the bus stop.
   b) change buses.
   c) walk to the library.
   d) on the left.

Page 77: Listening Questions

1) a) green spaces   b) clothes shops   c) train station
2) a) i) to go to the supermarket
      ii) Other supermarkets are too far from his home.
   b) i) She tries on new clothes
      The clothes are too expensive.
      ii) It's efficient to shop there. / You can find everything.
      It supports big brands rather than small local companies.

Page 78: Reading Questions

1) a) Clément
   b) Rachid
   c) Myriam
   d) Rachid
   e) Clément
   f) Myriam
2) B, C and E

Page 79: Writing Questions

1) a) J'adore | ma ville.
   b) J'aime aller | au château.
   c) Il y a un petit café | sur la place.
   d) La semaine dernière, | je suis allé(e) dans une nouvelle pâtisserie.
   e) Il y a toujours beaucoup de gens | au restaurant le samedi.
3) J'habite dans la banlieue d'une grande ville. | Ma maison se trouve | à côté d'un supermarché. | Notre quartier est idéal | parce qu'il est près du centre-ville | mais il est aussi calme et très sûr. | L'année dernière, les habitants | ont créé un nouveau jardin public. | J'aimerais rester ici | pendant plusieurs années.

Section Six — Environmental and Social Issues

Page 83: The Natural World

1) a) A and D   b) B and C

Page 85: Environmental Problems

2) a) He wants to protect the planet for the next generation.
   b) There were forest fires.
   c) It was a serious threat to the animals.
      There are fewer tourists visiting the country.
   d) He is worried about it.

Page 87: Equality and Social Issues

1) a) La faim est un problème | sérieux dans la société.
   b) L'identité de chaque personne | mérite le respect.
   c) C'était un choc | de voir la violence dans les rues.
   d) Je passe mon temps libre | à aider les autres.
2) a) a law on equality
   b) community safety
   c) prisons
   d) for a long time

Page 89: Listening Questions

1) a) forests
   b) animals
   c) plastic bags
2) a) A   b) C   c) B

Page 90: Reading Questions

1) a) Axel   b) Jade   c) Hugo   d) Jade
2) a) The president will continue | to fight against crime.
   b) Equality of the sexes is | essential for a fairer society.
3) B and D

Page 91: Writing Questions

2) Here are some examples of sentences you could have written:
   Il y a deux enfants et leurs parents.
   Ils marchent dans la forêt.
   Ils ont un gros chien.
   C'est l'automne.
4) Il est important de donner | aux gens des informations claires | sur les feux de forêt. | C'est un problème très sérieux. | La semaine dernière, j'ai donné de l'argent | à une organisation internationale | qui sauve les animaux en danger. | Je veux aider à protéger les bois et les arbres. | On doit faire plus de recherches | pour apprendre comment prendre soin de la nature.

Section Seven — Social Media and Technology

Page 95: Technology

1) a) False   b) True   c) True   d) False

Page 97: The Internet and Gaming

2) a) B   b) B   c) C

Page 99: Social Media

2) a) 3 hours
   b) He chats to his friends on social media sites.
   c) It is essential.
   d) It allows him to see his brother's photos.

Page 101: Listening Questions

1) a) C   b) B   c) B
2) a) sending messages
   b) You can learn new things online.
   c) learning Spanish
   d) They spend too much time in front of a screen.
   e) The influence of social networks.

Page 102: Reading Questions

1) a) Sarah   b) Jade   c) Toni   d) Jade   e) Toni
2) a) It is easier communicate / You don't feel alone.
   b) People can steal your information.
   c) They affected her self-confidence.

Page 103: Writing Questions

1) a) Ma sœur | n'utilise pas Internet.
   b) Je suis des influenceurs | sur les réseaux sociaux.
   c) Tu peux télécharger | des émissions gratuites.
3) Les jeunes d'aujourd'hui | sont la génération en ligne. | Ils ont beaucoup d'appareils, | mènent une vie virtuelle sur les réseaux sociaux, | et leurs compétences en ligne sont excellentes. | Cependant, ils ont aussi accès | à beaucoup d'informations sur Internet. | J'ai commencé à utiliser la technologie | quand j'avais trois ans, | et j'ai découvert qu'Internet est dangereux.

Section Eight — School

Page 109: School Life

1) a) Year 11
   b) She is interested in the natural world and likes doing experiments.
   c) The teacher is boring
2) a) i) useful in the future
      ii) his brother doesn't walk fast
   b) i) German
      ii) plays football in the playground

Page 111: School Pressures and Difficulties

2) a) J'aime beaucoup | la technologie.
   b) Cette année, | je suis en troisième.
   c) Les vacances commencent | en juin.
   d) Mon ami | lève la main.

Page 113: Listening Questions

1) a) A   b) C   c) A
2) a) B, C and F   b) B, D and F

Page 114: Reading Questions

1) a) the teachers / learning new things
   b) when students cause problems
2) a) B   b) C   c) B

Page 115: Writing Questions

1) Here are some examples of sentences you could have written:
C'est un cours de musique.
Il y a cinq élèves.
Les élèves portent un uniforme.
Un prof aide des élèves.
4) Notre emploi du temps est très strict. | Ce matin, nous sommes arrivé(e)s | à l'école à huit heures. | Nous avons passé toute la journée | devant un écran. | Parfois l'école est si fatigante | qu'il est difficile de se concentrer. | Je me sens stressé(e) et inquiet/inquiète, | parce que si je n'apprends rien, | je ne vais pas réussir.

Section Nine — Future Opportunities

Page 121: Education Post-16

1) a) En septembre, | je vais aller au lycée.
b) Je veux aller | à l'université de mes rêves.
c) Mon meilleur ami / Ma meilleure amie veut | faire une formation.
d) Nous avons l'occasion | de demander conseil sur les carrières.

Page 123: Career Choices and Ambitions

1) a) He wanted to work in a bakery.
b) He wants to have his own restaurant.
c) He works in the kitchen of a café.
d) The experience will be useful.
He doesn't earn a lot of money.
2) a) A and B b) A and C

Page 125: Listening Questions

1) a) Je suis <u>médecin</u> | pour <u>enfants</u>.
b) Je n'aime pas travailler | avec les adultes.
c) J'aime offrir du <u>soutien</u>. | C'est <u>pourquoi</u> j'ai décidé | de devenir <u>aidante</u>.
d) Ma mère est patronne, | et elle se sent toujours stressée.
2) a) Not being afraid of dogs / knowing how to ride a bike
b) Young people

Page 126: Reading Questions

1) a) My sister wants to be an actress.
b) She is not going to university.
c) She dreams of being famous.
2) I have just got my dream job. | After pursuing my passions, | I finally reached my goal, | and I can now say | that I am a headteacher. | However, the path | was not easy. | I worked very hard | to succeed in this field, | so I'm very proud of myself.
3) a) Worried / concerned
b) Doctor
c) Teacher
d) He no longer likes the music industry.

Page 127: Writing Questions

2) a) Mon frère va à l'université | cette année.
b) Ma mère travaille | comme prof.
c) Je veux gagner | beaucoup d'argent dans le futur.
4) Beaucoup de gens pensent | qu'il faut aller à l'université | pour trouver un bon métier, | mais je pense qu'ils ont tort. | Mon père dit toujours | que l'attitude est | aussi importante que l'éducation, | et je suis d'accord avec lui. | Cela dépend de ce qu'on veut | faire dans sa carrière.

Section Ten — Travel and Tourism

Page 131: Where to Go

1) a) She wants to go to France.
She wants to see the mountains.
b) She wants to go to Canada.
She wants to see her friend in Quebec.
c) She wants to stay in England.
She wants to visit museums.
d) He wants to go to southern Europe.
He wants to go camping.

Page 133: Accommodation and Travel

2) B, E and F

Page 135: What to Do

1) a) Two weeks
b) To improve her French
c) Any two from:
She will stay with a French family.
She will stay in a flat.
The flat is in an ancient building.
d) Any two from:
visit an interesting museum
go into the town centre
buy an ice cream in a café
e) at the weekend

Page 137: Listening Questions

1) a) A b) B c) C
2) a) a castle
b) bus / tube
c) make the most of the beautiful view of the landscape around the castle / discover lots of beautiful trails
d) taking photos in the building

Page 138: Reading Questions

1) a) Fathia b) Dorian c) Léa
2) a) They think it's too expensive to go alone.
b) work in a restaurant
c) You can learn another language.
You can earn a bit of money.

Page 139: Writing Questions

1) Here are some examples of sentences you could have written:
Il y a quatre personnes.
Ils sont à la gare.
Ils attendent le train.
Le train est bleu et jaune.
2) a) Je vais | en vacances.
b) Normalement, je préfère | voyager en avion.
c) Ma chambre d'hôtel | a une belle vue.
d) Hier, j'ai acheté | un billet à la gare.
e) Si je manque le train, | je peux prendre le bus.

Section Eleven — Nouns, Articles and Linking Words

Page 143: Nouns

1) le cadeau — les cadeaux
2) la piscine — les piscines
3) la maison — les maisons
4) le pays — les pays
5) la voiture — les voitures
6) le prix — les prix
7) la langue — les langues
8) le gâteau — les gâteaux

Page 144: Articles

1) L'homme a un peu de pain.
2) L'étudiant vient du Canada.
3) Je vais à la piscine.
4) Il va au marché.
5) Elle mange de la viande.
6) On a des légumes.

Page 145: Subject and Emphatic Pronouns

1) Il achète un billet. *He's buying a ticket.*
2) Le cadeau est pour toi. *The present is for you.*
3) Elle est plus contente que moi. *She is happier than me.*
4) Vous avez joué avec moi. *You played with me.*
5) Elle mange avec eux. *She eats with them.*
6) Il a envoyé la lettre lui-même. *He sent the letter himself.*

Page 146: Object Pronouns

1) Maria l'aime.
2) Je l'ai lu.
3) Je ne vous vois pas.
4) Elle lui a envoyé l'e-mail.
5) Ils nous parlent.
6) Il ne les visite pas.

Page 147: Relative and Interrogative Pronouns

1) C'est une grande maison.
2) J'adore vraiment ça.
3) Tu cours avec qui ? / Avec qui cours-tu ?
4) Qu'est ce que tu veux faire ? / Que veux-tu faire ?
5) l'hôtel où j'ai dormi
6) la nourriture que j'aime manger

Page 148: Indefinite and Adverbial Pronouns

1) Plusieurs ont fini leurs devoirs.
2) Tout le monde sait que c'est vrai.
3) Quelqu'un a acheté le livre.
4) J'y réfléchis.
5) Tu connais / Vous connaissez le château ? J'y suis allé.
6) Il y en a beaucoup.

Page 149: Conjunctions

1) Je voudrais un thé et une glace.
2) Si tu voles mon pain, je vais être triste.
3) Je veux sortir, mais je dois finir mes devoirs.
4) Comme il est tard, je vais me reposer.

Page 150: Prepositions

1) Je suis chez Nadia avec Tom.
2) La route passe sous le pont.
3) Je joue au football.
4) Il était en vacances pendant deux semaines.
5) Il y a un train dans deux minutes.
6) Je travaille à la boulangerie depuis six mois.

Section Twelve — Adjectives and Adverbs

Page 155: Adjective Agreement

1) une semaine régulière
2) un repas traditionnel
3) une fille triste
4) une porte bleue
5) les chiens dangereux
6) les nouveaux voisins
7) le premier jour
8) une star internationale

Page 157: More Adjectives

1) Mon père n'aime pas sa nouvelle voiture.
2) Tous tes amis habitent dans notre quartier.
3) Cet hôtel est grand.
4) Cette policière a leurs chats.

Page 158: Comparative and Superlative Adjectives

1) Théo est plus petit que Pauline.
2) Je suis plus jeune que toi / vous.
3) Julie est aussi riche que Léa.
4) Le printemps est meilleur que l'hiver.
5) Ses idées sont les pires.
6) Poole est la plus grande ville.

Page 159: Adverbs

1) tristement — sadly
2) négativement — negatively
3) sérieusement — seriously
4) généralement — generally
5) exactement — exactly
6) essentiellement — essentially
7) ordinairement — ordinarily
8) certainement — certainly
9) heureusement — happily / fortunately / luckily
10) actuellement — currently
11) évidemment — obviously
12) rarement — rarely

Page 160: More Adverbs

1) Je joue au foot là-bas.
2) Tu travailles tous les jours.
3) Souvent, je vais en ville en bus.
4) Il y a des animaux partout.
5) Je pars demain.
6) L'année dernière, je suis allé(e) en France.

Page 161: Comparative and Superlative Adverbs

1) Je travaille aussi vite que toi.
2) Lucie court plus souvent que Dorian.
3) Elle mange moins que vous.
4) Morgane chante le mieux.
5) Je nage le moins régulièrement.
6) Qui marche le plus rapidement ?

Page 162: Quantifiers and Intensifiers

1) Elle est très belle.
2) Elles ont beaucoup d'amis.
3) Il a un peu d'eau.
4) Le / La prof est vraiment vieux / vieille.
5) L'homme mange trop de fromage.
6) Sa maison est assez large.

Section Thirteen — Verbs and Tenses

Page 165: Verbs in the Present Tense

1) je parle
2) tu trouves
3) vous vendez
4) je réponds
5) elles finissent
6) vous commencez
7) on perd
8) nous remplissons

Page 166: Irregular Verbs in the Present Tense

1) nous devons
2) je veux
3) vous êtes
4) tu dois
5) elle va
6) ils font
7) elles peuvent
8) on sait
9) ils ont
10) nous faisons

Page 167: More about the Present Tense

1) J'aime manger.
2) Étudier, c'est ennuyeux.
3) Elles essaient de chanter.
4) Il continue à parler.
5) Il vient de partir.
6) Vous êtes ici depuis hier.

Page 168: The Perfect Tense

1) elles ont mis
2) je suis allé(e)
3) tu as dit
4) nous avons recyclé
5) elle est arrivée
6) il a pris
7) ils sont revenus
8) je me suis blessé(e)

Page 171: The Imperfect Tense

1) J'ai couru.
2) C'était amusant.
3) On rêvait.
4) Il était ennuyeux.
5) Ils ont mangé.
6) Elle a étudié.
7) Je jouais au foot.
8) J'achetais du pain.

Page 172: Talking about the Future

1) tu vas choisir
2) ils vont être
3) nous allons finir
4) tu vas regarder, tu regarderas
5) elles vont dire
6) vous allez faire
7) il va aller, il ira
8) elle va venir
9) je vais avoir, j'aurai
10) on va vendre

Page 173: The Conditional

1) vous amélioreriez
2) il goûterait
3) il mangerait
4) j'organiserais
5) elle irait
6) tu annoncerais
7) on serait
8) elle déciderait
9) ils s'identifieraient
10) nous chercherions

Page 174: Reflexive Verbs and Pronouns

1) il s'intéresse à
2) elle s'est mariée
3) tu t'entends avec
4) je vais m'habiller
5) elles se lèvent
6) nous nous échapperons

Page 175: Negative Forms

1) Je ne mange jamais de viande.
2) Il n'aime personne.
3) Je n'écoute plus.
4) Ils ne boivent que du thé.
5) Elle n'a ni chien ni chat.
6) Il n'est pas encore parti.

Page 176: Giving Orders

1) Finissez vos devoirs !
2) N'organisez pas de fête !
3) Écoute !
4) Ne buvez pas !
5) Ne pars pas !
6) Pars !
7) Dansons !
8) Mangeons !

Page 177: '-ing' Verbs

1) en aidant
2) en découvrant
3) après avoir mangé
4) en restant
5) en construisant
6) après avoir vu
7) après avoir choisi
8) en s'entraînant

Page 178: Impersonal Verbs and the Passive

1) Le chien est aimé par les étudiants.
2) Une vidéo est faite par l'influenceur / l'influenceuse.
3) Les vélos sont loués par la famille.
4) Les élèves sont adorés par le prof.
5) Le fromage est mangé par le garçon.
6) Un pantalon est acheté par Anna.

Higher Speaking Paper — Mark Scheme

It's very difficult to mark the practice Speaking Exam yourself because there isn't one 'right' answer for most questions. To make it easier to mark, record the exam and use a dictionary, or get someone who's really good at French to mark how well you did. Use the mark schemes below to help you, but bear in mind that they're only a rough guide. Ideally, you need a French teacher who knows the Edexcel mark schemes well to mark it properly.

Read aloud task (12 marks)

The read aloud task is divided into two parts. There are 8 marks available for reading the text aloud, and then 4 marks are available for answering the two compulsory questions.

Marks	Vocabulary
7-8	Pronunciation is consistently clear and comprehensible. Any lapses have no impact on the message.
5-6	Pronunciation is clear and comprehensible. Any lapses have minimal impact on the message.
3-4	Pronunciation is generally clear and comprehensible. Any lapses have little or no impact on the message.
1-2	Pronunciation is sometimes clear and comprehensible. Lapses occasionally make the message unclear/difficult to understand immediately.
0	No rewardable material.

Marks	Responding to the questions
2	Response fully communicated.
1	Response partially communicated with some ambiguity.
0	Does not meet the standard required for 1 mark.

Role play (10 marks)

In the role play, you'll be marked on how accurately you respond to spoken language. There are 2 marks available for each of the five tasks in the role play (10 marks in total).

Marks	Responding to the questions
2	Response fully communicated.
1	Response partially communicated with some ambiguity.
0	Does not meet the standard required for 1 mark.

Picture task (28 marks)

The picture task is broken up into three sections. 8 marks are available for your response to the content of the photo on the card, whilst 4 marks are available for answering the compulsory questions and 16 for the conversation.

Picture description task (8 marks)

Marks	Responding to the stimulus
4	You address all three bullet points. Your ideas are consistently developed. Your response is easily comprehensible.
3	You address all three bullet points. Your ideas are frequently developed. Your response is comprehensible.
2	You address two or more bullet points. Your ideas are generally developed. Your response is generally comprehensible.
1	You address two or more bullet points. There is some development of ideas. You response is comprehensible in some parts.
0	No rewardable material.

Marks	Grammar and Vocabulary
4	You use a wide range of relevant vocabulary and grammar. Your use of language is consistently accurate.
3	You use a variety of relevant vocabulary and grammar. Your use of language is mostly accurate.
2	You use some variety of relevant vocabulary and grammar. Your use of language is generally accurate.
1	You use occasional variety of relevant vocabulary and grammar. Your use of language is sometimes accurate.
0	No rewardable material.

Compulsory questions (4 marks)

There are two marks available for each question. If you only give a one-word answer, the maximum you can get for that question is one mark.

Marks	Responding to the questions
2	Response fully communicated.
1	Response partially communicated with some ambiguity.
0	Does not meet the standard required for 1 mark.

Conversation (16 marks)

Marks	Responding to the questions
10-12	You give consistently relevant responses to questions, developing your ideas throughout with consistently extended sequences of speech. Your response is easily comprehensible.
7-9	You give frequently relevant responses to questions, developing your ideas with frequently extended sequences of speech. Your response is comprehensible.
4-6	You give some relevant responses to questions, developing your ideas with some extended sequences of speech. Your response is generally comprehensible.
1-3	You give occasional relevant responses to questions, developing your ideas with occasionally extended sequences of speech. Your response is comprehensible in some parts.
0	No rewardable material.

Marks	Grammar and Vocabulary
4	You use a wide range of vocabulary and grammatical structures with frequent complex language. You show consistently successful use of past, present and future tenses and consistently accurate language.
3	You use a variety of vocabulary and grammatical structures with some complex language. You show frequently successful use of past, present and future tenses and accurate language.
2	You use some variety of vocabulary and grammatical structures with occasional complex language. You show generally successful use of past, present and future tenses and generally accurate language.
1	You use occasional variety of vocabulary and straightforward grammatical structures. You show some successful use of past, present and future tenses and some clear and accurate language.
0	No rewardable material.

You'll find mark schemes for the Speaking and Writing papers on p.230 and p.234.

Practice Exam — Higher Speaking Paper

Read aloud sample answers

1) Oui, j'aime passer du temps dans la nature. Les week-ends, nous allons souvent au parc national le plus près où il y a plein de fleurs.
2) Selon moi, les transports publics ne sont pas très pratiques. Normalement, c'est plus rapide et moins cher de prendre la voiture. C'est pourquoi il faut les améliorer.

Role play sample answers

1) J'aimerais acheter une chemise bleue de taille moyenne, s'il te plaît.
2) Est-ce que je peux l'essayer ?
3) Je déteste faire les magasins. Acheter des vêtements, c'est nécessaire mais c'est aussi ennuyeux.
4) Après, je vais aller au supermarché pour acheter du lait et puis à la poste pour envoyer une lettre à mon oncle canadien.
5) C'est combien, la chemise ?

Picture task sample answers

Picture 1: Sur la photo, il y a trois personnes qui sont en train de préparer un repas dans une cuisine. Il y a un homme qui utilise un couteau pour couper des légumes.

(a) Je voudrais travailler dans un supermarché car je veux un emploi où on peut parler à d'autres personnes.

(b) L'année dernière, j'ai pris un boulot d'été pour gagner de l'argent. J'ai travaillé dans un restaurant.

Picture 2: Il y a plusieurs étudiants dans une bibliothèque. Certains étudiants lisent un livre et une fille utilise un ordinateur portable. Une prof aide une étudiante — elle lui montre quelque chose dans un livre.

(a) Normalement, j'étudie dans la bibliothèque de mon collège — c'est très calme et elle a toutes les ressources dont j'ai besoin.

(b) Moi, j'ai choisi d'étudier le français, l'histoire et la technologie.

Sample answers to the optional example questions:

- Le problème principal à mon école, c'est les repas de midi. Ils ne sont pas très sains — il y a trop de frites et il faut avoir plus de légumes. J'ai écrit une lettre au directeur, mais il ne m'a pas répondu.
- Ma matière préférée, c'est les maths. Je suis fort(e) en maths car j'aime les matières qui ont des règles claires.
- Je n'avais pas de choix — à mon école, il faut absolument étudier une langue. Si j'avais un libre choix, j'étudierais l'histoire.
- Je ne sais pas encore ce que je vais faire l'année prochaine. Je dois prendre une décision bientôt : soit je continue mes études au lycée, soit je fais une formation pratique en cuisine. C'est très difficile de savoir que faire.
- Mon emploi idéal, c'est d'être président(e) d'une banque mondiale car on a l'occasion de voyager beaucoup et de gagner beaucoup d'argent.
- Quand j'étais petit(e), j'ai voulu être chanteur/chanteuse car c'est amusant. Cependant, je sais maintenant que très peu de personnes ont l'occasion de devenir chanteur.
- Oui, pour éviter de se sentir stressé, c'est très important de laisser son travail au bureau. Comme ça, la maison peut être un lieu pour se reposer et non un lieu de travail.

Practice Exam — Higher Writing Paper

Q1(a) — Sample answer

J'adore voyager. Dans ma ville, il y a beaucoup de choses à voir. Nous avons un château ancien, des magasins divers et de beaux parcs. Cependant, je préfère la campagne car il y a moins de personnes, de bruit et de déchets. L'année dernière, je suis allé(e) au Lake District avec ma tante, où nous avons fait de la natation dans un lac froid. C'était magnifique ! Cet été, je voyagerai à Paris — j'ai l'intention de visiter tous les lieux célèbres et de prendre un bateau sur la rivière.

Q1(b) — Sample answer

J'adore les plats sucrés, surtout le gâteau au chocolat. Malgré ça, je crois que c'est important d'avoir un régime sain, donc j'aime manger beaucoup de légumes aussi. Cependant, je déteste le fastfood car le goût n'est pas bon et je préfère soutenir les restaurants indépendants dans ma région. Hier, je suis allé(e) à un restaurant canadien qui vient d'ouvrir au centre-ville. C'était délicieux, quoique très cher. Ce soir, je vais essayer une nouvelle recette de poulet car mes amis vont venir manger chez moi.

Q2(a) — Sample answer

À cause des activités humaines, le niveau des mers est en train de monter, ce qui est une menace pour beaucoup d'animaux. Malheureusement, de nombreuses espèces vont disparaître. Évidemment, c'est une menace pour la prochaine génération d'êtres humains aussi.

Marcher plutôt que conduire, c'est une façon d'aider l'environnement, et c'est aussi un moyen de dépenser moins d'argent. Cependant, il faut partir plus tôt, et s'il pleut, ce n'est pas une option agréable.

Récemment, mon école a aussi agi pour aider la planète. Par exemple, elle utilise une compagnie qui fournit de l'énergie renouvelable. En plus, les profs nous ont encouragés à recycler nos déchets.

Dans ma région, il y a beaucoup d'occasions pour prendre soin de la nature. Le mois prochain, je donnerai de l'argent à une association qui protège les espèces en train de disparaître. Je vais aussi manifester contre la destruction de la forêt locale en écrivant au gouvernement.

Q2(b) — Sample answer

Comme la plupart des adolescents, je vais sur Internet pour jouer à des jeux, trouver des informations et utiliser les réseaux sociaux.

Cependant, je l'utilise le plus pour regarder des séries et des films sur des sites de streaming. C'est idéal car je peux regarder ce que je veux, quand je veux, où je veux, même si je ne suis pas chez moi. Par contre, il faut dépenser de l'argent, et quelquefois je regarde des séries au lieu de faire mes devoirs.

J'utilise souvent des réseaux sociaux — chaque jour cette semaine, j'ai passé une heure à regarder des vidéos et des photos. J'en ai aussi profité pour communiquer avec des gens à l'étranger.

La technologie de l'avenir sera très différente de celle d'aujourd'hui. Par exemple, les voitures vont être entièrement électriques. Selon moi, ce serait un monde meilleur.

Q3 — Translation

Mon sport préféré, c'est le basket parce que c'est passionnant. J'ai récemment commencé à jouer pour l'équipe de mon école, mais on perd souvent. La semaine dernière, je suis allé(e) regarder un match au stade — la foule était énorme ! Ma sœur m'a accompagné puisqu'elle n'avait pas de projets. Malheureusement, un joueur s'est blessé.

This is just a sample answer — there may be different ways to translate the paragraph that are also correct.

Practice Exam — Higher Listening Paper

Section A (Listening comprehension) — Mark Scheme

Question Number	Answer	Marks
1 (a)	A	*[1 mark]*
1 (b)	C	*[1 mark]*
1 (c)	A	*[1 mark]*
2 (a)	town centre	*[1 mark]*
2 (b)	farm	*[1 mark]*
2 (c)	fish	*[1 mark]*
2 (d)	bread	*[1 mark]*
2 (e)	makes you hungry	*[1 mark]*
3	A, C, E	*[3 marks]*
4 (a)	B	*[1 mark]*
4 (b)	B	*[1 mark]*
4 (c)	C	*[1 mark]*
4(d)	A	*[1 mark]*
5 (a)	he likes hot weather	*[1 mark]*
5 (b)	she really loves them	*[1 mark]*
5 (c)	visiting museums in Paris	*[1 mark]*
6 (a)	photos, articles	*[2 marks]*
6 (b)	relatives abroad	*[1 mark]*
7 (a)	it's essential for her mental wellbeing, it's hard to find time	*[2 marks]*
7 (b)	the team spirit is great, it's easy to be injured	*[2 marks]*
7 (c)	it helps you lose weight, you have less time to play video games	*[2 marks]*
8 (a) (i)	A	*[1 mark]*
8 (a) (ii)	A	*[1 mark]*
8 (a) (iii)	B	*[1 mark]*
8 (b) (i)	B	*[1 mark]*
8 (b) (ii)	B	*[1 mark]*
8 (b) (iii)	C	*[1 mark]*
9 (a)	B, C and E	*[3 marks]*
9 (b) (i)	the same job as their parents	*[1 mark]*
9 (b) (ii)	develop your knowledge of a subject	*[1 mark]*
9 (b) (iii)	if you don't want to spend money	*[1 mark]*
9 (b) (iv)	discover another culture / learn a new language	*[1 mark]*

Section B (Dictation) — Mark Scheme

Students will listen to a series of short extracts and will transcribe what they hear into French. Students will be rewarded for each individual word spelled appropriately and which demonstrates knowledge and understanding of Sound Symbol Correspondences (SSCs). The number of rewardable words will then be given a mark on a sliding scale of 1 to 10 as shown in the grid to the right.

Rewardable words include

- Words spelled exactly as in the transcript.
- Words that are spelt incorrectly but would still be pronounced correctly.
- Any spellings that do not change thepronuncation of the word and where the word is still recognisable.

Non-rewardable words include

- Misspellings due to incorrect application of SSCs, even if the word looks recognisable.
- Misspellings which are written phonetically, and which may contain appropriate SSCs, but which are so inaccurate that the words would be unrecognisable if seen on their own in isolation.

Below are the dictation sentences for this exam:

Sentence 1 Ma <u>tante</u> a de <u>jolies</u> <u>lunettes</u>.
Sentence 2 Mon <u>frère</u> et mon <u>neveu</u> sont <u>drôles</u>.
Sentence 3 Maintenant ma sœur est très grande.
Sentence 4 Nous allons acheter un chat.
Sentence 5 Mon oncle rêve de se marier.
Sentence 6 Il y a trop d'animaux chez moi. *[10 marks]*

Marks	Number of rewardable words
10	28-30
9	25-27
8	22-24
7	19-21
6	16-18
5	13-15
4	10-12
3	7-9
2	4-6
1	1-3
0	0

Total marks for Listening Paper: 50

Practice Exam — Higher Reading Paper

Section A (Reading comprehension) — Mark Scheme

Question Number	Answer	Marks
1 (a)	full of history	*[1 mark]*
1 (b)	unsatisfactory	*[1 mark]*
1 (c)	in the country	*[1 mark]*
2 (a) (i)	B	*[1 mark]*
2 (a) (ii)	A	*[1 mark]*
2 (a) (iii)	C	*[1 mark]*
2 (a) (iv)	B	*[1 mark]*
2 (b)	A	*[1 mark]*
3 (a) (i)	a party	*[1 mark]*
3 (a) (ii)	support	*[1 mark]*
3 (a) (iii)	avoid	*[1 mark]*
3 (b) (i)	A	*[1 mark]*
3 (b) (ii)	B	*[1 mark]*
3 (c)	she has too much to do	*[1 mark]*
4 (a) (i)	turn right	*[1 mark]*
4 (a) (ii)	**1.** go past the bakery **2.** turn left	*[2 marks]*
4 (a) (iii)	next to the post office	*[1 mark]*
4 (b)	A	*[1 mark]*
5 (a)	C, E, F	*[3 marks]*
5 (b) (i)	he can't decide which subject to pick	*[1 mark]*
5 (b) (ii)	his dad thinks it would be a better idea	*[1 mark]*
5 (b) (iii)	work as a volunteer	*[1 mark]*
6 (a)	B, D	*[2 marks]*
6 (b) (i)	he will go to a concert (with his family)	*[1 mark]*
6 (b) (ii)	on foot	*[1 mark]*
6 (b) (iii)	he hates them	*[1 mark]*
7 (a) (i)	A	*[1 mark]*
7 (a) (ii)	B	*[1 mark]*
7 (a) (iii)	A	*[1 mark]*
7 (b) (i)	shared information online (about reducing energy use)	*[1 mark]*
7 (b) (ii)	Any one from: recycle their rubbish / follow a vegetarian diet / use public transport to go to work	*[1 mark]*
8 (a)	Any one from: her children prefer it / it's tastier than vegetables.	*[1 mark]*
8 (b)	because of the influence of other young people	*[1 mark]*
8 (c)	the number of young people taking drugs	*[1 mark]*
8 (d)	it's difficult for young people to get medical advice	*[1 mark]*
8 (e)	it gives young people advice on taking care of their health	*[1 mark]*

Section B (Translation into English) — Mark Scheme

Marks	Responding to the Stimulus
9-10	The meaning of the original language is fully and appropriately transferred; any errors do not detract from the overall clarity of the message.
6-8	The meaning of the original language is mostly transferred appropriately. Occasional errors affect the clarity of the message, e.g. incorrect words, omitted words, inexact syntax.
3-5	The meaning of parts of the original language is appropriately transferred. Some errors prevent the message being conveyed, e.g. some use of incorrect words, omitted phrases, incorrect tenses.
1-2	Intermittent parts of the original language are appropriately transferred. Frequent errors prevent the message being conveyed, e.g. frequent use of incorrect words, omitted phrases, incorrect tenses.
0	No rewardable communication.

The answer below is a sample answer only, just to give you an idea of the way to translate it. There may be different ways to translate the paragraph that are also correct.

Every year, I go to France during the summer holidays. This summer, I would like to discover another francophone country. My friends and I are going to take advantage of a month in Madagascar. In order to get there, you have to go on the underground to the airport, then take the plane. The journey takes several hours. I have just booked an apartment in the capital city.

Total marks for Reading Paper: 50

Higher Writing Paper — Mark Scheme

Like the Speaking Exam, it's difficult to mark the writing exam yourself because there are no 'right' answers. Again, you ideally need a French teacher who knows the Edexcel mark schemes to mark your answers properly. Each of the writing tasks has a different mark scheme.

Question 1 (18 marks)

For this question there are four compulsory bullet points. There are 13 marks available for 'Responding to the stimulus' and 5 marks for 'Grammar and Vocabulary'.

Marks	Responding to the stimulus
11-13	You address all four bullet points. You frequently develop your ideas. Your response is comprehensible.
8-10	You address three or more bullet points. There is some development of ideas, and your response is generally comprehensible.
5-7	You address two or more bullet points. There is occasional, brief development of ideas, and some parts of your response are comprehensible.
1-4	You address one or more bullet point. You add little to no extra detail to your ideas. Limited parts of your response are comprehensible.
0	No rewardable material.

Marks	Grammar and Vocabulary
5	You use some variety of vocabulary and grammatical structures with some extended sentences and occasional complex language. You show generally successful use of past, present and future tenses, and your language is generally accurate.
3-4	You use occasional variety of vocabulary and grammatical structures with occasional extended sentences. There is some successful use of past, present and future tenses, and some accurate language.
1-2	You use a limited variety of vocabulary and grammatical structures with short, simple sentences. You show limited success in using past, present and future tenses, and limited accuracy in language.
0	No rewardable material.

Question 2 (22 marks)

For this question there are four compulsory bullet points. There are 17 marks available for 'Responding to the stimulus' and 5 marks for 'Grammar and Vocabulary'.

Marks	Responding to the stimulus
14-17	You address all four bullet points. You consistently develop your ideas. Your response is easily comprehensible.
11-13	You address all four bullet points. You frequently develop your ideas. Your response is comprehensible.
8-10	You address three or more bullet points. There is some development of ideas, and your response is generally comprehensible.
5-7	You address two or more bullet points. There is occasional, brief development of ideas, and some parts of your response are comprehensible.
1-4	You address one or more bullet point. There is limited development of ideas, and limited parts of your response are comprehensible.
0	No rewardable material.

Marks	Grammar and Vocabulary
4-5	You use a wide variety of vocabulary and grammatical structures with frequent extended sentences and complex language. You show consistently successful use of past, present and future tenses, and your language is consistently accurate.
2-3	You use some variety of vocabulary and grammatical structures with some extended sentences and complex langauage. There is some successful use of past, present and future tenses, and generally accurate language.
1	You use occasional variety of vocabulary and grammatical structures with occasional extended sentences and complex language. You show occasional success in using past, present and future tenses, and some accuracy in language.
0	No rewardable material.

Question 3 (10 marks)

The translation question is marked as a whole. There are 6 marks available for 'Responding to the stimulus' and 4 marks for 'Grammar and Vocabulary'.

Marks	Responding to the stimulus
5-6	The meaning of the original language is consistently and appropriately transferred; any lack of clarity is rare.
3-4	The meaning of most of the original language is appropriately transferred; the occasional message may be unclear or incomplete.
1-2	The meaning of some parts of the original language is appropriately transferred; the message sometimes breaks down or is incomplete.
0	No rewardable material.

Marks	Grammar and Vocabulary
4	You use consistently accurate vocabulary and grammatical structures.
3	You use generally accurate vocabulary and grammatical structures.
2	You use vocabulary and grammatical structures that are sometimes accurate.
1	You use vocabulary and grammatical structures with limited accuracy.
0	No rewardable material.

Index

Index

FES43